Olympic politics

Olympic politics

Christopher R. Hill

Manchester University Press
Manchester and New York

Distributed exclusively in the USA and Canada by St. Martin's Press

Published by Manchester University Press
Oxford Road, Manchester M13 9PL, UK
and Room 400, 175 Fifth Avenue, New York, NY 10010, USA

Distributed exclusively in the USA and Canada
by St. Martin's Press, Inc., 175 Fifth Avenue, New York, NY 10010, USA

British Library Cataloguing-in-Publication Data
A Catalogue record for this book is available from the British Library

Library of Congress Cataloging-in-Publication Data
Hill, Christopher R.
  Olympic politics / Christopher R. Hill.
    p.   cm.
  ISBN 0–7190–3542–2
  1. Olympics—Political aspects.   I. Title.
  GV721.5.H54   1992
  796.48—dc20   91–44101

ISBN 0 7190 3542 2 *hardback*
      0 7190 3792 1 *paperback*

Typeset in Great Britain
by Northern Phototypesetting Co Ltd, Bolton
Printed in Great Britain
by Bell & Bain Ltd, Glasgow

Contents

Illustrations

Acknowledgements

I have a great many people to thank for allowing me to interview them and for helpful advice. I conducted my interviews on the basis that the information obtained would not be attributed, but in most cases I was permitted to include my informants' names in these acknowledgements. I apologise to any whom I may have overlooked.

I am especially grateful to Her Royal Highness The Princess Royal (who is a member of the International Olympic Committee and President of the International Equestrian Federation) for receiving me.

His Excellency Juan Antonio Samaranch, President of the International Olympic Committee, was also kind enough to allow me to interview him.

The staff at the headquarters of the International Olympic Committee at Lausanne gave me unstinting help during a number of visits. I am particularly grateful to Maître François Carrard, Dr Karel Wendl and Madame Michèle Veillard.

I am very much indebted to the staff of the Organising Committee of the 1992 Games at Barcelona; the Manchester Olympic Committee, especially Bob Scott and Richard Parry, who were generous with their time and allowed me to consult documents at their offices; the International Amateur Athletic Federation, especially its General Secretary, John Holt; and to the late Victor Deacon, Honorary Archivist at Much Wenlock, Shropshire and his successor, Glyn McDonald, both of whom received me most courteously and guided me through the archives in their charge.

Others to whom I wish to record my thanks are: Albert Augusti, Shahbaz Beham, Miss Anne Beddow, Alfred Bosch, Guillermo Brugarolas, Joàn Brunet, Daniel Carbonell, Xavier Casadó, Miss Evie Dennis, Gunnar Ericsson, Bill Eadington, Carlos Ferrer, Raymond

Gazaer, Mrs Mary Glen Haig, Sir Arthur Gold, John Goodbody, Mademoiselle Miriam Gross, The Rt. Hon. Denis Howell, MP, Patrick Jourdain, Lord Killanin, David Miller, Josep Muñoz, Dr Primo Nebiolo, George Nicholson, Pedro Palacios, Charles Palmer, Richard Palmer, Michael Payne, Charles Randriamanantenasoa, Dr Harvey Schiller, Bernard Schneider, Sir David Scott, Alexandru Siperco, David Spanier, Howard Stupp, Leonard Steinberg, Andreu Mercé Varela, Mademoiselle Michèle Verdier, Josep Maria Vilaseca, George Walker, Madame Françoise Zweifel.

I am grateful to the Trustees of the Nuffield Foundation for their generosity in making me a grant in the early stages of the project and to Miss Pat Thomas, Deputy Director of the Foundation, for her wise advice.

Finally, it is a pleasure to thank Hugo Watson Brown, who read the whole typescript and suggested numerous improvements, as well as yet again master-minding the index, and Dawn Newbery, who was a patient and calming research assistant, and has an invaluable gift for organising material.

Acronyms

AAA	Amateur Athletic Association (UK)
AAU	Amateur Athletic Union (USA)
AIWF	Association of International Winter Sports Federations
ANOC	Association of National Olympic Committees
ARISF	Association of IOC-Recognised International Sports Federations
ASOIF	Association des Fédérations Internationales Olympiques d'Eté
BOA	British Olympic Association
COE	Comité Olímpico Español
COOB '92	Comité Olímpico Organisador Barcelona, 1992
DJP	Democratic Justice Party
EBU	European Broadcasting Union
ETA	Euskadi ta Askatsuna (Basque terrorist organisation)
FEI	Fédération Equestre Internationale
FIFA	Fédération Internationale de Football Association
FINA	Fédération Internationale de Natation Amateur
GAISF	General Association of International Sports Federations
GANEFO	Games of the New Emerging Forces
IAAF	International Amateur Athletic Federation
IF	International Federation
IOC	International Olympic Committee
KASA	Korean Amateur Sports Association
KOC	Korean Olympic Committee
LAOOC	Los Angeles Olympic Organising Committee
NOC	National Olympic Committee
PRC	People's Republic of China
SANROC	South African Non-Racial Olympic Committee

SLOOC	Seoul Olympic Organising Committee
TOP	The Olympic Programme
USFSA	Union des Sociétés Françaises de Sports Athlétiques
USOC	United States Olympic Committee

Chronology

Summer Olympic Games

1896 Athens
1900 Paris
1904 St Louis
1908 London
1912 Stockholm
1916 Cancelled (Berlin)
1920 Antwerp
1924 Paris
1928 Amsterdam
1932 Los Angeles
1936 Berlin
1940 Cancelled (Tokyo/Helsinki)
1944 Cancelled (London)
1948 London
1952 Helsinki
1956 Melbourne
1960 Rome
1964 Tokyo
1968 Mexico City
1972 Munich
1976 Montreal
1980 Moscow
1984 Los Angeles
1988 Seoul
1992 Barcelona
1996 Atlanta

Presidents of the International Olympic Committee

1894–1896   Demetrius Bikelas (or Vikelas) (Greece)
1896–1925   Baron Pierre de Coubertin (France)
1925–1942   Count Henri de Baillet-Latour (Belgium)
1946–1952   J. Sigfrid Edstrom (Sweden)
1952–1972   Avery Brundage (USA)
1972–1980   Lord Killanin (Ireland)
1980–   Juan Antonio Samaranch (Spain)

Selected dates mentioned in the text

776 B.C.   First ancient Games
A.D. 261 or 363   end of the ancient Games
1850   first Olympian Games at Much Wenlock, Shropshire, England
1859   first Greek Olympic Games
1863   birth of Baron Pierre de Coubertin
1865   foundation of National Olympian Association, Liverpool, England
1870   second Greek Olympic Games
1875   third Greek Olympic Games
1883   Coubertin's first visit to England
1889   fourth Greek Olympic Games
1890   Coubertin visits Much Wenlock
1894   International Athletic Congress, Paris
       International Olympic Committee founded with Demetrius Bikelas as President
1895   death of Dr William Penny Brookes
1896   Coubertin becomes President of the IOC
1906   'intermediate' Olympic games, Athens
1922   IOC recognises Chinese National Olympic Committee
1937   death of Coubertin
1945   division of Korea
1948   establishment of North and South Korea
1950   IOC grants provisional recognition to West German National Olympic Committee
1950–3   Korean War
1951   full recognition of West German National Olympic Committee
       National Olympic Committee of the USSR recognised

1952   USSR and West Germany participate in Helsinki Games
         People's Republic of China permitted to compete at Helsinki,
         although its NOC has not yet been recognised. Taiwan with-
         draws in protest
         Avery Brundage elected President of the IOC
1954   National Olympic Committee of People's Republic of China
         recognised as 'Olympic Committee of the Chinese Republic'.
         Taiwan's NOC still recognised as Chinese Olympic Com-
         mittee
1955   full recognition of National Olympic Committee of 'geo-
         graphical area' of East Germany
1956/60/64   joint East and West German teams compete at
         Melbourne, Rome and Tokyo Games
1956   People's Republic of China withdraws from Melbourne Games
         in protest at continuing recognition of separate NOC in
         Taiwan
1957   designation of National Olympic Committee of People's
         Republic of China changed to 'Olympic Committee of People's
         Democratic Republic of China'
1958   People's Republic of China withdraws from Olympic move-
         ment and from all international federations
1959   IOC decides that National Olympic Committee of Taiwan may
         not continue as 'Chinese Olympic Committee'
1960   Taiwan competes as 'Formosa' at Rome Games
         first Olympic television rights sold
         South Africa's last participation in the Games
1962   IOC grants provisional recognition to National Olympic Com-
         mittee of North Korea
1963   full recognition of North Korean National Olympic Com-
         mittee
1964   North Korea competes at Tokyo Games
1965   IOC grants provisional recognition to East German National
         Olympic Committee
1968   East German National Olympic Committee recognised as
         NOC of German Democratic Republic and competes
         separately at Mexico City Games
         confirmation of designation of Taiwan Olympic Committee as
         'Olympic Committee of the Republic of China'
1970   IOC withdraws recognition of South African National
         Olympic Committee

1971   expulsion of Taiwan from United Nations Organisation; admission of People's Republic of China

IOC resolves to reinstate People's Republic of China

1972   President Richard Nixon visits People's Republic of China

Avery Brundage retires as President of the IOC, Lord Killanin elected President

1973   Congress of the Olympic Movement, Varna

1974   Games of 1980 awarded to Moscow

1976   Canadian government refuses to admit Taiwanese team if 'China' appears in its title

1978   Juan Antonio Samaranch appointed Spanish Ambassador to USSR

Games of 1984 awarded to Los Angeles

1979   Soviet invasion of Afghanistan

1980   Juan Antonio Samaranch elected President of IOC in succession to Lord Killanin

IOC recognises National Olympic Committees of People's Republic of China and of Taiwan as 'Chinese Olympic Committee' and 'Chinese Taipeh Olympic Committee'

(February) President Jimmy Carter launches boycott of Moscow Games

IOC announces that Seoul is a candidate to host the Games of 1988

1981   Barcelona announces bid for Games of 1992

Congress of the Olympic movement, Baden-Baden

Games of 1988 awarded to Korea

1983   (September) Soviets shoot down Korean aircraft

1984   (May) USSR announces boycott of Los Angeles Games

1985   ISL takes over Olympic marketing on behalf of IOC

Madame Monique Berlioux 'resigns' as Executive Director of IOC

Birmingham adopted as British candidate for Games of 1992

1986   Games of 1992 awarded to Barcelona

1987   death of Horst Dassler, Chairman of ISL and of Adidas

North Koreans blow up South Korean aircraft in flight

1988   Manchester adopted as British candidate for Games of 1996

1990   Games of 1996 awarded to Atlanta

1991   IOC restores recognition of South African National Olympic Committee

IOC recognises National Olympic Committees of Estonia,

Latvia and Lithuania
Manchester adopted as British candidate for Games of 2000
(1994) Congress of the Olympic Movement, Paris

Introduction

Few enthusiasts of élite sport nowadays believe that it can be separated from politics, though there must be many who wish that it could. In fact they interlock at a number of different levels, the international, the national and, within sports organisations, the purely domestic. At the level of international politics it is impossible for sport to distance itself from the political questions which beset the world, especially questions relating to the recognition of states. This applies to all kinds of international sports organisations, but the necessary engagement with politics is especially obvious and important within the Olympic movement because of the extraordinary interest generated worldwide by the Olympic Games, the great amounts of money involved and the movement's aspirations to universality. The fact that it has outposts throughout the world renders it peculiarly vulnerable to the demands of international politics.

It might be thought that for the International Olympic Committee (IOC), the ruling body of the Olympic movement, to give recognition to a new National Olympic Committee (NOC), or to withhold it, would be no more important than any other decision by keen sports people about whether or not to compete with one another. However, the decision to recognise or not to recognise an NOC contributes to the far more important decision as to whether a territory with aspirations to recognition as a state (like East Germany after the Second World War) is to achieve it, or whether a country like South Africa, whose internal policies have been widely reviled, should continue to enjoy normal relations with other states. In such cases governments use sport as a weapon in the struggle, and sports people are bound to react.

At the second level, that of individual countries, sport and politics also interlock. Governments do not merely use sport as a means of projecting a national image abroad, but in order to achieve social and political objectives at home: these may include promoting racial harmony; improving conditions in the inner cities; keeping young people off the streets, or simply seeking to maintain a reasonable level of health among the general population. A common grievance among sports people in Britain is that not nearly enough is spent by central government on sport, and among educationalists its failure to give prominence to physical education in the curriculum of state schools is a cause of something approaching despair.

At the domestic level, within sports bodies, that is to say, the same processes may be seen at work as in national or international politics. When one studies the rise to power of Juan Antonio Samaranch, President of the IOC[1], or of Primo Nebiolo, President of the International Amateur Athletic Association, one could be examining the ascent of a conventional politician. Of course, a diagnosis of this kind is not unique to sport. Much the same could be said of the rise to eminence of any prominent man or woman, whether it be in the Church, journalism, business, the academic world or the armed forces. Similar processes of bargaining, alliance forming, luck, and idealism mixed with the desire for power are at work.

This, then, is a study in politics. Most of it concerns the events of very recent years, starting with the award to Moscow of the Games of 1980, but more remote events are briefly covered. The opening chapter gives an account of the ancient Games and of their revival in the 1890s by Baron de Coubertin. He too was no mean operator and without his political skills the modern Games might never have existed. The second chapter reminds the reader of some of the great issues of international politics which have necessarily affected the Olympic movement since Coubertin's day. It would never have been possible for the International Olympic Committee to ignore apartheid in South Africa, the Rhodesian rebellion of 1965, or, going further back in time, such questions as those posed by two territories, mainland China and Taiwan, each claiming to be the true China, the division of the Korean peninsula, or the problem of the two Germanies.

Chapters III and IV address the internal organisation of the movement, how power is exercised within it and how it is financed. Although these are internal matters they cannot be divorced from more obviously public concerns: men and women may rise within sport on merit, but their careers cannot be understood in isolation from the broader political background. For example, the USSR's late involvement in the movement, starting as recently as the Helsinki Games of 1952, inevitably politicised elections to the IOC's Executive Board, a trend which could not be resisted, given the movement's overriding interest in promoting its own universality and therefore in pleasing the states of the Soviet bloc. To discuss the financing of the Games necessarily provokes thoughts about whether they should now be seen more as a successful example of international capitalist entrepreneurship than as a festival of sport.

Chapter V discusses how and why cities vie with one another for the privilege of playing host to the Games and goes on to describe the unsuccessful attempts made by Birmingham and Manchester. It will be clear from this and later chapters that to understand why a city bids for the Games it is necessary to know something about the internal political situation in that country and about its international position.

Detailed studies of the politics of a series of modern Games are presented against this background analysis of the movement's power structure and finance. Moscow 1980 and Los Angeles 1984 are chiefly remembered for the boycotts organised by the United States and the Soviet Union respectively, and Chapters VI and VII examine those events in detail. The Seoul Games of 1988 (Chapter VIII) provide a prime example of a government which saw the advantages of the Olympics as a means of projecting itself worldwide and which masterminded the bid to host the Games for reasons unconnected with sport.

The Barcelona Games of 1992, which form the subject of Chapter IX, fall into a different category, since they have not yet happened, but they provide a study of peculiar interest because of the complicated politics of Spain, and because Barcelona's bidding campaign was conducted with enormous skill and confidence. Whether the 1992 games will be a success remains to be seen, but (unless they are marred by terrorism) the Olympic movement will certainly pronounce them a triumph, and even if they are not especially memorable from the participants' point of view, they will provide a television spectacular of unexampled splendour and audience appeal.

The final chapter examines some of the problems facing the Olympic movement and speculates about its future. The problem of which the movement is most conscious is, as it has been for many years, that of 'gigantism' – the Games' tendency to become ever bigger and more unwieldy. But there is room also for examination of what one might call a gigantism of the spirit, the over-estimation of the movement's importance, so noticeable at meetings of the power brokers of Olympism, and the corresponding forgetfulness that sport is in a sense a triviality. It is permissible when thinking about the future to think the unthinkable, and the book's concluding question is: Are the Olympic Games really necessary, or have they had their day?

Note

1   A Marquisate was conferred upon Samaranch by the King of Spain at the end of 1991.

I

Baron Pierre de Coubertin and the revival of the Games

The ancient Games were revived by Baron Pierre de Coubertin (born in Paris, 1 January 1863; died in Geneva, 2 September 1937) in 1896. This chapter describes Coubertin the man; briefly looks at some of the earlier festivals in the nineteenth century which described themselves as 'Olympic' and relates how Coubertin pushed through his own far more ambitious project.

Coubertin the man

Politics has been inseparable from the modern Olympic Games since the decision was taken at the Sorbonne in Paris in 1894 to revive them after a lapse of at least fifteen hundred years. Had the instigator of the decision, Baron Pierre de Coubertin, not been a natural politician of no mean skill, the decision might never been been taken, and even if it had been taken the Athens Games of 1896 might still never have been held without Coubertin's energy and determination.

Coubertin was an aristocrat, who could have taken to formal politics or to the army, but who decided to become an intellectual. In those days it was still possible for a man to be expert in a great variety of fields. Coubertin studied history, literature, education, sociology and many other subjects, and wrote voluminously on all of them.

His passion was for education, and in particular for sports education (*pédagogie sportive*), and in 1883 his first visit to England convinced him that Thomas Arnold's methods at Rugby School, where he had been Headmaster from 1828 to 1842, had been responsible for the great growth in England's power in the nineteenth century and should be exported to France.[1] Thereafter one of his major tasks was to persuade the French to introduce physical education in schools.

But he was not interested in just any physical education. His studies of classical history had convinced him that this aspect of education had reached its highest point in ancient Greece, where the gymnasia of Athens had created what he called a triple unity: between the old and the young; between different disciplines and between people of different types – the practitioner and the theoretician, the man of science and the man of letters. This union of many aspects of life was the central lesson to be learned from the Greek gymnasium, which was by no means to be confused with the modern type of gymnasium which was springing up everywhere.[2]

The original Olympic Games took place every four years at Olympia, in the Kingdom of Elis. They survived from 776 BC, when there was only one event, the 200 metres, until at least A.D. 261, and possibly until 393, when the Emperor Theodosius ordered the closure of pagan centres.[3] Coubertin's scholarship had a romantic tinge and with his idealised vision of Greece it was natural that he should come to believe that the Olympic Games represented the finest expression of sporting achievement and aspiration. He tells us that the religion of athleticism, which he celebrates in some splendidly purple passages, had its ceremonies at the Pythic, Nemean, Isthmic and other Games, but that the most illustrious were those held at Olympia.[4]

Though his prose was sometimes purple, his reasoning was hardheaded. Sport promoted physical health, which was essential if nations were to win wars – a powerful argument in a France still smarting from disastrous defeat in the Franco-German war. Sport also brought the classes together, which could only be desirable in the new age of democracy (by which he seems to have meant social equality). This is not to say that he was a warmonger, nor indeed a passionate democrat, but war was an occasional necessity, and democracy a fact of life. Furthermore, to bring the classes together was not the same thing as to mingle them.

It was not primarily because he was an internationalist that Coubertin pursued the Olympic ideal; rather, he saw this as the best way of promoting sport of the finest type, his efforts to balance intellectual and physical education in French schools having failed.[5] It seems that it was not until 1889 that he decided to try to revive the Games; thereafter he spent five years preparing the ground for the International Congress of sportsmen which took place in 1894.[6]

Coubertin has been much criticised on a number of counts. For example, David Young, an American scholar primarily interested in the ancient Olympic Games, says that he completely misunderstood them, and so based his case for the modern Games (of which Young thoroughly approves, though he thinks they often succeed despite their ideological base) on misconceived evidence. Young argues that Coubertin wrongly believed that the Games were limited to amateurs and, moving to broader ground, believes that he was in any case a part of a much more general nineteenth-century movement to take over sport from the working classes and place its direction in amateur, and upper-class, hands.

The second accusation may well have substance, if what is meant is that Coubertin was unconsciously part of that movement, but not if it is alleged that Coubertin was in any sense consciously trying to disadvantage the working class: the evidence is quite the other way. The question of amateurism is more complicated. He does indeed seem to have believed that the early Games were limited to amateurs (if one excludes their trainers, whom he saw as a harmless kind of professional), but he also deplores the gradual onset of profes-sionalism among the athletes, which in his view destroyed the games morally. At this point we enter a difficult dispute between specialists. On the one hand are those, like Young, who argue that the Games were for professionals from the very beginning: on the other hand scholars like Pleket (whose work Young greatly respects) believed that professionalism only became a factor in the Archaic period, conventionally held to have ended with the second Persian invasion of Greece in 480 BC.

The difficulty about coming to any conclusion is that the evidence is limited, but it appears to be common ground that the winners, although receiving no more than an olive wreath at Olympia and the other major festivals, were richly rewarded when they returned to their native cities. The point at issue is whether this happened from the beginning of the Games, or from some later period.

Coubertin's work predates this controversy. He may have been wrong to think that tnere had ever been a golden age of pure amateurism, but he certainly knew that the Games had eventually gone down hill. Yet he also propagated the entirely un-Greek idea that 'The important thing at the Olympic Games is not to win, but to take part; for the essential thing in life is not to conquer, but to struggle well'.[8] He may also have exaggerated the importance of the so-called 'sacred truce', which did not prevent wars or bring an end to one which had already broken out, but did have the more limited advantage of allowing athletes free passage to Elis for the Games.

On a more theoretical level, Coubertin may have been misguided in thinking that sporting contact between young people of different nationalities reduces the danger of war by promoting understanding. At least he did not believe that playing games together necessarily leads to people liking one another; indeed he thought such a belief infantile. But he did think that people could learn to respect one another, and that acquaintance must necessarily precede respect.[9] His successors in the Olympic movement have not always been so measured in their pronouncements. For example, Carl Diem said at the IOC's fiftieth anniversary that although the smoke of war had befogged the Olympic flame, it had not been put out. The profound point of the anniversary ceremony was to strengthen the certain truth that in future Olympism would continue to exercise its conciliatory power for the good of humanity.[10] The modern Olympic movement certainly sticks to this belief, though some of its members may do so in a spirit similar to that in which the Church of England remains attached to the Thirty-Nine Articles of Religion, which a Priest in that Church must sign.[11]

Although Coubertin insisted that the modern Games should follow what he believed to be the ancient example, and be limited to amateurs, he wrote in 1894 that English rowing had an out-of-date notion of 'amateur' and believed that the English oarsmen's exclusion of the working class was a monstrous aberration.[12] He would not allow work-people or anyone else to be paid for their sporting endeavours, but he thought it right that they should receive compensation for what would nowadays be called 'broken time' and used disrespectfully to refer to amateurism as 'this admirable mummy'.[13] Furthermore, although the 1894 Congress had reached a definition of amateurism, he seems to have believed that the definition should be open to change with circumstances. In an article published in 1909 he wrote that the movement should proceed very slowly towards a definition of 'amateur'.[14]

It is probable that Coubertin supported, to use a modern catch-phrase, 'sport for all' and at the same time believed in élite sport as the supreme test. His three passions can be summed up as love of country, education and love of sport. Many later commentators have rightly said that he misunderstood the Greek Games, and so had based the modern Games on false premisses. It is true that he misunderstood, or even invented, what he called Olympism, yet he was determined that the modern Games should be thoroughly modern. Like his current successors he was attached to ceremony, the Olympic Flame and flag and so on, and had a high idea of the respect due to the personages of the Olympic movement, yet in much of his thinking he was entirely down-to-earth. He would not have disagreed with those who say that in evolving new guidelines the modern movement has no need to be the prisoner of the past. He seems also to have been disinterested to an outstanding degree and after his retirement from the presidency in 1925 he never attended the games again.

The forerunners: 1 Much Wenlock

Even in the sixteenth century there had been English 'Olimpick' festivals and Coubertin's were not the first Games in the nineteenth century to regard themselves as in the Olympic tradition. Games had been held in Greece in 1859, 1870, 1875 and 1889 (the last two were not at all successful) and from 1850 annual 'Olympian Games' had been held at Much Wenlock, in the English county of Shropshire.

It may seem surprising that a small town in Shropshire, with about 2,500 inhabitants a hundred and fifty years ago, and not many more now, should have played any part in the foundation of the modern Olympic Games. Nevertheless, a number of authorities[15] agree that Dr William Penny Brookes, the moving spirit of the Much Wenlock 'Olympian' Games, had some influence on Coubertin's thinking, and Britain's Princess Royal, a member of the modern IOC, has lent her name to this view.[16]

Brookes was a fighter for causes. He was, in the usage of the day, a gentleman, which not all surgeons were, and so had access to leading figures in the county. The forerunner of the Olympian Society was the Agricultural Reading Society, which he founded in 1841, and for which he obtained subscriptions from 725 people. It was intended for all classes – though there is no record of who actually used the library – but one purpose of encouraging people to read was to help them to decide how to vote after the extension of the franchise in the Reform Act of 1832.

It was also necessary to keep people out of ale houses, with which Much Wenlock was very well supplied for its small population, and to encourage games. The Society therefore established an Olympian 'class' (meaning 'section') in 1850.[17] (There were also a philharmonic

class, art class, etc.) The Olympian class led to the formation of the
Olympian Society, which in turn organised annual Olympian Games.
These at first were more like traditional village jollifications than
conventional athletics meetings, but the programme gradually
became more sophisticated. As the Games became more established
Brookes was able to interest distinguished national figures, and he was
never reluctant to approach grandees of the highest rank.

Like Coubertin, he had a passionate interest in physical education
in state schools, where he thought it absurd that farm labourers
should have compulsory drawing lessons but no physical training, and
he used the Wenlock Olympian Society as the vehicle through which
he propagated his views.

In 1871 the committee was able to congratulate the members of the
Society

on the recognition for the first time of the importance of physical training in
our National Elementary Schools by the Committee of the Council on Education, in Article 24 of the Code of Regulations just issued, which states that
Attendance at drill, under a competent instructor, for not more than two
hours a week, and twenty weeks in the year, may be counted as school
attendance.

This was no more than a first step, for it did not make drill
compulsory. In any case Brookes did not think highly of drill,
compared with athletics.

Although your committee are of opinion that so small an amount of bodily
training will not be sufficient to preserve in early life the physical stamina of
the people, yet they regard it with satisfaction as a first instalment in the right
direction, and feel thankful that a branch of education which they have
advocated for so many years has at last been adopted by the State.[18]

Many quotations may be found to illustrate Brookes's conviction of
the virtues of physical education. For example:

The encouragement of outdoor exercise contributes to manliness of character.
I say contributes, for true manliness shows itself not merely in skill in athletic
and field sports, but in the exercise of those moral virtues which it is one of the
objects of religion to inculcate.[19]

Again, he says:

'Every year it is getting more difficult to decide what children who are
educated at the expense of the State ought to be taught', and goes on to argue
that England should follow the Swiss example and introduce gymnastics in
schools, partly by way of preparation for war.[20]

Ten years later Brookes writes that he has been struck on various visits to France by the population's physical degeneracy and as usual he had not been afraid to approach the highest authority: 'I wrote to the Emperor pointing out the dangerous consequences to France of a continued neglect of physical education.' A gymnasium was established, but 'it was too late! The Franco-German war showed the French that a nation cannot, with impunity, neglect the bodily traning of its people. England should take a warning from this disaster' . . .[21]

How horrified Brookes and Coubertin would have been by the British government's suggestions in the summer of 1990 that sport might be dropped from the compulsory curriculum. In the words of Sir Roger Bannister (noted neurologist, Master of Pembroke College, Oxford and the first man to run a mile in under four minutes):

This reverses the trend of more than a century in which sport has been an integral part of school activity, in many cases setting a life-long pattern.

It is no exaggeration to say that Britain's enlightened attitude to school sport has been the envy of many other countries. The object of sport at school is enjoyment for all, by the mastery of skills and co-operative effort, not to mention obeying the rules.

But the effect does not end there. The medical profession, faced with evidence of declining fitness in children, is mustering more and more studies which show that sport and exercise in childhood help to reduce the likelihood of heart disease, one of the greatest sources of chronic ill health and mortality in our society. How ironic that this might be thought the moment to drop physical education from the compulsory curriculum. An own goal?[22]

In 1862 leading lights of the Liverpool Athletic Club held an 'Olympic Festival' and in 1865 they founded a National Olympian Association (NOA), with the intention that annual Games should be held in turn in each of England's major cities. However, unlike modern cities, which vie with each other from all over the world to stage the Games, English cities of those days did not have enough enthusiasm for the idea ever to take off. Furthermore, the National Association was disregarded by the athletic 'establishment' of Oxford and Cambridge. Indeed, it appears, as the historian of the Amateur Athletic Association has shown, that the Amateur Athletic Club, the AAA's predecessor, was established as a riposte to the NOA.[23]

Brookes had seen the importance of the Olympic Games as early as 1859, when the Wenlock Olympian Society gave £10 to be presented to the winner of a race at the Athens Games of that year. When in 1877 he successfully applied to the King of the Hellenes for a silver cup to the value of £10, he showed his readiness to co-operate with the National Olympian Games by having it presented to the winner of the Pentathlon at the National games, rather than seeking to keep the glory of the royal gift for the Wenlock festival. As a local newspaper reported (perhaps in rather exaggerated terms): 'some years ago the late King of Greece applied to the founder of the Wenlock society, W. P. Brookes Esq., for information as to how the society was conducted, the object being to establish one similar in the country which Wenlock itself had endeavoured to emulate.' The paper believed that the present King was showing his gratitude by giving a cup in return.[24]

Brookes was soon afterwards to express the hope that the King of the Hellenes would visit Much Wenlock. He may not have had any serious expectation that this would happen, but the fact that he expressed the hope illustrates his willingness to fly high.[25] For many years, long before Coubertin had hit upon the idea, Brookes had been urging the revival of the ancient Games upon the Greek government. Correspondence in the Wenlock archives shows that he was pressing this idea upon the Greek Minister in London, Mr Gennadius, as early as 1880, the year in which Gennadius became an honorary member of the Society, though he seems never to have been able to visit Much Wenlock.

In January 1881 Brookes, as Treasurer, and William Lawley, Secretary, announced:

Your committee has suggested the holding of an International Olympian Festival of Athens, when the present critical state of affairs in Greece is ended . . . The proposal has been favourably received by Greeks resident in England, and will, no doubt, be cordially responded to by the authorities at Athens, and by the principal Athletic Associations of Great Britain, many of whose members would gladly avail themselves of an opportunity of visiting the classic land of Greece: of making an acquaintance with its people; of inspecting the interesting and important archaeological discoveries recently made, at a great cost, by the German Government and nation; and of contending in a generous rivalry with the Athletes of other nations, in the time-consecrated Stadium of Athens.[26]

This was no doubt written after Brookes had received Gennadius's letter of 18 November 1880. He wrote very cordially, but had to say that, after consultation:

while congratulating you upon all your Society aims at, and the most excellent proposal you now make to us, we deeply regret that in the present troubles and critical circumstances of the Kingdom it would not be possible to carry out in a befitting manner the scheme you propose. If, as we must hope, later on a more settled and satisfactory state of affairs be established in the last[?], then I have every reason to believe that such a proposal would meet with a ready and cheerful response.[27]

Clio, a Greek paper, refers back to the exchange of prizes:

Dr Brookes, this enthusiastic Philhelline, is endeavouring to organize an International Olympian festival, to be held in Athens, from which much good will arise in many respects and, we have no doubt that the Greek Government will give every facility for its realization.[28]

Brookes kept up the campaign, and it seems that he had an ally in Gennadius, though the uncertain political state of Greece made the revival of the Games problematic. In June 1886 he wrote to Brookes:

I quite agree with you that what has lately happened in Greece was for the best. It was of very great importance that we have shown we can put on the field an important force which proved its ability to fight well.

But these events [?] have made the periodical keeping of the Olympian games difficult and of late they were not regularly kept. A meeting[?] will take place next year I think.[29]

As for Brookes's relationship with Coubertin, it appears that Brookes took the initiative in approaching him, since in January 1890 Coubertin referred to interesting documents received from Brookes (with the implication that they had arrived unsolicited), one dealing with tilting, and the other giving details of an experiment carried out by Brookes some years earlier. In this experiment he had taken twelve boys: subjected six to a regime of drill, and the other six to gymnastics, and shown that the latter group's muscular development significantly outshone that of the former.[30]

Thereafter Brookes and Coubertin exchanged a number of letters, and in October 1890 Coubertin paid a visit to Wenlock, where a special festival was held in his honour. Despite pouring rain he enjoyed himself, an oak was planted in his honour, and after the visit he wrote a complimentary article in the *Revue Athlétique*.[31] In 1891 he became an honorary member of the Olympian Society. A cordial letter from Coubertin to Brookes in July 1892 is interesting, not only because it shows that they were by now on quite close terms, but also

because it says something about the Union of French Athletic Sports
Societies (USFSA) which Coubertin was using as the base from which
to float the idea of reviving the Games, and gives an insight into his
views on amateurism. He apologises for the delay in answering
Brookes's last letter, but has been terribly busy. His Union has
recently reached sixty-two member societies with about 7,000 members, compared with seven societies, sixty-two with 800 [700?] two
years ago, and at their last international meeting some of the best
English runners and cyclists had taken part. 'The only trouble we
have is with reference to professionalism as in country towns money
prizes are given very often for bicycle races in which our men are
sometimes tempted to compete. Of course we don't allow it.'[32]

The prospect of the 1896 Games was received with enthusiasm by the
Much Wenlock Olympian Society. On 24 May 1894 Brookes read to
the members the programme of the International Athletic Congress to
be held in Paris on 17–24 June 1894 at the Palace of the Sorbonne on
the subject of 'Amateurism and Professionalism in Athletics' and on
the establishment of international Olympian festivals, with letters
relating to the same from de Coubertin.

The members present expressed their decided opinion that amateurs only
should be allowed to compete. They were also unanimously and enthu-
siastically of opinion that the proposed establishment of international
Olympian festivals, to be held in rotation by all nations desirous of joining the
movement, will be one of the grandest and most beneficial institutions of
modern days, as it will tend to increase the bodily and mental vigour of the
people and to promote friendly feeling and intercourse between the different
nations of the earth.

They believed that there should be no delay. The first Games should
be in Paris in 1895, and thereafter they should be held annually:
otherwise, if ten nations joined the movement, each would be host
only once in forty years.[33] Clearly, Brookes was not without honour in
his own country, for at the 1895 Much Wenlock games R. J. More,
M.P., said that it was mainly thanks to Brookes that the Olympian
Games were to be renewed at Athens in the following year, and
afterwards at Paris and London.[34]

   Brookes, who was by now aged eighty-five, was too frail to attend
the 1894 Congress, but he was included in the list of honorary delegates. In December 1895, in a letter warmly congratulating Coubertin
on his engagement to be married, Brookes wrote, 'The Greek Govern-

ment should I think, gladly acquiesce in the honour France wishes to confer upon Greece by holding the first festival at Athens' and goes on, with his usual practicality, to suggest that Coubertin 'write to Baron Courcel, your Ambassador to London, and ask him to request the Greek Ambassador to London, Athos Romanos, to use his influence with the wealthy Greeks in England, and solicit their pecuniary support . . .'[35]

It is impossible to say how much influence Brookes had on Coubertin, but it is obvious that he had some. He had presented a prize to the Athens Games in 1859, four years before Coubertin was born, and had been actively working for the revival of the Olympics at least by 1880, when Coubertin was seventeen. To ask for a cup, as Brookes did in 1877, does not in itself indicate a desire to revive the ancient Games, but it does show a lively interest, and even if Brookes's active lobbying dates only from 1880 it seems virtually certain that he was seeking to revive the Games well before the same idea had occurred to Coubertin. However, that is not to say that Coubertin got the idea from Brookes, of whom he appears not to have heard until Brookes wrote to him in 1890.

The most that can be said with certainty is that they were similar men with many ideas in common. They shared a passion for physical education: some of the words used by Coubertin, especially when he writes of the need for a healthy population in case of war, echo those of Brookes; both were political animals, and no doubt Coubertin's admiration for Thomas Arnold of Rugby overflowed into other aspects of English life. Coubertin may not have been much given to acknowledging debts, but he was generous in his article about his visit to Wenlock, where he wrote that 'if the Olympic Games that Modern Greece had not yet been able to revive still survive to-day, it is due, not to a Greek but to Dr W. P. Brookes'.[36]

The forerunners: 2 Greece: the Games of 1859 and 1870

Greece owed the Games of 1859 and 1870 to Evangelios Zappas, a rich merchant of Greek origin living in Romania. He was one of the many nineteenth-century humanists and intellectuals who were passionate about Greece, and wanted to see it regain its place as leader of the western cultural world. He was born in the village of Lavovo, near Ioannina, in 1800, became a Major in the army and had been involved in Greek liberation movements before becoming an extremely active farm administrator and then landowner in Romania.

On 10 January 1852 the German archaeologist Professor Ernst Curtius of the University of Berlin gave a rather romantic lecture in which he stated that the Games would be revived. This came to Zappas's ears and he proposed to King Otto I (who had been installed as King of the Hellenes by the French and Germans in 1829, after much of southern Greece had been liberated from the Turks), that an Olympic contest be held. Since it was to be entirely financed by Zappas, Otto agreed and in 1858 Zappas gave shares and money to the Greek government to establish an Olympic Trust Fund, whose purpose was to organise competitions at four-year intervals, on the occasion of Greek industrial and agricultural fairs. The first festival, a combination of fair, exhibition and athletic events, took place at Athens in 1859. Zappas's intention to repeat the Contest every four years came to nothing, a failure which caused him great unhappiness in his last years. Nevertheless, when he died in 1865 he left the greater part of his immense fortune to the Olympic Trust Fund, in order that it might restore the Games. His request that a stadium be built at Athens was not acted upon, but in 1870 the second competition took place on a site outside Athens which had been acquired by the Fund.[37]

Later Games were held in 1875 and 1889, but it appears that they were insignificant. However, those of 1870 were serious enough for there to be some dispute about whether Coubertin's Games should be seen as the beginning of something entirely new or as the continuation of a pre-existing series. Those who wish to magnify the purely Greek achievement and correspondingly to downgrade Coubertin's, believe that Zappas's efforts and the enthusiasm which the Games evoked meant that the modern Olympic movement had been born years before Coubertin's Congress of 1894. Young goes so far as to claim that Coubertin feigned amnesia about these earlier Games. He states that the Greek press regarded Coubertin as a thief when he claimed the credit for reviving them, since they had already been revived in 1859. 'The Greeks fought to keep the Games, but Coubertin spirited them away to Paris.'[38]

It is an exaggeration to say that Coubertin was amnesic about Zappas and his brother Constantine, for he records that the glorious name of the Olympic Games had been applied to artistic, industrial and athletic events, thanks to the brothers' munificence. But, Coubertin argues, his own project was different, because it was international, whereas those of Zappas resembled the ancient Games in drawing athletes only from the Greek world.[39] Much later he wrote that there existed in Athens a permanent Commission to administer the Zappas Foundation, and that he and his collaborators had counted on it as the embryo of the future organisation. At the same time he further underlines the difference between the brothers' achievements and his own plans by pointing out that their wish that athletic events should be held in the Zappeion, an exhibition building which they had financed, had been frustrated by the Romanian government having seized part of their heritage, so preventing their Will being put into effect.[40]

The Congress of 1894

In 1894 Coubertin arranged an international Congress, at which the decision was taken to revive the Olympic Games. However, it has been alleged that he misled the delegates by causing them to think that they were to attend a conference primarily on amateurism, at which the Games would be of relatively minor importance.[41]

To say that he misled the delegates may be an exaggeration, but he certainly displayed the neat political footwork which remains such a noticeable feature of the Olympic movement today. His own account of the genesis of the Congress, in a book published in 1931, only six years before his death, gives a full and frank account of the matter. Its tone is often almost frivolous; without a doubt he looked back with pleasure at the finesse that he had shown.

Coubertin recounts that he used the fifth anniversary of the Union des Sociétés Françaises de Sports Athlétiques (USFSA) in November 1892 to float the idea of reviving the Games. He had expected almost any response to the speech in which he argued for their revival, except the one that it in fact received. There was applause and no opposition, but also, he complains, no understanding of his desire to revive the essence or principle of Olympism. Looking back, one can see that this failure need not have been surprising, because, as he goes on, in those days sporting organisations found it extraordinarily difficult to collaborate. A man was a fencer or an oarsman or a cyclist, but did not have the Olympic ideal of being simply a sportsman.

The winter of 1892 to 1893 passed without his idea catching on at all, whereas he had expected it to make enough of an impression to assure the success of an international Congress. It was this lack of

public interest in Olympism that led him initially to make amateurism
the focus of the Congress. His next step was to cause the USFSA to
decide at its General Assembly in the summer of 1893 that a Congress
should be held and to approve a preliminary programme. In his
speech to the General assembly of the USFSA Coubertin explained
why the question of amateurism needed study but did not on this
occasion again directly advocate the revival of the Olympic Games (as
he had done in the previous November), although he did refer to the
stringent conditions of amateurism that they imposed. This time his
emphasis was on the need for the Union to settle the question of
amateurism for its own purposes, in order that it might be able to
strengthen its internal organisation, widen its influence in the French
provinces, and establish relations with foreign unions.

He argued that money was threatening to corrupt athleticism: bets
were struck; professionals did not run for the sake of physical and
mental strength in the service of their country, but in order to earn as
much as possible. Furthermore, it had to be said that if the athlete
was, for example, a cyclist, money was not lacking, for once a cyclist
was well known he could obtain subventions from bicycle manufacturers and from organisers of cycling meets. (These practices
would now be called sponsorship and appearance money.) There had
also grown up, almost everywhere, a class of individuals whose right
hand certified their amateur status, while the left accepted the metal of
corruption under the counter. The students of England and America
would not accept this corruption of their ideals (the English reference
is to the young Oxford men who had established the Amateur Athletic
Association), and the Union's own leading position gave it the
authority required to hold the international Congress that had been
arranged for 1894.

Coubertin was disappointed that his great idea still failed to catch
on after the USFSA had adopted it. He spent four months in the USA
at the end of 1893, but found no one excited about his project except
Professor W. M. Sloane of Princeton, who had given a dinner at which
there had been goodwill and interest but evident expectation of
failure. He received the same impression, but even more markedly, in
London in February 1894. Nor was there any interest in Germany,
despite the efforts Coubertin made to draw the Germans in. Indeed
these efforts made matters worse, because the French gymnasts were
furious at his overtures to the Germans, and threatened to withdraw if
the Germans did join.[42] As it turned out, there were no German

representatives at the Congress, as Coubertin rather acidly observed.[43]

The programme adopted by the USFSA included eight Articles, (that
is, headings for discussion), six on amateurism, one on betting and the
last on the possibility of re-establishing the Olympic Games. (We may
note in passing that, so far as is known, betting has never been in
evidence at the Olympics, although certain bookmakers will take bets
on events in which they have sufficient expertise to be able to judge the
odds. However, it had been very much a feature of athletics meets in
England, and Coubertin must have been aware of this, as he was of the
general deterioration of the Olympic ideal in England.)
    The suggestion that Coubertin misled the delegates to the Congress
rests upon the fact that there were two programmes for it. The first
had been agreed in the summer of 1893 and printed in January 1894,
when it was sent out to athletic and other sporting associations all over
the world. The second, Coubertin records, was published at the
beginning of 1894. It contained the dates and place of the Congress,
11–24 June (eventually it lasted from 16–23 June) at the Sorbonne,
named eight Vice-Presidents and added two new Articles to the earlier
list. The most important new development, he says, was that the list
was now divided into two sections, thus giving far greater prominence
to the objective of reviving the Olympic Games.[44] The first section
consisted of the first seven of the original eight Articles; the second
contained the original eighth Article and two new ones, providing for
Olympic rules and the establishment of a committee to run the
Games. It was this enlarged agenda which appeared just after the
Congress in the Olympic Committee's first official bulletin.[45]
    It seems, therefore, that Young may well be right when he suggests
that delegates learned only from their admission tickets that the
Congress was to be so much concerned with the revival of the Games,
for although the ten-Article version had been ready at the beginning of
1894 it was not printed until May.[46] Coubertin is no doubt correct
when he recalls that the letters of invitation referred to a Congress for
the re-establishment of the Olympic Games, but if they were sent out
as late as the end of May there may have been a number of delegates
who did not receive them in advance. Be that as it may, Coubertin
claims to have known within hours of the beginning of the Congress
that there would be no opposition to his project.[47]
    The guiding trinity throughout the whole operation were

C. Herbert, Secretary of the Amateur Athletic Association 'for
England and the British Empire'; W. M. Sloane, for the American
continent, and Coubertin himself for France and western Europe. His
two colleagues were crucial because Herbert had an organised propaganda network through the AAA and Sloane dominated American
athletics to the extent that, as Coubertin had noticed in 1889, no one
could do anything without him.[48]

The delegates divided into two commissions on the Games – and
on amateurism – and the report of the commission on the Games
was accepted without opposition at the final session. The President of
the commission was D. Bikelas, of the Société Panhellénique de
Gymnastique (who became the first President of the International
Olympic Committee) and its Vice-Presidents Sloane, R. Todd, dele-
gate of the International Cyclist's (sic) Union and Baron Carayon la
Tour of the Société Hippique Française.

The commission on the Games met the conditions on which
Coubertin had always insisted. The Games were to be held at four-
year intervals; they were not to imitate the ancient Games, but to be
exclusively modern in character – what mattered was the spirit of
Olympism rather than the specific nature of the events; the Games for
boys between the ages of twelve and eighteen were not to be reproduced: in the absence of birth certificates they had given great trouble
to the judges. Coubertin was also to have full responsibility for the
designation of an international committee whose members would
represent Olympism in their countries.

That the first Games should be at Athens in 1896 had not been in
Coubertin's original plan, as he had not expected an enfeebled Greece
('les forces juvéniles de la Grèce ressuscité') to be capable of organising them. He had thought of holding them at Paris in the first
years of the twentieth century, but he had been charmed by Bikelas
into changing his mind, although even Bikelas had been somewhat
nervous about Athens's ability to arrange so important an event.

As for the commission on amateurism, the general principle of
amateurism was established, but the report of the commission was not
easily agreed, and provoked a good deal of discussion on report-back
to the full Congress. There was general disapproval (even expressed
by the delegates from England, and from Australia, where similar
restrictions obtained) of the (English) Amateur Rowing Association's
exclusion of labourers from membership, and a definition of 'amateur'
was accepted which omitted this provision. It was also agreed that a

distinction must be made between reward and compensation (for loss of earnings), and that, very exceptionally, unions, federations and societies might allow encounters between amateurs and professionals, provided that the prizes offered were not in money. The question of gate-money (Coubertin uses the English expression) preoccupied the commission, and it was agreed that in no circumstances should any part of it be paid directly to athletes, but only to their parent associations. However, the possibility of those associations passing on compensation to the athletes was not excluded.

There were some exceptions to the prohibition of money prizes. These were in yachting, horse-racing and archery. The item caused especially lively discussion, as many delegates thought it unfair to release the rich from rules which still bound the poor. Some delegates thought the difficulty so great that they wanted to limit the Congress's competence to purely athletic sports, but it reached the general conclusion that money prizes were not indispensable in any sport. No amateur in one sport could be a professional in another and in all sports except fencing Olympic competitions were to be organised only by amateurs.

A subject which worries many in the Olympic movement today raised its head, namely the question of heats. The Congress decided that in each country, and in every sport, there should be preliminary contests, so that only true champions should take part in the Olympic Games themselves.[49] Other principles were established which still guide the Olympic movement. The members of the International Olympic Committee were to be the representatives overseas of Olympism, rather than their countries' representatives on the committee and each country was to establish a National Olympic Committee.

One principle which did not survive long was that, although the IOC's administration was to be permanently in Paris, the presidency of the Committee should revolve, passing after each Games to the country which had been chosen to host the next.[50] Under that rule Bikelas was the first President, and Coubertin took over after the Athens games of 1896, as the Games of 1900 were to be in Paris. However, Coubertin was then asked to continue as President, and, as we have seen, remained in office until 1925.

The Games of 1896

According to Coubertin's own account, the King of the Hellenes had telegraphed to the 1894 Congress that he favoured the idea of holding the Games at Athens. Nevertheless, Coubertin experienced considerable difficulty in persuading the Greek government actually to follow the Congress's wish and hold them. A committee had been promptly set up in Paris to organise the Athens Games and, as has been noted above, it had counted on the permanent commission which administered the Zappas Foundation to provide an organisation in Athens. However, the Prime Minister, Charilaos Tricoupis, was determined that the Games should not be held in Greece.

The Prime Minister's opposition was made known through intermediaries. A letter of 1 November 1894 to Coubertin from Etienne Dragoumis, a member of the Zappeion Commission, says that Greece is very honoured to be asked to hold the Games, but that it is a new country, where much remains to be done, and that it cannot afford them. He suggests that it would be much better to attach them to some great international festival, such as the one that is to be held in Paris in 1900. He refers to Paris's great resources, and suggests that 1900, the beginning of a new century, would be a good starting date for the Games.

Coubertin was wily enough to have a second string (Budapest), in case the Greeks refused to hold the Games, and even mentioned in the *Bulletin* that this alternative existed, no doubt to give the Greeks a coded warning that he was serious.[51] But he was not immediately successful. On a visit to Athens in November 1894 he spent his first day leaving cards, and on the second Tricoupis came to see him at the Hotel Grande Bretagne, where Coubertin was receiving the French chargé d'affaires. It is not clear whether the Prime Minister called by appointment, nor whether Coubertin had timed the French diplomat's visit with that in mind: it must, in any case have been something of a coup for Coubertin to have the Prime Minister call on him, rather than the other way about. He records that Tricoupis was cordial but still refused to accept the Games.

At the same time a political row was brewing in Greece about the Games. The people who most wanted them were the small businessmen and the cab drivers. Coubertin avoided commenting to the press, but accepted an invitation to give a lecture arranged by the literary society Parnassus.[52] He spoke to an audience of seven hundred, 'from all classes of Athenian society' and, having explained the Paris Congress's thinking about the Olympic Games, ended with a eulogy of modern Greece, which received enthusiastic applause. He had also taken the precaution of going to see the Crown Prince (who had accepted the presidency of the organising committee), and Prince Nicholas, the King's third son. Both had promised active and enthusiastic support.

Coubertin's lecture was well received by the newspapers. As a result Tricoupis markedly changed his tune. He still refused to commit the government, but his attitude became benevolent, and he authorised the Zappeion Commission to help organise the Games. The next step was to set up a fund-raising committee, although Coubertin noted that it was not greatly needed. However, the picture was not entirely satisfactory, since the Crown Prince, who was acting as Regent (because his father was away in Russia for Alexander III's funeral), did not think that, as Regent, he could go to its first meeting, on 1 November 1894, despite the enthusiasm that he had expressed. Nor was any help forthcoming from the Zappeion Commission.

Coubertin recalls that, once he had left Athens for Paris, one of his Vice-Presidents worked against him, and the committee left to the Prince the decision about whether the Games would be held, expecting that he would decide against them. However, he left the decision in the air, saying that he wanted time to think. This annoyed Tricoupis greatly, and Coubertin believed that it had an influence on his fall from office in 1895.

The Prince then took over the committee and reconstituted it, appointing as Secretary-General a former Mayor of Athens, Timoleon Philemon, who set up a 'véritable ministère Olympique'. Everyone wanted to join the 'ministère Philemon' and gifts of money poured in, not just from Greece, but from Greek colonies in Marseilles, Alexandria and London. Special stamps were issued, whose sale yielded more than would have come from the lottery that the government had refused to allow.

Meanwhile Coubertin was extremely active. As none of his Greek collaborators knew anything about the design of cycle-racing tracks he studied the one at Arcachon, and sent a preliminary sketch to Athens. He was also under pressure from the Greeks to tell them exactly how many visitors and competitors to expect at the Games. He had had to prepare the invitation list himself, and the Greeks, who, he comments, naturally thought the whole world was as interested as

they were, were astonished that he could not give them the
information, fourteen months in advance.

Indeed, attracting visitors and persuading athletes to participate
was not plain sailing. The archers would take no part, because they
did not wish to lose their independence and appear to be an offshoot of
the French National Olympic Committee. There was powerful opposition among Frenchmen, who wanted revenge for 1870, to international Games involving the Germans. So deep was the hostility that
'The French sporting press virtually ignored the Games, not only in
1896 but also in several succeeding meetings.'[53] There were few
French visitors, and their athletes needed subventions to get them
interested. The response from Sweden and Hungary was good, but
not from Belgium, thanks to a hostile campaign by the gymnasts'
federation, and in Britain there was sympathetic scepticism.

Coubertin worked out the programme, with the aid of experts, eliminating the sports that seemed inadequate, because in those days there
were no international federations (except the Cyclists, founded in
1892). He went on directing the programme until he decided that he
could hand over the technical details to such federations as had grown
up meanwhile.[54] In all other cases the rules were those of a national
association (for example, the English Amateur Athletic Association),
or were devised specially for the Olympic Games by one of the existing
associations. Coubertin regretted that polo, football and boxing were
omitted from the Athens programme, the last because the Paris
Congress had judged it an uncivilised sport. However, cricket was to
be included.[55]

Another hostile campaign, this time in Germany (which, it will be
remembered, had taken no part in the 1894 Congress), was based on
an interview which Coubertin was falsely said to have given, in which
he was alleged to have said that he would do everything he could to
stop the Germans participating in the Games, or coming to Athens.
However, a correspondent in Berlin wrote to Coubertin that he
thought his excellent letter of denial would be shown to the Kaiser:
'no one is unaware of how anxious His Majesty is to maintain good
relations with France' (original in French). A few days later the
German National Olympic Committee relented and eventually
Philemon, who had been infected by the German hostility, also got
over his irritation.

As the preparations advanced Coubertin was piqued to discover that, despite his years of effort, he was no longer needed in Athens. No one, he complains, mentioned him again, because the Greeks had become sure of success, and everyone conspired to forget France's part in reviving the Games. After all the trouble he had taken to persuade them, the Greeks were now delighted to have the Games, and assumed that they would continue to hold them every four years. Coubertin naturally decided that this was a quite unreasonable ambition: he would probably have thought the same in any case, but he would have been superhuman not to have been affected by the Greeks' undiplomatic behaviour.

Athens, he reasoned after the Games, had attracted visitors from all over Greece, but few foreigners (despite the efforts of Thomas Cook, who had been appointed official travel agents to the Games); there was no rail line to the rest of Europe, and there were few boats. He also thought that there would be endless political problems, which he did not specify, if Athens were permitted to retain the Games permanently. In short 'to locate the revived Games definitively and exclusively in Greece would be the suicide of my achievement,' (original in French).

The King had hinted at having the Games permanently in Greece, and the press wanted a law to that effect, arguing that Coubertin was stealing Greek property, and interrupting a series of revived Games which had begun in 1859. So serious was the situation that some IOC colleagues thought the IOC would have to dissolve itself. Coubertin, however, came up with a skillful compromise. He suggested to the Prince that there should be pan-Hellenic Games spaced between the Olympics. The Prince had thought of this too, and the King liked the idea, but the press were irritated, and Coubertin got some abusive letters.[56]

The only intermediate Games were held at Athens in 1906. They may even have saved the modern concept of international sport, because they were a success, whereas the Olympic Games that followed them in London in 1908 were 'scarred by loud and bitter charges of cheating and professionalism hurled back and forth between the British and the Americans'.[57] Be that as it may, they also fulfilled Coubertin's objective. As Diem says, having realised that he could not stop the Greeks from being convinced that they should permanently host the Olympics he had arranged the Athens Games as a palliative, but they provoked so much protest from other countries that no more was heard of the idea. Nobody wanted a parallel series of games – nor wished them always to be held in a Mediterranean country.[58]

Philemon's own account, in a booklet published shortly after the 1896 Games, of the politics behind them more or less corroborates Coubertin's version, except that he goes into far more detail over the difficulty of raising funds. The Crown Prince was convinced that Greece, however poor, must go ahead with the Games. The only solution was to raise funds from wealthy Greeks, both at home and abroad, but the moment was not propitious, because there had recently been earthquakes and other calamities in Greece. 'Many wealthy persons', he records, 'turned a deaf ear to the appeal while others stubbornly turned down the appeal, declaring that the matter was comic and destined to failure and the money would be spent in vain.'[59] In the end they collected three times as much as had at first been thought necessary, so to this extent Coubertin is correct when he says that contributions flowed in. However, the contributions were made slowly, but the stadium had to be rebuilt immediately. The answer was an appeal to George Averoff, who had already built the Athens Polytechnic, the Military Academy, the juvenile prison and other public buildings. Philemon went to see him in Alexandria, armed with a letter from the Crown Prince, and Averoff saved the day by paying for the stadium's renovation.

Philemon ends his account with a paean of praise to the Greek populace and manages to mention Coubertin only once. The King was even less gracious and did not mention him at all in his speech at a great banquet at the Palace in honour of the foreign athletes. (An American attended in bicycling shorts and only the Hungarians wore the regulation dark suit.) By contrast Coubertin himself proudly took credit, in his introduction to the booklet, for the revival of the Games.

'I claim its paternity with raised voice and I would like to thank once more here those who assisted me to bring it into wellbeing; those who, together with me, think that athletics will emerge greater and ennobled and that international youth will draw from it the love of peace and respect for life.'[60]

These first Games of the modern era were of course small beer compared with the vast circus that is now the norm. They included nine sports, forty-three events, 311 participants (230 of them Greek) from thirteen countries.[61] But they certainly seem to have generated great enthuasiasm in Greece coupled with a feeling that the Games belonged to Greece as of right. That continuing feeling is generally believed to have led the Athens team bidding for the centenary Games of 1996 into a state of over-confidence amounting almost to arrogance, which was one of the reasons for Athens's losing the contest to Atlanta.

Notes

1 For his views on Rugby see Coubertin's *L'Education en Angleterre: Collèges et Universités*, Paris, 1888. The chapter on Rugby is reprinted in Norbert Mueller (ed.), *Pierre de Coubertin: Textes Choisies*, Zürich, 1986, I, pp. 48–56.

2 For a fuller exposition of Coubertin's thinking see Marquis Melchior de Polignac's speech 'Baron Pierre de Coubertin' made at the IOC's Session in Stockholm in June 1947 to mark the tenth anniversary of his death. *Bulletin du Comité Olympique* (new series), 6, September 1947, pp. 12–15.

3 For details of the ancient Games see M. I. Finley and H. W. Pleket, *The Olympic Games: the First Thousand Years*, London, 1976, pp. 13 and 43 and *passim*.

4 This example is typical of his more flowery style of writing: Les temples, ce seront les *gymnases*, foyers de vie municipale assemblant adolescents, adultes, vieillards autour de cette préoccupation d'exalter la vie humaine qui est à la base de tout l'hellénisme et se reflète si nettement dans la conception d'un au-delà crépusculaire ou domine le regret du séjour terrestre.' 'Pédagogie Sportive', *Textes Choisies*, II, p. 33. (Reprinted from *Pédagogie Sportive*, Paris, 1922, pp. 11–24.)

5 'Pierre de Coubertin', a speech by Carl Diem to be delivered at the fiftieth anniversary celebration of the IOC at Lausanne, 17 and 18 June 1944, p. 6. (The text was printed in advance, and the speech duly delivered as planned.)

6 Polignac, p. 13.

7 David C. Young, *The Olympic Myth of Greek Amateur Athletics*, Chicago, 1984, especially pp. 89–102. He refers to several works by Pleket, in particular 'Games, Prizes, Athletes and Ideology', in *Arena*, 1, 1976, pp. 49–89. For a reference to the harmless professionalism of trainers in ancient times see Coubertin's *Mémoires Olympiques*, Lausanne, n.d., but 1931.

8 There is a version of this famous remark in John J. MacAloon's exhaustive study of Coubertin and the Origins of the Modern Olympic Games, *This Great Symbol: Pierre de Coubertin and the Origins of the Modern Olympic Games*, Chicago, 1981, p. 5.

9 'Demander aux peuples de s'aimer les uns les autres n'est qu'une manière d'enfantillage. Leur demander de se respecter n'est point une utopie, mais pour se respecter il faut d'abord se connaître.' Quoted by Diem, p. 13.

10 'Les fumées de la guerre ont obscurci l'éclat de la flamme, mais elles n'ont pu étouffer le feu olympique . . . Le sens profond de cette cérémonie est d'affermir la certitude qu'a l'avenir également l'olympisme manifestera sa force conciliatrice, pour le bien de l'humanité.' *ibid.*, p. 1.

11 I owe this nice observation to Christopher Richardson, lately head of Classics at Cranleigh School.

12 'C'est à coup sur une abérration que de refuser a un ouvrier la qualité d'amateur et d'assimiler le travail manuel a un acte de professionalisme. La discordance est aigue entre cette législation vétuste et notre siècle democratique. *Textes Choisies*, II, p. 560. (Reprinted from *Revue de Paris*, 15 June 1894, pp. 170–84.)

13 Diem, p. 6. Coubertin refers to amateurism as 'cette admirable momie' in *Memoires Olympiques*, p. 12.

14 *Revue Olympique*, May 1909, pp. 67–8, reprinted in *Textes Choisies*, II, pp. 576–7.

15 For example, Don Anthony, 'One Hundred Years of Olympism in Shropshire', typescript, January 1990.

16 See the Princess Royal's foreword to Sam Mullins, *British Olympians: William Penny Brookes and the Wenlock Games*, London, 1986. The President of the International Olympic Committee (IOC), Juan Antonio Samaranch, paid tribute to Brookes in his speech at the IOC's Session at Birmingham in June 1991. *Olympic Review*, 285, July 1991, p. 308.

17 Minute of 25 February 1850.

18 Olympian Society, *Annual Report* for the year to 1 March 1871.

19 *The Shrewsbury Chronicle and Shropshire and Montgomeryshire Times*, 19 October 1877, Minute Book 2, p. 14. Cuttings and other documents are pasted into the Society's Minute Books, which are preserved at the Much Wenlock Corn Exchange.

20 *The Standard*, 30 September 1878, Minute Book 2, p. 28.

21 *National Physical Recreation*, March 1888, Minute Book 2, p. 135.

22 Sir Roger Bannister, letter to *The Times*, 7 August 1990.

23 Peter Lovesey, *The Official Centenary History of the Amateur Athletic Association*, London, 1979, p. 17–21.

24 *The Shrewsbury Chronicle and Shropshire and Montgomeryshire Times*, 28 September 1877.

25 *ibid.*, 19 October 1877.

26 *Address* for the year 1880 to the committee of the Olympian Society, Minute Book 2, pp. 52–3.

27 Gennadius to Brookes, Minute Book 2, p. 59.

28 Original cutting from *Clio*, June 13/25 1881, at Minute Book 2, p. 65, and translation at p. 66.

29 Gennadius to Brookes, 23 June 1886, Minute Book 2, p. 138.

30 *Revue Athlétique*, vol I, 1, 23 January 1890. Minute Book 2, p. 144. Reprinted in *Textes Choisies*, II, pp. 78–84.

31 *Revue Athlétique*, vol. I, 12, 25 December 1890. In July 1990 the Princess Royal, in her capacity as President of the British Olympic Association, attended the Games held to mark the centenary of Coubertin's visit.

32 Coubertin to Brookes, 20 July 1892, Minute Book 2, p. 206.

33 *Minutes* of meeting of the Olympian Society, 24 May 1894, Minute Book 2, p. 218.

34 *The Wellington Journal and Shrewsbury News*, 8 June 1895, Minute Book 2, p. 229.

35　Brookes to Coubertin, 14 December 1895, IOC archives, Lausanne. Brookes, who died on 10 December 1895, misdated the letter. Internal evidence shows that he intended to write 1894.

36　*Revue Athlétique*, 25 December 1890. Translation (cyclostyled) by Michael Gillions, sometime Head of Modern Languages at the William Brookes School, Much Wenlock. It is curious that Brookes's gift to the 1859 Games was a cup, since letters from Sir Thomas Wyse, H.M. Ambassador at Athens, refer to it as a money prize, and an enclosure to his letter of 15 July 1859 states that the winner of the race 'sponsored' by Much Wenlock received $281^2/_{100}$ drachmas in addition to the 100 drachmas received by the winners of other events. If Sir Thomas was right, it appears that Brookes was underwriting the professionalism which he so much deplored. (Wyse's letters are in a letter book of the Wenlock Agricultural Reading Society.)

37　In the preceding two paragraphs I have drawn especially on Young, *op. cit.*, and on M. I. Finley and H. W. Pleket *op. cit.* I am also most grateful to Dr Karel Wendl for sight of some unpublished notes on Zappas dated 12 January 1990.

According to Finley and Pleket, Curtius had been tutor to the future Wilhelm I, who, with Friedrich Wilhelm IV, had been in the audience at the 1852 lecture. Two years later, when Wilhelm I came to the throne of the new united Germany, the Germans agreed to bear the cost of a full-scale Olympic excavation. From 1875 to 1881 much was discovered under Curtius's direction, and promptly published each year, so that people like Coubertin were able to follow the progress of the dig.

38　Young, pp. 28 and 71–2 for the view that Coubertin continued an existing tradition. According to Young, pp. 32–4, a few people had complained that some labouring men had competed in the 1870 Games, so that those of 1875 were reserved for educated youths only. They were universally judged a failure. For the 'equally disastrous' Games of 1889 see Young, pp. 40–3.

39　*Bulletin du Comité International des Jeux Olympiques*, 2, January 1895, p. 3.

40　Pierre de Coubertin, 'Une Compagne de Vingt-et-un Ans (1887–1908)', Paris 1909, from which extracts are reproduced in *Textes Choisies*, II, pp. 115–23 and 131–47. This reference p. 131.

41　See, for example, Young, pp. 179–81.

42　*Mémoires Olympiques*, and Coubertin's speech to the 1893 Congress of USFSA, *Les Sports Athlétiques*, vol. 4, 172, 13 July 1893, pp. 2–4, reprinted in *Textes Choisies*, II, pp. 99–103.

43　*Bulletin*, 2, p. 4.

44　Coubertin, *Mémoires Olympiques*, pp. 13–15.

45　*Bulletin*, 1, July 1894, pp. 1–2.

46　Young, p. 63. Young goes a long way towards clearing up the confusion between the circular of January 1894, in which Coubertin merely referred to the desirability of re-establishing the Games, and the definitive programme of the following May, which included the ninth and tenth Articles.

47　*Mémoires Olympiques*, p. 18.

48 *Bulletin*, 1, July 1894, p. 1 and *Mémoires Olympiques*, p. 13.
49 *Bulletin*, 1, p. 4 and *Mémoires Olympiques*, pp. 19–20. The reference to 'les forces juvéniles' is at p. 19.
50 *Bulletin*, 2, October 1894, p. 1 and *Mémoires Olympiques*, p. 21.
51 *Bulletin*, 3, January 1895, p. 2.
52 The fact that he made the speech is rather blandly recorded in *Bulletin*, 3, p. 2, with extracts at p. 4.
53 Finley and Pleket, p. 5.
54 Diem, p. 8.
55 *Bulletin*, 3, pp. 1 and 2.
56 Except where otherwise indicated the preceding passage is based on Coubertin's 'Une Compagne de Vingt-et-un Ans (1887–1908)', pp. 131–47. See also *Mémoires Olympiques*, pp. 28–42. According to Gaston Meyer the King had done more than hint. Advised by Philemon and backed by a petition from the American athletes he had publicly suggested at the closing banquet in 1896 that Coubertin should fall in with his wishes or resign. Coubertin, however, had pretended not to understand. Gaston Meyer, 'Paris 1900' in Lord Killanin and John Rodda (eds.) *The Olympic Games 1984*, London, 1983, p. 57.
57 Young, p. 75. John Rodda gives this view qualified support, but adds that the 1906 Games turned out to be disappointing because many events were not contested. 'Athens 1906' in Killanin and Rodda (eds.), p. 67. It is noteworthy, as an indication that the Greeks had become reconciled to not being permanent hosts to the Games, that when Lord Desborough announced that the 1908 Games were to be held in London he was able to add that a message of good wishes had been received from the Greek Crown Prince. *The Daily Telegraph, letter from Lord Desborough and editorial comment, 24 November 1906. (Cutting in Dr Brookes's scrapbook, inserted between items dating from 1864.)*
58 Diem, p. 9.
59 The booklet is ponderously entitled *The Olympic Games in 776 BC to 1896 AD: the Olympic Games of 1896*, by The Baron de Coubertin, Timoleon I. Philemon, N. G. Politis and Charalambos Anninos. It was originally printed in 1896 in Greek and French by Charles Beck in Athens and H. Lesaudier in Paris and appeared in a facsimile edition, with an English translation, in 1966. Philemon's contribution is at pp. 111–20 and the quotation at p. 116 (English version).
60 Pierre de Coubertin, Introduction to the above, p. 110.
61 Otto Szymiczek, 'Athens 1896' in Killanin and Rodda (eds.), p. 54. Finley and Pleket give slightly different figures, stating that there were ten sports, forty-two events and 285 participants and add that the gymnasts were the only athletes to compete as a team.

II

The primacy of politics in the Olympic movement

We have seen that without Baron de Coubertin's political instincts and skills the Olympic Games might not have been revived and that had not his self-esteem been as vulnerable as the next man's they might have remained perpetually in Athens. Since those far-off Games of 1896 almost every celebration of the Olympics has been fraught with politics. The Games of 1916, 1940 and 1944 were not held at all, and after the Second World War West Germany and Japan did not compete until 1952, when it was thought that the bitterness of mass destruction had sufficiently subsided.

The Olympic Games have not been alone in their political involvement, but their great public exposure has meant that the stakes have been higher and the need for circumspection correspondingly greater than in other sports organisations. Nevertheless, all sports have had to take a view on questions of international politics. In bridge (known as a 'mind sport' in some countries) where some sixty nations are represented in the world championships, the problem of how to deal with the enmity between Israel and numerous other countries has been solved by ensuring that nations which will not compete against Israel are drawn in separate qualifying pools, with the hope, so far fulfilled, that two incompatible nations will not both qualify for the later stages.[1]

Just as it is not possible for sports people to abstract themselves from politics, so it is impossible to keep politicians out of sport if they can discern some advantage in making use of it. It would not, for example, have been reasonable to expect to persuade a politician like President Richard Nixon, or groups of private individuals like SANROC (the South African Non-Racial Olympic Committee) not to use sport as a political instrument. The battle against apartheid was strengthened by the well-judged campaign of SANROC to force international sports federations to expel South Africa and it would have been pointless to have asked SANROC not to use the sporting weapon which lay to hand. Some teams made the decision, no less political, to go ahead with tours of South Africa despite their governments' advice. The fact that governments had to give such advice (most famously in the shape of the statement made in 1977 by Commonwealth Heads of Government, known as the Gleneagles Declaration), when many of them would no doubt have much preferred to 'keep sport out of politics' demonstrates how powerful were the forces tapped by SANROC.

Sport may look like a continuation of war by other means but, as a leading sports administrator, Sir Athur Gold (who has experienced both sport and war), has wisely said, it is not difficult to decide which of the two one prefers.[2] However, some sports people go so far as to argue that sport actually promotes peace. If this is taken to mean that athletic competition promotes a camaraderie which inhibits hostility, there is not much evidence to support it in top level sport, and some against. High level sport is now so closely linked with large sums of hard cash that there is little room for friendship, and investigation of the idea that interaction on the sports field produces friendly feelings has shown that the thesis is by no means necessarily true, at any level. One author goes so far as to describe the relations between Olympic athletes as 'an incidental by-product of these quadrennial political festivals where athletic events happen to take place'.[3]

On the other hand, it is clearly true that sporting contacts are from time to time used by governments as the prelude to contact at a more formal level. One has only to remember President Richard Nixon's 'ping-pong diplomacy' which paved the way for his visit to China in 1972 and to the opening of diplomatic relations between the United States and China on 1 January 1978, or the new willingness of the two Koreas to speak to each other since the Seoul Olympics of 1988.

The Olympic Games may be an effective way of bringing the youth of the world together, though if that were their sole aim it could be far better achieved by spending a fraction of their cost on scholarships. However, nearly every celebration of the Games has been marked by acrimony or worse and the recollections of contretemps or disaster long outlive the warm glow of competitive interaction. A catalogue would be tedious, but it is worth remembering that other Games than those held in Berlin in 1936 have provoked international outrage. For example, 1968 saw a massacre by the Mexican government of young people who thought the Games a waste of money. Israeli athletes were murdered by Palestinians at the Munich Games of 1972, when the outgoing President of the International Olympic Committee, Avery Brundage, decided that 'The Games must go on'. In 1976 numerous African states boycotted the Games in protest against a rugby tour of South Africa undertaken by a New Zealand side. The protesters demanded that the IOC should bar New Zealand from the Games, which it of course had no reason to do, since rugby was not even an Olympic sport.[4]

The IOC has not sought political involvement, but has had it thrust upon it. South Africa's suspension from the movement (it last took part in the Games at Rome in 1960) is probably the issue known to the widest public, but in their time the problems of the two Chinas and the two Germanies, both now settled, caused as much anguish. Such issues as whether Rhodesia should continue to be recognised by the IOC after its rebellion in 1965, or whether the IOC should recognise NOCs from both North and South Korea, attracted rather less public attention, but were no less difficult to solve.

The IOC's conduct of policy has generally been consistent, statesmanlike and above all slow. It believes that political questions must be settled by politicians, so that its leaders frequently protest against the use made by politicians of sport, while themselves being obliged to act politically. Its overall objective has been to preserve the movement's universality, if necessary by postponing choice. In those terms, South Africa was a failure of Olympic diplomacy, because in 1970, after many years of negotiation, the decision could no longer be put off to withdraw recognition from its NOC, thereby expelling the Republic from the Olympic movement. Though expulsion was in some eyes a failure, South Africa's reinstatement in 1991 is by many seen as a triumph. The two Chinas were a qualified success because in the end both the mainland and Taiwan remained in the movement (after a long period of withdrawal by the mainland) and the two Germanies an unqualified success, because both parts of the country, once admitted, were kept in the movement through thick and thin.

The remainder of this chapter develops further the account of the questions of the two Germanies and the two Chinas, as examples of the Olympic movement's involvement in international politics since the Second World War.

The two Germanies

In 1950 the International Olympic Committee provisionally recognised the West German Olympic Committee. It seems likely that the IOC was influenced by a letter written to Lord Burghley by the British High Commissioner a few days earlier, in which he expressed the most earnest hope that the new Federal Republic of Germany might be allowed to compete in the Helsinki Games of 1952. The provisional recognition given in 1950 did not, however, commit the IOC to allow West German participation at Helsinki: that decision was to be taken a year later at Vienna.[5]

At the Vienna Session (that is, the IOC's annual full meeting), which was also memorable for the introduction of the Soviet member, Constantin Andrianov, and with him the first interpreter, the West German NOC received full recognition, but there was considerable debate about whether it was a new body, or whether it had continued to exist through the war. The main point of the debate was to decide whether the pre-war German IOC members should be allowed to remain in office, or whether new ones should be elected to symbolise Germany's break with the past. One of them, the Duke of Mecklenburg, solved the problem by retiring because of age, so that discussion focused on Dr Karl Ritter von Halt. No one attacked him personally, but there was lively feeling that a new member was needed. One argument used was that such a move would convince the athletes that a new spirit was abroad. On the other hand, the IOC's establishment was strongly in favour of von Halt. The American Avery Brundage, the IOC's President 1952–72, described him as a perfect gentleman, with whom he had taken part in the Stockholm Games of 1912, and J. Sigfrid Edstrom, the IOC's President, refused to put the question to the vote, simply declaring that von Halt remained a member. Protests led him to defer a final decision until after the discussion of East Germany's status, but he got his way, and von Halt (who had been elected in 1929) remained a member until 1964.[6]

The question of the East German NOC had only impinged upon the IOC when separate East German federations sought international affiliation. The Executive Board of the IOC had sent out a circular to international federations (IFs) in 1949 recommending the re-recognition of German and Japanese federations, but the recommendation provoked unease at the Session in Copenhagen in the following year, because it did not reflect the general feeling of the IOC membership.[7] It appears that the IOC then urged the international federations to delay their decisions until it could consider the German question in full session at Vienna in May 1951.[8] At Vienna the discussion of whether or not the East German NOC should be recognised was lively. Some members argued that the basis of the Olympic Charter was its duty to bring the youth of the world together and that they should assist the two Germanies to reunite. The IOC was not, after all, one member said, discussing the recognition of a state, but of an NOC. However, another said that NOCs could not be recognised unless they were based in 'regular' states. The Soviet Union naturally wanted an independent NOC for its satellite and Andrianov, although a new member, took a full part in the discussion, arguing that both Germanies must be equally treated, but other members thought that to recognise two German NOCs would be to entrench the division between them – and by implication between the two Germanies.

Edstrom announced after long debate that East German representatives were waiting in the next room (it is not clear whether the generality of members were expecting them, or whether Edstrom was indulging in a theatrical gesture) and after an interval it was announced that the IOC's Executive Board and representatives of both Germanies were to meet at Lausanne a fortnight later. The Board was to have full powers, including removal of West Germany's recognition if necessary. Meanwhile the two sets of German representatives were to negotiate, so that the Lausanne meeting might not be required.[9] Agreement was reached at Lausanne that a united German team would be formed, but was immediately repudiated by the East Germans.[10]

A richly farcical second attempt was made at Copenhagen, in the hope that East Germany would be able to compete in the Helsinki Games of 1952. Edstrom, Brundage and Otto Mayer, the Chancellor of the IOC (the title was later changed to Executive Director, although Monique Berlioux described herself as Director-General) made a special visit to Copenhagen, where they and the West Germans arrived punctually for a 9 a.m. meeting. However, the East German delegation, which was known to have been in Copenhagen at least since 2 p.m., did not respond to several telephone calls, so that at 6 p.m. the IOC and West Germans left in an extremely disgruntled state, and naturally found it difficult to take the East Germans seriously in future. In the absence of any agreement it was, of course, not possible for them to compete at Helsinki. It appears that the East Germans arrived late in Copenhagen because they had had to travel via Prague, but were prevented from keeping their appointment largely by fear of their government (compounded by exhaustion), although in that case it is not clear why they ever undertook the journey at all.[11]

One of the most important discussions of the German question was held at the IOC's session at the time of the Helsinki Games. Several members spoke in favour of recognising East Germany's NOC, and Edstrom recalled the precedents of Bohemia, whose NOC had been recognised although the territory had been an integral part of the Austro-Hungarian Empire, and of Finland, which had been self-governing but annexed to Russia.[12] Brundage was, as one might expect after his experience at Copenhagen, extremely opposed to the East German Olympic authorities, whom he described as irresponsible, and von Halt recounted that all efforts to reach an accommodation with the East had failed. Every possible concession had been made, including allowing the East's team to have its own team managers, umpires, uniform, and separate lodgings, but they had refused to parade with the West.

Von Halt also had no objection to international federations affiliating local East German branches and indeed some had already done so, although most were waiting on a decision by the IOC.[13] Thus the IOC was in a dilemma, for if it delayed a decision the IFs might be pushed into going ahead without it, thereby weakening the IOC's authority. Yet it would not have been unreasonable for them to do so, for some IFs must have feared that their own authority would be weakened if they delayed recognition and thereby encouraged states to sponsor athletes directly, without reference to the appropriate IF. Once provisional recognition had been granted to East Germany's NOC, many international Federations did follow the IOC's lead. For example, Burghley, who was both President of the International Amateur Athletic Federation (IAAF) and a member of the IOC, persuaded the East and West Germans into a single athletics federation, but with two addresses. But, as with the two Chinas, not all international federations followed suit, because the call from the IOC for co-operation was seen by some of the international federations as a threat.[14]

So disillusioned was Brundage with the East Germans that he asked Andrianov to negotiate with them on the IOC's behalf.[15] At the next session Brundage referred to the torrent of abuse hurled at the IOC in the East German press, but Andrianov was able to report that the East German NOC, although unrecognised, was functioning normally and that it would be wrong for the IOC to deprive East German youth of the possibility of Olympic sport, or to keep East Germany out of the 1956 Games. He added that the President of the East German NOC had wished to attend in person to present his apologies for the bad press coverage, but had been unable to obtain a visa to travel to Athens.

Von Halt reminded his colleagues of his deep commitment to a united German team, but thought that the IOC must be bound by the principle that NOCs are independent and autonomous, and considered the East German NOC a striking example of the opposite. Von Halt himself did not feel that he could resume negotiations after the attacks to which he had been subjected, including faked photographs (of what he does not say). The East German NOC was refused recognition by 31 votes to 13.[16]

At Paris in 1955, the year in which the Soviet Union released East Germany from its status as the Soviet Zone of Germany and recognised it as a sovereign state, the East German NOC was provisionally recognised, but only on condition that it co-operated in forming the single team on which the IOC insisted. Brundage reviewed the history of the IOC's unhappy relationship with East Germany. He had told its representatives that he did not think the IOC would wish to deal again with the individuals who had repudiated the Lausanne agreement, but that it might reopen the question if the NOC were reorganised and represented by more responsible delegates.

A few days earlier the NOC had duly been re-formed and a meeting had been held at which Brundage had said that he would recommend provisional recognition once a united team had been formed to compete at the Melbourne Games of the following year. The East Germans, however, had said that in view of their definite promise to co-operate with West Germany they expected immediate recognition. It was agreed by 27 votes to 7 to grant provisional recognition 'on the understanding that, should it prove impossible to form a united team from both Germanies for the Melbourne Games this recognition will lapse automatically. It is understood that after the reunification of Germany, the IOC will recognise one German Olympic Committee, standing for the whole of Germany.'[17] It would have been difficult for the IOC to grant recognition on any other terms, given that the West

German response to the Soviet Union's recognition of East Germany
had been to enunciate what came to be known as the Hallstein
Doctrine, whereby West Germany refused to maintain or to enter into
diplomatic relations with any country that recognised East Germany.

So successful were negotiations between the two Germanies that
they were able, against all expectations, to enter a joint team for the
winter Games at Cortina d'Ampezzo as well as for Melbourne later in
the year. The athletes were to share flag, emblem, uniform and
lodgings; the head of the contingent was to be drawn from the larger
team, and the best athletes were to be chosen from both sides (it
sounds, therefore, as if the trials themselves were not mixed).
Brundage enthused 'We have obtained in the field of sport what
politicians have failed to achieve so far.' He was, however, displeased
by East German newspaper articles warning their athletes not to lose
sight of the political question.[18]

The provisional recognition of East Germany continued and the
Germans competed as a joint team at Rome in 1960 and Tokyo in
1964. There were many difficulties. In 1962, as a consequence of the
erection of the Berlin Wall in the same year, both the French and the
Americans refused visas to East Germans for world championships.
The IOC's response was to point out that French, American and
Canadian cities were bidding for the Games of 1968, and to threaten to
reject them if their governments did not mend their behaviour. East
Germany continued to ask for separate recognition, though with
assurances that if it were not granted it would still compete on the
current terms. NATO wished the joint team to continue, but the West
Germans were also beginning to want a separate team of their own.[19]

When the question, having been deferred from Tokyo, was discussed at Madrid in 1965, the President said that complete recognition of the East German NOC would imply two separate teams being
entered for the winter and summer Games of 1968 at Grenoble and
Mexico City. The latter presented no problem, but he believed that
for Grenoble NATO would refuse visas to East Germans. Thus, if
Grenoble were unable to receive the East Germans it would be necessary to hold the winter Games elsewhere. The French Prime Minister
Georges Pompidou had agreed that if the Games were granted to
Grenoble, the French Government would 'grant entry to all teams
under existing conditions'. The IOC had interpreted this to mean 'in
accordance with IOC rules', but the French were now saying that they
had intended a united German team as before. However they relented

and allowed entry to a separate East German team using Olympic identity cards.

A further cause of urgency was that, now that political reunification of the two Germanies was barely on the cards, twenty out of twenty-four international federations were demanding separate teams for 1968. Indeed, as Guttmann records, the IAAF had played an important part in undermining the agreements that there should be a joint German team by recognising a fully independent East Germany in 1964 and allowing separate teams to compete in the European Championships in 1966. A vote was taken, and the IOC agreed by a very large majority, with only five dissenting votes, that as East Germany would no longer accept a joint team 'the West German Olympic Committee will revert to affiliation for Germany and the East German Olympic Committee is fully affiliated for the geographical area of East Germany'. (This use of the term 'geographical area' – sometimes the word 'territory' is used – neatly avoids commitment as to the legal status of East Germany.) At Grenoble and Mexico City there would be separate teams, marching under the same banner, with the same anthem and emblems. A new affiliation for Berlin would not be considered. East Berlin was included in East Germany and West Berlin in West Germany.

The German question was laid to rest at the Mexico city session of the IOC in 1968, when it was agreed that the name by which East Germany referred to itself, the German Democratic Republic, would be adopted in Olympic parlance.[20]

Lessons of the German question

The German story illustrates a number of characteristics of the Olympic movement. First, the IOC felt able to take a strong line with East Germany for many years. The forces that persuaded it to abandon its insistence on a joint team for the two Germanies were in part internal to the movement and in part external. Internally, the international federations' interest lay in affiliating East German federations, and as time went on they increasingly did so. The IOC was therefore faced with its usual problem: if it gave a lead it might act precipitately and be accused of acting in too overtly political a manner; if it delayed indefinitely, the IFs might take decisions without waiting for the IOC, thereby undermining its authority within the world of sport.

Externally, the IOC was strongly influenced by the prevailing belief

that it would not be long before Germany was reunited. This
gradually became an unlikely outcome, partly because East Germany
had made such effective use of sport as a means to establish a separate
national identity in the eyes of the world. The West German Government had also abandoned the Hallstein Doctrine and even given up, at
least in the short term, the objective of reunification in favour of an
Ostpolitik which normalised relations with the whole of eastern
Europe. The process culminated in an exchange of letters in
November 1972 recording the two Germanies' intention to co-ordi-
nate their requests for membership of the United Nations, followed in
December by a 'Treaty on the Basis of Relations between the Federal
Republic of Germany and the German Democratic Republic'. It is
true that the treaty was accompanied by a letter from West Germany
stating that 'this Treaty does not conflict with the political aim of the
Federal Republic of Germany to work for a state of peace in Europe in
which the German nation will regain its unity through free self-
determination', but this can at the time have hardly been seen as more
than a prudent reservation without much real force. The Treaty led in
March 1974 to a protocol by which the two states agreed to exchange
'Permanent Representations'. These, although not called embassies,
were more or less indistinguishable from them.[21]

Once the policy of normalisation had been firmly established, there
was no point in the IOC's continuing to press for a joint German
team at the Olympic Games, or to stick to its routine proviso that
agreements made would automatically lapse once Germany was
reunited. Indeed to do so would have been to blow futilely against the
wind of politics. Instead the IOC made prudent use, as it did in the
Chinese case, of the distinction that it had invented between a
'territory' and a country.

But in the long run both the IOC and the West German government
have proved right, for Germany has been reunited with startling speed
and suddenness.

The two Chinas

The first Chinese IOC member was elected as long ago as 1922, and
the IOC thereby recognised the Chinese NOC.[22] In 1932 China sent
one athlete to the Los Angeles Games, but at the Berlin Games of 1936
they had fifty-four participants in seven sports. In 1948 at London
they managed twenty-six, in five sports. A further IOC member had

been elected in 1939.

General Chiang Kai-shek was a signatory of the Charter of the United Nations in 1947 and China received one of the permanent seats on the Security Council. At that stage Taiwan was no more than a province of China, which is the status still officially accorded to it by Beijing, and there was no question of its having any independent existence as a state. After the war between nationalists and communists most (or at least some: the accounts vary) of the NOC fled to Taiwan in 1951 and continued to be recognised. According to Brundage it had simply changed its address, and the change had been duly registered.[23] However Killanin (who was to become President of the IOC in 1972, after the Munich Games) states that there is no trace at Lausanne of the change ever having been recorded.[24] Meanwhile, in the Cold War the USA and its allies and the United Nations recognised what we now call Taiwan as the 'Real China' and went along with its claim to sovereignty over the whole of China, although that is not unlike recognising the 'government' of the Isle of Wight as having jurisdiction over the whole of Great Britain. Of course the Soviets and their satellites recognised the mainland, which adopted the name 'People's Republic of China' (PRC).

On the Olympic front nothing was heard at Lausanne for some years after the Second World War. But in 1952 the President (Edstrom) told the IOC Session that the All-China Athletic Committee had informed him that it supervised all sport in China and functioned as an NOC, and that he had told the committee how to proceed in order to be recognised. The Taiwanese were also signalling their interest in the Olympics, for Erik von Frenckell (the IOC member in Finland) said that he had recently been told by the Chinese (i.e. Taiwanese) Minister in Helsinki of his surprise that the Chinese Olympic Committee had not been invited to the forthcoming Games, which were to be held in Helsinki later in the year.[25] Brundage thought the first step should be to establish contact with the Chinese members, one of whom lived in New York and the others in Hong Kong and Shanghai.[26]

Since both Chinas had said that they intended to send athletes to the 1952 Games at Helsinki, the Helsinki Session was faced with an awkward decision. On the one hand there was the rule of only one NOC per country, and Taiwan (often referred to as Formosa) was already recognised; on the other, if there were two distinct governments in China, should not both their territories be allowed to participate in the Games? Twenty-two members voted for no Chinese team being invited to Helsinki, and twenty-nine for both, for those events for which they were recognised by federations. Brundage acknowledged that the IOC was breaking its own rules by allowing participation by a territory without an NOC, but argued that the circumstances were exceptional.[27] Much time and eloquence were expended, but in the event the discussion had been a farcical waste of energy. Only one athlete from the PRC presented himself at Helsinki, and none from Taiwan, which withdrew in protest once it had learned of the resolution to admit the PRC despite its lack of an NOC.[28]

In 1954 the IOC at last recognised the NOC of the People's Republic, while maintaining its recognition of Taiwan's. The Beijing committee was known as the 'Olympic Committee of the Chinese Republic', changed in 1957 to 'Olympic Committee of the People's Democratic Republic of China' and Taiwan retained the title 'Chinese Olympic Committee'. Since the rules stated that there could be only one NOC per country, the IOC might be thought to have been implying recognition of two countries by recognising two NOCs, but it got over the difficulty (as it did later in the case of the two Germanies) by introducing the idea of recognising territories under the control of an NOC, rather than insisting that an NOC have a nation behind it.

At the beginning of 1956 the third Chinese IOC member, Shou Ti-tung, who had been elected in 1947 and who supported the Beijing government, asked that the Taiwan Olympic Committee be erased from the list of NOCs. This proposal got short shrift from the President, Avery Brundage, who said that it was out of the question to exclude Taiwan on political grounds. Later in the year the PRC withdrew from the Melbourne Games in protest at Taiwan's continuing membership and in 1958 it withdrew from the Olympic movement and from all international federations. Shou Ti-tung resigned from the IOC with an abusive letter dubbing Brundage 'a faithful menial of US imperialists'. (The Taiwanese members remained in office until the mid-1950s.) That summer the PRC bombarded Quemoy and Matsu and the United States despatched reinforcements to Taiwan.[29] Thereafter the PRC was lost in the throes of the Great Leap Forward and the Cultural Revolution, and played no part in Olympic affairs for some years.

Of course the communist bloc IOC members wanted Taiwan expelled and the PRC reinstated. In 1959 the IOC agreed that the

Taiwan committee could not continue under its present name, since it did not administer sport on the mainland. It would therefore be struck off the register under that name, though if it chose to reapply for admission under another the application would be considered.[30] This decision was generally misunderstood by the press, which thought Taiwan had been expelled, with the result that there was uproar in the USA.

In 1960 it was reported to the IOC that the Taiwanese NOC had proposed that, as it was recognised by the United Nations as the Republic of China, its NOC should be known as the Olympic Committee of the Republic of China. This was accepted for the future, but the Taiwanese were told that at the Rome Games they must compete as Taiwan (Formosa).[31] The team duly carried a name board 'Formosa' during the opening parade, but displayed a placard 'under protest'.[32] In 1968 the name 'Olympic Committee of the Republic of China' was reaffirmed by the IOC.

The PRC's return to the fold

In 1971 the United Nations recognised the PRC and expelled Taiwan, giving Taiwan's seat on the Security Council to the PRC. In 1972 President Nixon visited China, the way having been prepared by 'ping-pong diplomacy' – an officially blessed visit by an American ping-pong team.

Events in the Olympic world marched in tandem. In 1971 the IOC resolved that the PRC would be welcome back if it respected Olympic rules, although it also laid down that Formosa would not be excluded. The mainland Chinese began to rejoin international federations, in order to build up to the five required for Olympic eligibility, a policy which posed problems for federations of which Taiwan was a member. If they decided to make the major shift in policy involved in recognising the PRC they risked endless squabbles between the two Chinas. If they did not, they would cut themselves off from competition with the mainland.

The dilemma was particularly difficult for federations which had a rule against competition with non-members, as was well illustrated in 1973, when the American State Department wanted to sponsor ten swimmers to go to the PRC. But the Amateur Athletic Union, which governed swimming in the United States was a member of FINA (the international swimming federation), which did not recognise the

PRC, and did not allow competition against non-members. The result was that if the swimmers had competed against the Chinese the AAU would have had to suspend them or itself be suspended from FINA and in that case no US swimmer would have been able to take part in any international event. The Senate, which was already holding hearings on American sport, asked FINA to make an exception, which it could not do. In the end the storm in a teacup had been for nothing: the ten swimmers had nothing to lose because they had already decided to end their swimming careers, and so were able to carry out the visit to China.

The Chinese question was much discussed at the Varna Congress of the Olympic movement in 1973, the first since 1930. In October 1973 the Asian Games Federation voted to admit the PRC to the Tehran Asian Games and to expel Taiwan. This was proposed by Japan and Iran. Thereupon some international federations said they would withdraw from the Asian Games if the PRC were admitted at the expense of Taiwan. After the Varna Congress the IOC warned the Asian Games Federation that it risked the loss of IOC patronage if it expelled Taiwan, but the IOC did not in fact withdraw its patronage because it wanted to develop sport in Asia, and many international federations agreed with Taiwan's expulsion.[33] It may seem illogical, as Geoffrey Miller comments, for the IOC not to have withdrawn its recognition, but the decision has to be seen in the context of Killanin's conviction that by one means or another China must be brought back into the Olympics. Killanin records that he even arranged for Chinese representatives at the Asian Games to attend an Olympic seminar, a gesture of acceptance which he believes they understood.[34]

Killanin also reveals that discreet contacts had been maintained with the mainland behind Brundage's back all through the 1960s. Eventually he got wind of them, and responded in 1970 by forcing the election to the IOC of a Taiwanese member, Henry Hsu, in 1970. This he did by falsely informing the session that Hsu's election had been recommended by the Executive Board. However, even if the election had gone to a vote the wily Brundage would have won, since he had a majority of the IOC members behind him.[35]

By April 1975 the PRC was in membership of the required number of international federations, and applied for IOC membership, stipulating however that it would only join if Taiwan were expelled. The strength of its political case lay in its now being the Chinese member of the United Nations, although the IOC was naturally reluctant to admit that a sporting decision should be governed by political arguments. The immediate decision to be made was whether the PRC should be allowed to participate in the 1976 Games at Montreal. There was considerable discussion at the session in May 1975, when Alexandru Siperco, the Romanian member, proposed that Beijing's NOC be recognised as the sole representative of China; that the recognition of Taiwan be withdrawn and that the mainland be assisted to frame its statutes in a form acceptable to the IOC in time for the 1976 Games. Dr Hsu pointed out that it was unprecedented for an applicant to attach conditions to its application; that the Taiwanese government was recognised by many states, including the USA, as the government of China and that it was clear that the mainland did not control sport in Taiwan. In any case, he demanded to know, how could the IOC expel an NOC which it had recognised for fifteen years?[36] In the same month, at the IOC's meeting with the NOCs, forty-two delegates spoke. Twenty-five favoured dual membership; seventeen wanted Taiwan to be expelled and there were vitriolic Chinese attacks on Brundage and the IOC.[37]

The Montreal crisis

No immediate decision was taken. Killanin announced his intention to visit both Taiwan and the PRC, but the situation was raised to new heights of crisis by the Canadian government. Canada had adopted a one-China policy in 1970 and recognised the PRC as the sole representative of all Chinese. It would not accede to the Chinese request to refuse entry to the Taiwanese team, but did say that the word 'China' must not appear in its name, and that it might not use its flag or anthem. At the Montreal Session, where the Chinese question occupied the IOC for days (they seem to have spent far more time on it than on the African boycott) there was considerable indignation.

Killanin had first to apologise to the assembled members for the late circulation of information, which had been delayed because fifty activists demanding the independence of the Jura had occupied the headquarters at Lausanne and removed the Director and staff from the premises. Having got this embarrassing explanation over he pointed out that the Canadians were in breach of the undertaking given in 1970, when they had been awarded the Games, that no recognised member country would be denied entrance. He had had no inkling of their intention to refuse entry to the Taiwanese team until

28 May. James Worrall, the senior Canadian member, was mortified by his government's attitude, and said that he and the Canadian NOC would never have supported Montreal's candidature if they had known that their government would behave as it had.

Some members of the IOC argued strongly that the Games should be cancelled, but it was eventually decided to go ahead with them, by 57 votes, with 9 abstentions. Some thought the Games should be moved to the United States or Mexico, which was considered impracticable, or to hold them without the Olympic label, which it was thought would weaken the IOC's control. It was also suggested that the opportunity should be taken to stop the practice of marching under national flags and to invite all NOCs to use the Olympic flag instead, but this idea, which if pursued would have represented a major step back towards the traditionalists' conception of the Games, made no progress once it became clear that at least some NOCs would reject it: indeed, Killanin thought that it would give NOCs an excuse not to participate in the Games.[38]

The Canadian decision was very unpopular in the United States. Ronald Reagan and President Ford intervened, with an eye to the Presidential race, in Ford's case very possibly producing the opposite effect to that which he had intended by strengthening the Canadian Government's resolve. According to Killanin the United States Olympic Committee (USOC) had been instructed to follow its government's policy and withdraw from the Games if Taiwan did not compete, and such a withdrawal would have invalidated the television contract. It is not clear why Killanin should have thought that the United States government was in a position to instruct USOC, but the American member Roosevelt did say that if the United States team were to go home it would be difficult to keep the US government out of USOC's administration in future.

The Taiwanese refused the IOC's offer to permit it to march in the opening parade as Taiwan Republic of China, under the Olympic flag, and threatened to withdraw, which made the IOC fear that others might follow their example. However, after Killanin had negotiated with the Canadian government the latter agreed that Taiwan might retain its own flag and anthem, provided its team paraded as 'Taiwan'. This was a break through, and Killanin believed that Taiwan should have accepted the compromise. However it refused and the Canadians would not allow the counter-compromise proposed by Taiwan that they parade as 'Republic of China – Taiwan'. By 11 July all efforts had been exhausted: the Executive Board of the IOC gave in and said it would propose to the full IOC that Taiwan should compete as 'Taiwan' under the Olympic banner and the IOC approved the Executive Board's recommendation by 58 to 2, with 6 abstentions.[39]

The Canadian government remained unrepentant in the face of uproar in the United States and general disapproval throughout the Olympic movement. It insisted that it had given plenty of warning of its intention to exclude the Taiwanese. Its policy had been adopted in 1970, and it had refused to allow Taiwan to attend the World Cycling Championships of 1974 and the pre-Olympic boxing, both at Montreal. One charge was that the Chinese had threatened to go elsewhere for their wheat. The government flatly denied this (and Killanin accepts that the charge was mistaken) and said that in any case Canada only supplied 1.5 per cent of the PRC's wheat.

Espy comments that the IOC should have known that there would be trouble in store at Montreal. 'To be unaware of Canada's consistent policies, or to believe that the IOC was somehow invincible and supranational, showed serious lack of political acumen.' Yet the Canadian action over something so trivial as a name destroyed everything the athletes had worked for.[40]

In fact the Taiwan team solved everything by packing its bags and going home the day before the Games.

Solutions

The solution was only temporary. In 1977, by now determined to settle the Chinese question before it could pose any threat to the Moscow Games, Killanin paid his delayed visit to China (but put off his visit to Taiwan until after a crucial Session at Montevideo in April 1979). In 1978 three members of the IOC (Lance Cross of New Zealand, Roy Bridge of Jamaica and the Romanian, Alexandru Siperco) followed, although Siperco went only to the PRC. According to Killanin his government had forbidden him to visit Taiwan.[41]

Juan Antonio Samaranch, who succeeded Killanin in 1980, makes his first major appearance in the saga in 1978, when he reported at Athens on his own recent visit to the PRC and said that the IOC must do everything in its power to allow the PRC to be recognised. As a first step the NOC of the Republic of China should be asked to change its name. The Marquess of Exeter (formerly Lord Burghley), who, having been President of the IAAF from 1946 to 1976, was well versed in the China question, agreed that only one of the Chinas could be called 'China', but pointed out that there were precedents for dependent territories having their own NOCs, such as the American Virgin Islands and Puerto Rico. Dr Hsu made a significant, though little remarked, concession by observing that both parts of the divided country were entitled to recognition.[42] However much his government was still insisting on all or nothing, he at least was prepared to recognise reality.

At Montevideo Killanin reported that he had visited China without much success and Cross reported on his team's visit to China and Taiwan, giving five reasons why he could not support the recognition of a single NOC for the two Chinas. One of the difficulties at Montevideo was that the IOC could not get Taiwan and China together round the same table. Taiwan caused the difficulty, in a way reasonably, since its delegation insisted that its purpose in coming to Montevideo had been to consult the President. However, Killanin subjected the delegation to quite harsh questioning, implying that the Taiwanese were playing politics with what should have been a solely Olympic question. This was of course, true, although Killanin also understood perfectly well that the PRC was making political capital from the whole issue, and was not really so naive as to believe that a question so fraught with politics could be kept on a 'purely Olympic' level.

Nevertheless, at Montevideo some signs of compromise began to appear, possibly in response to João Havelange's remark that it would be to the glory of the Olympic movement if there could be two Chinese IOC members, one from the PRC and one from Taiwan. Mr Ho, for the mainland, made the crucial point that the PRC would only accept the title 'Chinese Olympic Committee' for itself, but would accept 'Chinese Taiwan Olympic Committee' for Taiwan, with the proviso that the Taiwanese committee would be regarded as a local body with delegated powers, and that the compromise would be temporary. Frantisek Kroutil of Czechoslovakia referred to the opposition of both Austria and Hungry in 1912 to Bohemian participation in the Games, which had been solved by the Bohemian team marching at a distance behind the Austrian team, and with its own flag. Perhaps the two Chinas could do something similar? The observation was pertinent (if somewhat esoteric), since this was the first time that the PRC had shown any willingness to allow Taiwan's NOC to include the word 'China' in its title. Beside that change of position, all talk of delegated powers and temporary measures was mere face-saving.

Killanin persuaded the Executive Board to accept a resolution, which proposed to 'reintegrate' the Chinese Olympic Committee and to 'maintain recognition of the Olympic Committee whose headquarters are located in Taipeh'. All matters pertaining to name, anthem and flag were to be the subjects of further study. When this resolution was presented to the full IOC it was (no doubt to Killanin's considerable annoyance) amended from the floor, so that the motion finally carried at Montevideo, by 36 votes to 30, recognised the Chinese Olympic Committee located in Beijing and maintained recognition of the Chinese Olympic Committee located in Taipeh. Thus, both bodies were to be permitted to describe themselves as Chinese. The Executive Board was authorised to solve the problems associated with names, anthems, flags and constitutions.[43]

The matter was remitted to the next meeting of the Executive Board, which met at Nagoya in October 1979. Killanin, who had at last visited Taiwan on his way to Nagoya, was by now thoroughly tired of the Taiwanese manoeuvrings, and considered that 'the course ahead was to get China back in and let Taipei remain members, if they wished, on our terms'.[44] After the Nagoya meeting a postal vote was taken on a resolution that the PRC's NOC be recognised as the Chinese Olympic Committee, with the PRC's flag and anthem. The emblem and statutes had been approved. Taiwan's NOC was to be known as the Chinese Taipeh Olympic committee, with a different anthem, flag and emblem from those used at present. They were to be approved by the Executive Board by 1 January 1980 and its statutes submitted by the same date. The ballot paper was sent to all 89 members, and brought 81 responses: 62 in favour; 17 against and two spoiled papers. In his memorandum accompanying the ballot papers Killanin urged members to forget the various political pressures which had been brought upon them. In this he showed some inconsistency, since in the preceding paragraph of his memorandum he had reminded them that Avery Brundage had used the argument that the government in Taiwan, and not that in Beijing, was recognised by the United Nations. The situation was now, Killanin said, reversed, and he asked members to bear in mind the precedent created by his predecessor.[45] In April 1981 it was reported that the name, flag and emblem of the Chinese Taipeh Olympic Committee had been approved.[46]

C

The international federations and China: the example of the IAAF

The problems faced by the international federations in their dealings with the two Chinas were exactly similar to those of the IOC. For example, the IAAF, the most important of the international federations (though football might dispute the title), had been aware of the problem for years, and had in part got over it by allowing member federations to take part in competitions where the non-member PRC were taking part. In 1976 the IAAF had sent an angry telegram in support of Taiwan's participation in the Montreal Olympics, in which it affirmed that 'Our member is recognised as the sole governing body for athletics in the country or territory'.[47]

The question became active in 1978, the year in which the political wind changed decisively when the United States dropped its recognition of Taiwan and switched to the PRC. By then nine IFs recognised the PRC and sixteen were still loyal to Taiwan.[48] Some IFs were torn apart over the issue, for example the cyclists, whose woman President had caused great offence to some members by accepting a personal invitation to Taiwan. The IAAF had recognised the PRC in 1954 and Taiwan in 1956, whereupon the PRC had resigned. The decision facing the IAAF in 1978 was whether to admit the PRC to full membership, at the price of expelling Taiwan. The federation was naturally reluctant to expel a member which had been in good standing, first as Taiwan and since 1970 as the Republic of China, ever since 1956. On the other hand China was still adhering to its policy of not belonging to any international federations of which Taiwan was a member, and the IAAF did not want to cut itself off from the athletes of the world's most populous country.

There were major discussions at the IAAF's Council in April and October 1978 and at three meetings in 1979. According to Primo Nebiolo, who was to become President of the IAAF in 1981, Killanin was waiting on a decision from the IFs and it was agreed that the Republic of China (meaning, of course, its NOC) should be asked to change its name to Taiwan. The problem was to find a way to let Taiwan athletes compete which was acceptable to China. It was argued that before expelling Taiwan they should find out whether China wished to join the IAAF but Nebiolo, with his eye on the Moscow Olympics, was in favour of expelling Taiwan, not playing for time. It was finally agreed, by 7 to 5, with 2 abstentions, to expel Taiwan if China applied. The action would not be intended to be punitive, but would be taken in order to allow the PRC to provide opportunities for the overwhelming majority of Chinese athletes. A further motion, to recommend to Congress that the PRC be the sole Chinese representative, was just carried, by 9 votes to 10.[49]

The IAAF's decision naturally encouraged the PRC to believe that, if enough other IFs followed its lead, Taiwan would automatically lose its recognition by the IOC because it would lack the necessary five international affiliations. Taiwan, however, did not take its troubles lying down. As its relations with the United States and other nations fell away so it became ever more important for it to gain what international political mileage it could from sport, and the IAAF was soon notified that the Taiwan Athletic Association intended to issue a writ in England alleging that the IAAF Congress had acted *ultra vires*, and would seek an injunction against its suspension.[50] The action was successful and at its meeting at Dakar in April 1979, the IAAF Council, whose defence had been that it should never have admitted Taiwan in 1956 and was seeking to rectify the mistake by expelling the territory now, learned that the court had ruled that the Republic of China Track and Field Association remained a member of the IAAF with all the rights and privileges of membership, and that the Congress resolution was void and of no effect. The court had not yet given an injunction, as it had thought it very likely that the IAAF would act on the declaration. The IAAF's lawyers advised against an appeal and considered that the judgement should be accepted. The costs so far amounted to about £12,000. The decision provoked consternation among the Council members, who seem genuinely not to have understood why an international body should be subject to English jurisdiction just because of its residence in England.[51]

The Council learned at its meeting in Montreal in August 1979 that the IOC's Executive Board now wanted to recommend that there should be a Chinese Olympic Committee and a Taiwan Olympic Committee, on condition that the latter had a new anthem and flag. This was two months before the Executive Board actually took the decision at its Nagoya meeting, and the IAAF decided to await the result of that meeting. If the recommendation were adopted as foreseen, then the IAAF would be able to recommend its Moscow Congress to follow suit, and in that case there would be no need to appeal against the English court.[52] In due course the IAAF was able to follow the IOC's line and the crisis was at an end.

News of the London court's decision was received at the beginning of the IOC's Montevideo meeting, where sympathy for Taiwan was reinforced by fears that it might also sue the IOC in the Swiss courts. In fact two cases were attempted. One, brought in Lausanne by the Taiwan Olympic Committee, 'could not' in Killanin's words, 'be proceeded with because of legal technicalities'. Another, brought by Henry Hsu, the IOC member in Taiwan, was still pending when Killanin handed over to Samaranch, and was dropped thanks to the latter's diplomacy.[53]

More recent events

Killanin was naturally disappointed that both Chinas boycotted the Moscow Games, but he records with pleasure that their representatives sat together and talked amicably at the Baden-Baden Congress of the Olympic movement in 1981.[54] However, the PRC's sporting relations with the rest of the world have had their ups and downs.

In 1983 the PRC severed all sports ties with the United States in retaliation for the asylum given to their tennis player Hu Na. Samaranch did not think this would affect the PRC's participation in the Los Angeles Games, and to the great joy of their organiser, Peter Ueberroth, he turned out to be right. Overall, Ueberroth says, the relationship had been good, although in 1982 the float of the oil company ARCO (a sponsor of the Games) in the Rose Bowl parade had flown the Taiwan national flag instead of its Olympic flag, and had not flown a PRC flag at all. PRC had immediately stopped ARCO's off-shore drilling rights for several months.[55] Such difficulties notwithstanding, the PRC's Olympic credentials have become so well-established that Zhenliang He, who was elected to the IOC in 1981, reached the Executive Board in 1985, and has since held numerous other posts, including the Vice-Presidency of the Board since 1989.

Despite the massacre of students in Tiananmen Square in 1989, there was never any danger of a boycott of the eleventh Asian Games in September 1990. As David Miller wrote in a justifiably emotional article, the Games would go ahead without the slightest twinge of conscience for the students who had died for democracy in Tiananmen Square. 'Sport, as always, rises above tragedy in a euphoria of self-interest.' A senior official of the Hong Kong Olympic Committee had even described the China situation as 'nothing serious'.[56] In September 1989 the Chinese Olympic Committee announced that it would bid for the Games of 2000.[57]

The two Germanies and the two Chinas are prime examples of the inability of the Olympic movement and sport in general to avoid involvement in great questions of international politics. Sometimes the involvement entails the expenditure of inordinate amounts of time and energy on essentially trivial contentions, such as the precise name to be accorded to an NOC. Yet those trivial-seeming questions are often symbols of deeper disputes, so that by giving way a contestant may lose ground at a more genuinely important level. In any case time-wasting is often elevated by diplomats to an art of meticulous petifogging, and in this respect Olympic officials do not differ from their governmental equivalents.

Notes

1   I am indebted for this observation to Patrick Jourdain, Editor, The International Bridge Press Association.

2   I am grateful to Sir Arthur Gold for permission to quote this remark.

3   Roman Czula, 'Sport as an Agent of Social Change', *Quest*, 31, 1979, p. 48. See also, for example, C. Roger Rees, 'The Olympic Dilemma: Applying the Contact Theory and Beyond', *Quest*, 37, 1985, pp. 50–9; Richard G. Sipes, 'War, Sports and Aggression: an Empirical Test of Two Rival Theories; (extracted from a 1973 article in *American Anthropologist* in D. Stanley Eitzen (ed.), *Sport in Contemporary Society: an Anthology*, New York, 1984 (first edn 1979)), pp. 46-57.

4   The Olympic movement's involvement with the major international issues of modern times has been well documented in Richard Espy, *The Politics of the Olympic Games*, Berkeley, 1979. (Reprinted with an *Epilogue 1976–80*, 1981.)

5   44th Session, Copenhagen, 15–17 May 1950, *Minutes*. General Robertson's letter is at Annexe 3.

6   45th Session, Vienna, 7–9 May 1951, *Minutes*.

7   44th Session, Copenhagen, *Minutes*.

8   Espy, p. 33. I have made extensive use of Espy's valuable sections on the German question.

9   45th Session, Minutes.

10   50th Session, Paris, 13–18 June 1955, *Minutes*. Espy, p. 34, adds that the East Germans were demoted by their government for having made the agreement. If this is correct Brundage's frequent diatribes against the East German representatives may have been less than fair.

11   46th session, Oslo, 12–13 February 1952, *Minutes*, and Espy. p. 35.

12   Neither Austria nor Hungary had wished Bohemia's NOC to be recognised, but it had been allowed to take part in the 1912 Games. See p. 48.

13   47th Session, Helsinki, 16–27 July 1952, *Minutes* and Espy, p. 52.

14 Espy, pp. 52–3.

15 48th Session, Mexico city, 17–18 April 1953, *Minutes*.

16 49th Session, Athens, 11–15 May 1954, *Minutes*.

17 Paris, 1955, *Minutes, loc. cit.*

18 51st Session, Cortina d'Ampezzo, 24–5 January 1956, *Minutes*.

19 Espy, pp. 76 and 78–9.

20 63rd Session, Madrid 6–8 October 1965, *Minutes*; Espy, p. 108 and Allen Guttmann, *The Games Must Go On: Avery Brundage and the Olympic Movement*, New York, 1984, pp. 156–7.

21 The documents are conveniently assembled in *Documentation Relating to the Federal Government's Policy of Détente*, Bonn, Press and Information Office of the Government of the Federal Republic of Germany, 1974.

22 Another account states that the China National Amateur Athletic Federation was recognised in 1924 as the Chinese NOC. Confusingly, the Olympic Directory gives the date of the mainland NOC's foundation as 1910. I have made use in this section of two summaries of the Chinese question as it affected the Olympic movement, one in English and the other in French, both kindly made available by the archivist of the IOC, Dr Karel Wendl. I have also drawn heavily on Espy, and on the relevant sections of Geoffrey Miller's *Behind the Olympic Rings*, Lynn, Massachusetts, 1979 and Allen Guttmann, *The Games Must Go On*.

23 55th Session, Munich, 24–8 May 1959, *Minutes*.

24 Lord Killanin, *My Olympic Years*, London, 1983, p. 109.

25 An IOC member is always referred to as the member *in*, rather than *for* a certain country, to underline the now somewhat mythological view that members are akin to ambassadors of the IOC to their countries, rather than those countries' representatives on the IOC.

26 Oslo Session *Minutes*, 12–13 February, 1952.

27 47th Session, Helsinki, 16–27 July 1952, *Minutes*.

28 IOC summaries. Espy, p. 37, adds that the mainland team arrived too late to compete. According to Brundage, as reported in the *Minutes* of the 48th Session, Mexico City, 17–18 April 1953, far more than one mainland athlete took part at Helsinki, since he states that Chinese athletes had participated in swimming and football. Both appear to be mistaken. The Chinese arrived too late to take part in the opening ceremony, judging by the list of participating countries in *Bulletin du Comité Olympique*, 34–5, September 1952, p. 50, but the *Official Report* of the organising committee of the Helsinki Games does not record any Chinese participation in football, although it does list a lone Chinese swimmer.

29 Espy p. 45; Geoffrey Miller p. 162; 51st Session, Cortina d'Ampezzo, 24–5 January 1956, *Minutes*.

30 Munich, 55th Session, 25–8 May 1959, *Minutes*.

31 57th Session, Rome, 22–4 August 1960, *Minutes*.

32 Espy, p. 66, says the display of the protest placard was momentary. However, it continued for long enough to be photographed. Killanin regrets that no disciplinary action was taken against the Taiwanese NOC for this political demonstration in the Olympic arena.

33 Espy, pp. 147–50.

34   Geoffrey Miller, p. 166; Killanin p. 113.

35   Killanin, p. 111.

36   76th Session, Lausanne, 21–3 May 1975, Annexes to *Minutes*, pp. 64–7.

37   Espy, p. 151.

38   78th Session, Montreal, 13–19 July 1976, *Minutes*.

39   Espy pp. 152–3; Montreal *Minutes*; Killanin, p. 134.

40   Espy, p. 155, Killanin, p. 133.

41   Killanin, p. 113.

42   80th Session, Athens, 17–20 May 1978, *Minutes*, Annex 37, p. 112.

43   81st Session, Montevideo, 5–7 April 1979, *Minutes*.

44   Killanin, p. 114.

45   Resolution and memorandum reprinted in *Olympic Review*, 145, November 1979, pp. 626–9.

46   *Olympic Review*, 162, April 1981, p. 211.

47   IOC, 78th session, Montreal, 13–19 July 1976, *Minutes*, Annexe 4, p. 63. The IAAF, like the IOC, prudently allowed itself, following a change in its rules in 1968, to recognise territories as well as countries.

48   Geoffrey Miller, pp. 166 and 170.

49   IAAF Council meetings, Seoul 14–16 April 1978 and San Juan, Puerto Rico, 3–4 October 1978, *Minutes*.

50   IAAF Extraordinary Council, London, 19 January 1979. (The Taiwanese NOC had previously sued the International Badminton Federation, whose headquarters, like those of the IAAF, were in England. Geoffrey Miller, p. 169.)

51   IAAF Council, Dakar, 26–8 April 1979, *Minutes*.

52   IAAF Council, Montreal, 2–4 August 1979, *Minutes*.

53   Killanin, p. 116.

54   *ibid.*, p. 110.

55   *The Times*, 9 April 1983 and Peter Ueberroth, *Made in America*, London, 1986, p. 232.

56   *The Times*, 21 September 1989 – David Miller, Beijing.

57   *ibid.*, 22 September 1989.

III

Power and authority in the Olympic movement

The Olympic movement consists of the International Olympic Committee (IOC), the National Olympic Committees (NOCs) and the international federations (IFs), with their many regional associations and offshoots, all existing in a state of sometimes uneasy, and always delicate, symbiosis.

The IOC is a self-electing, self-regulating body, consisting on the whole of individuals (mostly men, with a few women since 1981) who are rich or well-born or powerful, or all three. As in other regulatory bodies whose members are unpaid (Britain's Jockey Club is a good example) the need has been felt in recent years for more members who are young and businesslike enough to make effective contributions to the growing committee work, and efforts have been made to find people who fit these requirements.

Nevertheless, of the ninety-two members at the beginning of 1989 fifty-five were aged sixty or over.[1] Juan Antonio Samaranch, the President since 1980, reached his seventieth birthday in July 1991, and the punishing routine of constant meetings and travel that he sets himself has taken its toll. It was expected that he would retire after the Barcelona Games of 1992, but there have been rumours that he will offer himself for yet another term, or perhaps until after the next Congress of the Olympic movement, to be held in Paris in 1994 – an offer that his colleagues would find difficult to refuse.

Since its foundation in 1894 the Committee has had only seven Presidents, several of whom have been larger than life in one way or another. In modern times the American Avery Brundage has been perhaps the most remarkable. A man of ruthlessly authoritarian and reactionary opinions, he ran the movement almost as a private hobby from 1952 until his retirement at the end of the Munich Games of

1972. In those days the movement's staff and activities were far less extensive than at present, and Brundage was able to finance it largely from his own fortune. Although the movement was not rich when Lord Killanin succeeded Brundage at the end of the Munich Games the IOC was able to pay his expenses: he was the first President to be unable to forgo them, although, like all Presidents, he served without salary.

Killanin is a shrewd and amiable peer who, as his memoirs show, had a high estimation of the importance of his office and a strong sense of protocol. He did not attempt to control the IOC's day-to-day business, but left much of it to his full-time Executive Director, Madame Monique Berlioux, who (when there were still no women members of the IOC) ran the headquarters in Lausanne, while Killanin continued to operate from his fairly modest house in Dublin.[2]

President Samaranch

Juan Antonio Samaranch, who had long had his sights on the Presidency, achieved his heart's desire in 1980, immediately after the Moscow Games. His management style has been entirely different from Killanin's; soon after his election he took up residence in Lausanne, and concerned himself with every detail of Olympic life. There was no room for Madame Berlioux, who was opposed to the growing commercialisation of the movement, under a President who was presiding over the developments that she so much deplored. They got continually on each other's nerves, but she survived for a surprisingly long time, until finally Samaranch sacked her, with virtually no notice, though with a generous retirement package, at the IOC's session in East Berlin in 1985. Samaranch used Richard Pound (a young Canadian tax lawyer who had been elected to the IOC only in 1983) to inform Madame Berlioux that she was to 'resign'.[3] Her nephew, Alain Coupat, survived as Samaranch's *chef de cabinet* until 1989, since when the President has relied increasingly on his new part-time Director-General, François Carrard, who before his appointment was already the IOC's lawyer.

A new President does not take up office until the end of the Games which mark the commencement of a new Olympiad (the four-year period ending with the Games) in which he is elected, so that it was Killanin, rather than Samaranch, who had to deal with the American boycott of the Moscow Games. However, Samaranch's life as President has not been easy: he had to heal the wounds in the movement after Moscow and limit the damage caused by the Soviet boycott of the Los Angeles Games of 1984. Furthermore, the Games of 1988 were a source of nightmarish uncertainty from the moment in 1981 when Seoul was chosen to host them.

Samaranch has suffered even more keenly the ups and downs of his native Barcelona's preparations for 1992, although it is often thought that his life's greatest triumph was to see Barcelona win the nomination. (Of course he had played no overt part in winning the Games for his native city, but he had propagated the idea as long ago as 1978 or 1979, while he was still ambassador in Moscow, in conversations with Narcis Serra, the then Mayor of Barcelona, who later became Minister of Defence). However, once Barcelona was chosen, the city's slow progress gave him constant anxiety, which led him frequently to express his worries to the Prime Minister, and even to the King. He may look forward to these Games as the summit of his career, yet he can seldom be free from the fear that terrorism, bad luck or incompetence may render them a fiasco.

History will no doubt establish Samaranch as the IOC's pivotal President. He has been unkindly described by distinguished *Times* journalists as (like the post-war Labour Prime Minister, Clement Attlee), someone who might emerge from an empty taxi, and as probably the only man in the world who looked like his passport photograph.[4] He may also, as has often been said, be too concerned with public relations, yet his background in business, politics and diplomacy prepared him ideally for the demands of his highly political office and he has presided over fundamental changes in the movement's nature. The wealth now associated with top-level sport has brought about a proliferation of interest groups within the movement, all competing for the spoils, and the finesse with which Samaranch has placated and controlled the IFs and NOCs and managed to maintain the IOC's position at the movement's centre has earned him worldwide admiration.

Samaranch had a successful career in both local and national politics under General Franco; he seems to have belonged to no particular faction within the Falange, but to have seen his political career as in a sense non-political, because it was concerned with sport. Some politicians of those days have faded away, but Samaranch avoided the mistake of thinking that he could simply continue as a member of the political class after the death of Franco and the restoration of the monarchy in 1975, and instead has made his name in sport and business.

Samaranch's business career, largely in banking, made it possible for him to indulge his passion for sports administration. There has been no difficulty in combining the two: even as President of the IOC he has been active in business, and in 1990 became chairman of the largest savings bank in Spain, through a merger between the Caixa de Pensiones (then the third largest) and the Caixa de Barcelona.

Samaranch, a great devotee of roller hockey, which is to be a 'demonstration sport' at the Barcelona Games in 1992, attended the Olympic Games for the first time in 1952, became a member of the Spanish Olympic Committee in 1954 and its President from 1967 to 1970. Some accounts say that it had been his dream from youth to become President of the IOC, and that he had worked for it tenaciously, even to the extent of learning foreign languages as an adult. However, he was not well known in sporting circles outside Spain, until in 1966 Brundage proposed him for membership of the IOC. He rose quickly in the movement, as Brundage had forecast, serving as a member of the Executive Board from 1970 to 1978 and as a Vice-President from 1974 to 1978.

In 1977 he was appointed Spain's first ambassador to the Soviet Union. At that time there were commercial and cultural relations between the two countries and, with his passion for news, Samaranch may have realised sooner than most people that full diplomatic relations were about to be established. It is generally considered that he asked the King of Spain for the appointment in order to build up his position as an eventual President of the movement. He was able to do this by staying close to the Soviet preparations for the 1980 Olympics, which could so easily have been spoilt by President Carter's boycott, and at the same time being physically close enough to Lausanne to stay in touch with what was going on at the Olympic movement's headquarters. Although he had never before been a diplomat, it could still be said that his was a suitable appointment, in that, thanks to his sporting interests, he was one of the few Spaniards who had Soviet contacts. He worked hard as ambassador, helped Moscow to organise Games which were successful, barring the boycott, and made good friends in Moscow and in the Soviet bloc generally, particularly with Serge Novikov, one of the nine deputy Prime Ministers of the Soviet Union and later head of the organising committee for the 1980 Games.

In 1980 Samaranch fended off other candidates (of whom the most serious was Marc Hodler, an IOC member since 1963 and President of the Swiss Ski Federation since 1951), and was duly elected President of the IOC in succession to Lord Killanin.

He also, according to Aris, seems to have opened the Soviet bloc to Adidas (the sports gear manufacturers), aided by Horst Dassler, the chairman of Adidas, and João Havelange, President since 1974 of the international football federation, FIFA. Aris says: 'Dassler and Havelange not only taught Samaranch an immense amount about the nature of Sportsbiz [a useful term invented by Aris] but they helped him get his job . . . It was Dassler who delivered the Third World while Havelange controlled the Latin bloc.'[5]

According to an unsigned profile of Havelange in *The Independent*, another of the businessmen who helped Samaranch up the ladder was Colonel Marceau Crespin, an old Gaullist with strong sports connections, who was head of Coca-Cola in France (and who is also said to have assisted the rise to power of Jean Marie Balestre, the high priest of motor racing). According to this account, Samaranch's final push came after an interview between Havelange, the King of Spain and the Spanish organising committee for the 1982 World Cup at which Havelange gave the first pay-off for the Third World votes which had enabled him to defeat Sir Stanley Rous for the presidency of FIFA. Havelange's victory had been brought about by the expansion of the World Cup from sixteen to twenty-four teams, in order to make African and Asian participation possible. It had been known that the expansion would raise the World Cup's costs and lower its profits, but the arguments goes that these disadvantages were worth while for the King and Samaranch, because Samaranch gained Third World votes in return for backing the expansion. All this may present a startlingly labyrinthine picture, but it has become the common change of speculation about sports politics.[6]

IOC Membership

Election to the IOC is an honour much desired by men and women who have made their names in the practice and administration of sport. The duties are not demanding, except for those who take a serious interest in committee work. But even for those who are not much involved in central administration there are meetings to be attended of such bodies as ANOC (the Association of National

Olympic Committees) and the regional associations of NOCs and the IFs which provide interest, as well as pleasant outings and the opportunity to see old friends and associates. Furthermore, sports administration is for some of its practitioners an occupation somewhat akin to publishing in providing a combination of creativity, hard-headed business and vicarious excellence. One cannot forever go on running races, or riding them, but one can go on as an administrator into old age.

Membership of the IOC does not in itself bring financial rewards, although it has often been alleged that such firms as Adidas could 'deliver' votes in the competition to host the Games. Bidding committees have been said to offer jobs to relations of undecided members, or to hold out such inducements as free surgical operations. The journalist David Miller, commenting on a meeting which was to take place in Lausanne to discuss how the bidding process could be simplified and abuses eliminated, recounts how a minority of members will make money by taking a round-the-world ticket to visit the bidding cities, and then send a bill to each city for a first class fare from their home bases.[7] At a trivial and uncorrupt level, any well-travelled member will accumulate numerous presents, and will usually feel able to keep them (though Britain's Princess Royal sets an example by accepting nothing). Some of the presents are attractive, many hideous, and some, like banners and commemorative medals, are harmless mementos.

However, although for the majority of members there is no financial reward, even the rich enjoy free travel. Since the main power of the run-of-the-mill IOC member is to vote for the host cities for the summer and winter Games, the proliferation of candidates since Seoul (whose only rival was Nagoya in Japan) means that the member who believes it to be his or her duty to visit all the bidding cities can have an agreeably busy schedule, and be treated like a Prince along the way. Of course, not all members enjoy travelling: some cannot afford the time to visit all the bidding cities, and so may decide to visit none; again, the Princess Royal is an example. Others are infirm or too heavily occupied with other business, and for them travel may well be a sacrifice, rather than a pleasure. Nevertheless, the power to award the Games to a supplicant city is not to be despised, and if the current plans to cut down the number of visits paid by members are successful there may be protests.

In principle a member operates without regard to political considerations, though in many cases the claim is obviously false. Furthermore, we have seen in Chapter I that a member (again in principle) does not represent his country on the IOC, but is the IOC's representative to his country. Both these pieces of mythology lend some plausibility to the idea, in itself a good one, that the IOC should not terminate a member's tenure just because he or she is out of favour at home. Even the Tunisian member Mohamed Mzali, a former Prime Minister who lives in exile in Paris, has not fallen foul of the rule that a member must normally live in his or her own country, presumably because it is hoped that he will be able to return there.

Naturally enough, the distribution of IOC membership between countries and the manner of members' election are bones of contention. At present many countries are not represented at all, and most of those that have held the Games are allotted two members. There is thus ample room for disaffection among the unrepresented and, although the official line is that significant expansion of the IOC would make it impossibly unwieldy, one report suggests that Samaranch has admitted the possibility that all NOCs will eventually have IOC members by saying that the process will take twenty-five or thirty years.[8]

It appears that Samaranch has virtually sole say about who is to be proposed for membership, and it is almost unknown for one of his candidates to be rejected. So tight is his control that some stronger-minded members complain that there is no opportunity to debate a candidate's suitability, and that nominations just go through 'on the nod'. This may be part of what the Princess Royal had in mind when she told David Miller that she saw the IOC as a one-man band.[9] Of course the President will take extensive soundings, as may be seen from Denis Howell's account of why he was passed over in favour of Mrs Mary Glen-Haig, when Samaranch's enquiries apparently extended as far as the Duke of Edinburgh.[10] However, the President's control over nominations to the IOC seems not to be a new phenomenon: one reason for Killanin's papers remaining under seal until his death is that they contain so much correspondence about possible members. At least Killanin consulted, whereas, as he told Aris, before his presidency 'What normally happened was that the president made decisions off the top of his head which were then ratified by the full session of the IOC. It was run like an international jockey club.'[11] One might add that, although the comparison may be unjust to the Jockey Club of the 1990s, Samaranch's Caixa de Pensiones is perhaps a not dissimilar institution to the IOC as described by Killanin.

The Executive Board and commissions

It is not surprising that day-to-day business has to be left to an Executive Board – it is not possible to envisage a committee of ninety members being an effective decision-making body. Membership of the Board is greatly prized, both by those members who see it as the highest office to which they can aspire, and by some who have their eyes on the succession to Samaranch. The Board is elected by the Session and elections, although fiercely contested, are strongly influenced by Samaranch. However, although he can help his friends to make their careers within the movement by assisting them to gain office in such bodies as the ANOC or by nominating them to IOC commissions (as committees are called), he cannot bank on having his own way at the Board. Both its, and his, freedom of manoeuvre is also limited by the need to have a good geographical spread among the members.

The President's power is even greater when it comes to commissions, since the Olympic Charter reserves to him the right to set them up, determine their membership and terms of reference, decide when they shall meet and dissolve them when he considers that they have served their purpose.[12] Appointments to these bodies are highly valued, and are therefore useful pieces of patronage, for although they do not bring financial reward they do offer opportunities to travel, and within the extended Olympic family they confer a prestige which is often prized more highly than money. Often an appointment to a commission may serve to keep an experienced Olympian close to the centre of the movement; for example, after Charles Palmer had been defeated by Sir Arthur Gold for the chairmanship of the British Olympic Association, Samaranch appointed him to the powerful Programme Commission of the IOC, which decides which sports are to be included in the Games. The appointment may not have pleased all his British colleagues, but it would clearly have been foolish to waste his talent.

At a more exalted level the gift of the gold medal of the Olympic Order represents patronage which seems to be appreciated even by heads of state, though it must be said that the choice of recipients has sometimes been unfortunate. At Baden-Baden Amadou Mathar M'Bow, then Secretary-General of UNESCO (with which the IOC has had troublesome demarcation disputes), received it; subsequent recipients have included Nicolae Ceauşescu of Romania (1984) and Erich Honecker of East Germany (1985).

When he travels Samaranch is treated with a deference at least equivalent to that accorded the Secretary-General of the United Nations, especially in poor countries, which owe so much to the IOC's fund for sports development, known as Olympic Solidarity. In Korea he became an extraordinarily popular figure because he was seen as the saviour of the Games for Seoul, who had triumphed over the protests that the decision to hold them there had provoked. His popularity was marked by the announcement in September 1990 that he had been awarded the first 'Seoul Peace Prize' of £300,000, which he at once donated to the new Olympic museum's construction fund.

Throughout the movement Samaranch's web of patronage and influence maintains him as a virtually unchallenged monarch, but such a network of influence does not sustain itself automatically: it requires constant maintenance and the judicious choice of friends. Those friends must not only be made within the IOC, but in the NOCs and IFs, which themselves, as Samaranch's own career illustrates, provide ladders to power in the world of sport. It is often unkindly said that Samaranch surrounds himself with a 'Latin Mafia': indeed, he is believed to have no use for Anglo-Saxons, whom he calls 'Sassenachs' and has been heard to ask 'What have the Sassenachs ever done for sport?' The names most frequently associated with him are those of Mario Vázquez-Raña, João Havelange and Primo Nebiolo. Raña is independently rich from the ownership of newspapers in Mexico, but the other two have made their own ways. Until 1991 (when Raña was elected by only a small number of members and with many opposing him) only Havelange was a member of the IOC, but all of them take their positions extremely seriously. For example the IOC put out a press release on 30 October 1990 merely to record the fact that Samaranch had received Havelange, and that they had 'discussed subjects concerning their two organizations in an atmosphere of total cooperation and friendship'.

In the crises of Olympic life it is noticeable that these men (especially Raña and Nebiolo) are in Samaranch's entourage. For example, after Moscow announced its boycott of the 1984 Games, these two accompanied Samaranch to an acrimonious meeting of the Soviet bloc sports leaders at which he sought to reassert the unity of the Olympic movement: in 1980 and 1984 Raña was the IOC's intermediary with President Fidel Castro of Cuba; Raña's ANOC issued the supportive 'Mexico Declaration' in 1984, when the award to Seoul of the 1988 Games was coming under fire; Nebiolo was early in his support of Barcelona's candidacy for 1992 and Havelange was described by John Goodbody as 'an outrageously enthusiastic supporter'. Samaranch could, according to this account, afford to remain neutral because Havelange was doing the lobbying for him. Samaranch had even had to restrain Havelange's enthusiasm for promoting Latin officials when in 1982 it looked as if Anglo-Saxons were going to lose effective representation on the Executive Board, and Samaranch had to ensure that an American was elected to it in order to preserve appearances.[13]

The three pillars of the Olympic movement

There is a constant tension about the balance of power between the IOC, the International Federations (IFs) and the National Olympic Committees (NOCs), particularly over the choice of host cities for the Games, which is decided entirely by IOC members, though with the benefit of ample advice.

It is even said that the IOC is redundant and that the IFs and NOCs could adequately run the Olympic movement between them. This may seem a surprising assertion, since one great source of power to the IOC is that it decides which IFs are to be recognised, and which are to take the further step of being admitted to the programme of the Olympic Games. Both these steps are eagerly desired by IFs, because they immediately make a sport better known and more popular, and so increase its ability to raise funds.

However, it can equally well be argued, and sometimes it is even hinted by the Presidents of such important federations as the IAAF, that without the IOC, IFs would simply concentrate on their own World Championships and the Games would fall away. A step towards seriously weakening the Olympic Games was taken when the campaign long waged by Primo Nebiolo, President of the IAAF, to hold IAAF World Championships every two years, instead of four, came to a successful conclusion at the IAAF's Congress in Tokyo in August 1991. Meanwhile the IOC replies to any suggestions that it could become redundant that, although without it the IFs might benefit in the short term, in the long run the world of sport would collapse into chaos, because there would be no supreme regulatory body.

The NOCs join with the IFs in complaining about the IOC's power. Though neither they, nor the IFs, contest the IOC's ownership of the Games, so long as the Games continue, they do believe that they should have more say in the IOC's decisions by being given greater representations on the Committee. Complaints have been heard for at least the past ten years, to the effect that every NOC should have a seat on the IOC. More recently similar suggestions have emanated from the IFs, on the ground that their members are the people most directly affected by the choice of city. A further demand voiced by the IFs is that they should have some share in the IOC's marketing income from the TOP programme (to be discussed in Chapter IV). This complaint is not shared by the NOCs, which already participate in the pro-gramme.

Certainly, IFs could break away from the Olympic movement if they wished, though it would only be worth while for the richer ones to do so. It must therefore be asked why they in fact remain within the movement. The reasons, no doubt, are partly matters of calculation, and partly idealistic or even irrational. On the one hand the sports administrator who contemplates going it alone knows that he may not succeed, and that in breaking away he will forfeit for ever the chance of becoming an IOC member himself. (This must be a powerful factor in Nebiolo's thinking, since it is generally supposed that his dearest ambition is to achieve IOC membership.) On the other, there is the intangible magic of history; the fact that the IOC has prestige of a unique kind in the world of sport; an attachment to the ideals upon which the Olympic Games were founded.

There may not be much evidence that élite sport promotes friendship between peoples – perhaps more is gained from the twinning across Europe of small provincial towns – yet it may be that the old ideals still have a powerful atavistic force. The reasons for the potential rivals' continuing (if uncertain) loyalty are complex but, whatever they are, the IOC does not stay at the top of the sport-ing pyramid without continuous effort. The process is political. It demands resources, which are channelled worldwide through Olym-pic Solidarity, an understanding of human motivation and the prudent manipulation of power.

The IFs' concern for greater representation on the IOC is to some extent motivated by a desire for personal aggrandisement on the part of the leading personnel in these bodies and that is a motive which cannot be argued away. But it also rests upon a genuinely felt need for the technical aspects of the various candidates cities' bids to be more expertly evaluated than, it is said, they are at present, and here there are plenty of counter-arguments available.

For one thing, not all IF Presidents are in favour of such a change in the composition of the IOC. When it chooses a host city the IOC has at its disposal the reports prepared for it by the IFs and NOCs, as well as those of its own evaluation commission, not to mention the information and opinions gained from the numerous formal and informal contacts which take place between IOC members and figures in other organisations, and from such reports as may be rendered by Samaranch's personal emissaries. Many IOC members (a few of whom are already Presidents of IFs) are in any case expert in at least one sport, and it is hard to see that they would benefit by having further sources of advice built in to the structure of their committee, when they can so easily obtain it as things stand. The clinching arguments may be, first, that significant enlargement would make the IOC still more unwieldy than it is at present, so accelerating the tendency for power to be concentrated in a few hands, and secondly that the ordinary members would strongly resist the dilution of their power to choose between rival bidding cities, the only real power left to them.

Two aspects of the IOC's response to threats to its dominance have been to consult the IFs and NOCs more fully than in the past and to follow a policy of divide and rule, by recognising a plethora of organisations through which the interests of the IFs and NOCs are articulated. The ANOC brings all the NOCs together, and has itself spawned local associations in Africa, the Americas, Asia, Europe and Oceania. The federations have the Association of Summer Olympic International Federations (ASOIF), and its winter equivalent, AIWF. There is even an association of all federations which have been recognised by the IOC, whether or not they have been admitted to the Games (ARISF) and a General Association of International Sports Federations, which contains all IFs, whether recognised or not (GAISF).

There may be something to be said for all these bodies, since without them common interests might not be formulated, nor effective pressure groups formed. But a movement devoted to spending money economically might decide that the regional associations of NOCs could just as well meet at the same time as ANOC's main meeting, or just before it, as hold special conferences of their own. Similarly, it is hard to see what would be lost by re-amalgamating the associations of summer and winter federations, although it is certain that rival caucuses would persist within them.

The IOC and the host cities

With the Games' growth there has arisen the necessity to consolidate its power over the movement by obtaining guarantees on behalf of the host city, which have generally been given by governments. Although it has not until recently been totally clear what exactly was being guaranteed, the essential point from the IOC's point of view has been to protect it from liability if the Games made a loss. It has even been argued that the point of a guarantee is its commercial soundness, rather than its source, and that there is no reason in Olympic law why a city should not offer a guarantee from a major company, instead of from its government.

The IOC has also strengthened the contract which every bidding city is required to sign, despite opposition from the old guard, in advance of the decision as to which city is to hold the Games. The contract confirms the IOC's ownership of the Games and the right to exploit them (which is in any case laid down in the Olympic Charter): it confirms the division of television rights between the local organising committee and the IOC and the latter's share in the marketing programmes and ultimate control over them. It also contains a clause approving the separate contract between the IOC and its marketing company, ISL, to sell the Games, the details of which are not made known to the candidate cities. The formulation of detailed contracts began with the Games of Los Angeles in 1984 and Seoul in 1988, but these were signed after the Games had been awarded. However, under Samaranch the new procedure was adopted of signing in advance by all the cities competing to hold the Games of 1992.

Naturally, candidate cities have been unhappy with these arrangements, but have felt unable to combine to resist them for fear of antagonising the IOC. The reasoning behind the IOC's firmness is that it has been found that cities have ignored aspects of the contract once the Games have been awarded, or interpreted it in ways unacceptable to the IOC, and the purpose has been to ensure that the IOC's interpretation will prevail in future. There was a nice example at the June 1990 meeting of ANOC, when NOCs were demanding from Barcelona more free facilities than it was prepared to give. Right was probably on Barcelona's side, but Vázquez-Raña, the President of ANOC, remarked bitterly on the humility with which candidate cities approached the IOC and the arrogance with which they behaved once the Games were in the bag.

This chapter has shown that the Olympic movement is a hotbed of politics, as the passenger on the Clapham omnibus has always suspected. Yet it would not be fair to blame the movement. Like any sub-culture it breeds its own rivalries and power blocks and, as in any large organisation, much of the managers' energy is spent on keeping all the potentially conflicting interests in some sort of balance.

Notes

1 Four were over eighty; seventeen in their seventies; thirty-four in their sixties; twenty in their fifties; eleven in their forties and six in their thirties.

2 Lord Killanin, *My Olympic Years*, London, 1983.

3 Neil Wilson, *The Sports Business: the Men and the Money*, London, 1988, p. 16.

4 *The Times*, 17 July 1980, John Hennessy, Moscow and *The Times*, 16 December 1988, Simon Barnes.

5 Stephen Aris, *Sportsbiz: Inside the Sports Business*, London, 1990, p. 160.

6 *The Independent*, 9 June 1990.

7 *The Times*, 9 January 1991.

8 *ibid.*, 9 October 1984, David Miller, Delhi.

9 *ibid.*, 18 October 1989.

10 Denis Howell, *Made in Birmingham: the Memoirs of Denis Howell*, London, 1990, pp. 290–1.

11 Aris, p. 158.

12 *Olympic Charter 1991*, clause 24:5.

13 *The Times*, 24 October 1986, John Goodbody.

IV

Financing the Games

This chapter examines some aspects of the complicated subject of Olympic finance. It discusses the movement's rise to riches with the growth of income from the sale of television rights and the ways in which that income is divided. There follows an account of the IOC's marketing programme, introduced in order to reduce dependence on television. The chapter concludes with sections on the powerful United States Olympic Committee (USOC) and its dissatisfaction with its share of the income from television, and on the part played in the Olympic movement by Adidas, the firm of sports gear manufacturers which has played a great part in its commercial development, and has even been thought capable of influencing the choice of host city for the Games.

The rise to riches

Samaranch often says that the IOC has 'semi-diplomatic status', but in fact it is recognised in Swiss law as an international Non-Governmental Organisation. It is therefore something like a non-profit-making sports club, whose international dimension gives it certain tax advantages and allows it to employ foreigners without the usual necessity, very strict in Switzerland, of obtaining work permits for its employees.

Without access to a four-year cycle of IOC accounts (which are not published) it is not possible to arrive at an overall view of what it is worth, because much of the money held in its accounts will eventually be paid out to IFs and to Olympic Solidarity for the benefit of NOCs, and its own share of television rights is only counted as income after the final payment has been received from the various television companies. However, one indicator of the IOC's economic wellbeing is that by 1987 it was able to pay the final instalment of the $13 million spent on the extension to its headquarters in Lausanne, a beautiful, indeed magnificent, but not ostentatious building beside Lake Geneva, designed by one of the Mexican IOC members, Pedro Ramirez Vazquez. There, and in some other buildings in Lausanne, a staff of a little over a hundred work, many of them exceedingly hard, in an atmosphere which to an outsider seems harmonious, even familial.

When one surveys its current influence it is hard to remember that in its early days the IOC was not a rich organisation. In 1952, at its Oslo Session, Lord Burghley asked that provision should be made for television, and that the number of cameramen be restricted. He was told that negotiations were already taking place with an American firm, and that the rules for cameramen would be the same as at the London Games of 1948.[1] In 1955 the IOC's President, Avery Brundage, informed the Paris Session that estimated receipts for the year were 31,000 Swiss francs, against estimated expenses of 45,000. Although he was exceedingly rich, and had treated the Olympic movement as a hobby, he said that the IOC could not continue to spend 50 per cent more than it received and that the matter was to be put in the hands of the Executive Board.[2] At the Cortina Session in 1956 Lord Burghley picked up the same theme again and said, speaking from his experience as President of the IAAF, that many international federations

suffered from the same evil as the IOC, namely from want of money. Were it possible for us to obtain subsidies [from television companies] on a friendly basis, we could let the International Federations reap the benefit of this. The latter in their turn, may feel more inclined to give us satisfaction in the matter of the world championships.

(He was referring to the IOC's fear that some IFs might organise world championships in the same year as the Olympic Games.)[3]

The attitudes expressed in the 1950s would nowadays be seen as naive, but television soon began to turn the Olympic movement into a business, though at first the sums raised were trivial by modern standards. The first rights were sold in 1960 to the American network CBS for $440,000, which allowed it thirty-five hours' coverage of the winter and summer Games. None of this came to the IOC, and even when ABC paid $4m for the summer Games of 1968 in Mexico the $150,000 given to the IOC was an *ex gratia* payment. Thereafter it changed its rules to protect its ownership of the Games and their exploitation, and when Killanin succeeded Brundage in 1972 at the end of the Munich Games, it had $2m in hand (a loan from the Munich organising committee), which had grown to over $45m by 1980, when Samaranch became President.[4]

It had been agreed that from 1972 the organising committee should receive two-thirds of the television rights and the IOC one-third, of which it would pass on one-third to the National Olympic Committees and a third to the international federations. The IOC received over $2m as its share for 1972 (and a further $945,000 for the winter Games) and so was able to pay off its debt to Munich and to survive until 1976.[5] After Munich the IOC was well enough off to allow it not to touch the sums promised for the summer and winter Games of 1976 at Innsbruck and Montreal until after those Games had been staged. It was therefore not necessary for insurance to be taken out against the Games not taking place, whereas this had been necessary before Munich, because the IOC had had to spend some of the money in advance.[6]

ABC paid only $7.5m for Munich. In those days 'The telecasts still garnered relatively small audiences, and the advertising community could barely stifle a yawn.' The Munich kidnappings turned the Games into major news and 'Even commercial advertisers realised a grisly profit: they had paid low rates in anticipation of the usual low Olympic ratings and were the unintended beneficiaries of the skyrocketing audiences as the crisis wore on'. ABC bought the Montreal rights for $25m, Roone Arledge, the head of ABC's negotiating team, having made use of what became known as 'the ABC closer'. That is, he made a much higher offer than ever before, but allowed only twenty-four hours for its acceptance or rejection.[7]

Even in 1984, according to Peter Ueberroth, who was shown its accounts by the Australian member, David McKenzie, the IOC's net worth was very little.[8] Although there is a dearth of figures, and the sources conflict, it is clear that the IOC's real wealth (ignoring any sums that it holds on behalf of IFs and NOCs) is very recent. But with the Games' growth as a television spectacular the IOC has behaved prudently and steadily taken more power unto itself, in order to protect its share of the proceeds.

Since television has been the backbone of the IOC's new wealth its leaders have become understandably nervous lest the market collapse and leave the movement in unaccustomed poverty. If the television rights did not sell, the Games would hardly be 'the Games', and to sell the American rights for a record sum has become the ultimate status symbol for organising committees. Seoul did everything it could to set a record, including publishing misleading figures in its *Official Report*. Thereafter the IOC believed that the ceiling had been reached; Pasqual Maragall, the Mayor of Barcelona, thought he knew better, and turned out to be right. Yet another record was set.

The division of the spoils

The sale of television rights benefits the whole movement. The general principle has been established, as was noted above, that the host city retains two-thirds of the proceeds and that the IOC receives the remainder, passing on a third of its share (that is, a ninth of the total) to the international federations and a third to NOCs through the Olympic Solidarity fund. The latter is disbursed partly in the form of subventions to assist with the expense of sending teams to the Games and partly on projects, such as training coaches, for the general improvement of sport in the recipient countries.

Although the principle is established, there is room for argument about the details. We have already seen that Associations of International Federations and National Olympic Committees proliferate in the movement. Much business is generated in all these bodies by competition for office within them, which naturally absorbs a great deal of political energy. Their other principal reason for existence is to safeguard the division of the proceeds of the Games. Although these consist mainly of television rights, an increasing contribution is made by advertising revenue obtained from firms licensed to use the Olympic symbols on their products.

The contributions made by Olympic Solidarity towards sending the teams to the Games are the same for all NOCs, but ANOC and its subsidiaries naturally lobby for them to be increased. In 1992 each NOC will receive a basic subsidy of $8,000 and $800 for each athlete up to six. The training projects underwritten by Olympic Solidarity are allocated on merit, but an element of political calculation does enter into the division of the percentages of the budget destined for the different continents. For example, Africa receives a steadily increasing percentage, to the chagrin of the Europeans. Such interests have to be defended, but it is doubtful whether the process has been made more effective by the creation of five offshoots of ANOC.

The issues within and between the associations of winter and summer federations also relate to money. The summer federations nowadays divide equally the portion of the television proceeds allocated to them by the IOC, but formerly the IAAF took the lion's share with 25 per cent, because of the high proportion of revenue from ticket sales generated by athletic events. This was whittled down to 20 per cent at the Moscow Games, and drastically reduced at Los Angeles, when Primo Nebiolo agreed, just before his election as President of the Association of Summer Olympic Federations (ASOIF), that the IAAF should receive no more than any other summer federation. (The reduction did not take effect immediately: as an interim measure it was agreed, on the initiative of the yachting federation, that the IAAF should receive the same amount as at Moscow, £1.2m). There has been speculation that if Nebiolo were to lose the presidency he would press for the restoration of what some regard as IAAF's rightful share in the television rights, but the smaller federations correctly identified their own interests when he came up for re-election in 1989 and only six of them voted against him. No doubt there were some sighs of relief, even from people who disapproved of him as President, and the possibility of a painful renegotiation was averted.

The Olympic Programme (TOP)

The 86th Session of the IOC at Delhi in April 1983 had decided that the movement was becoming too dependent on television. On 1 June 1985 the IOC, with the organising committees of the 1988 summer and winter Games at Seoul and Calgary, and the United States Olympic Committee (USOC) jointly handed marketing over to ISL. This company was 51 per cent owned by Horst Dassler, chairman of Adidas, the manufacturer of sports equipment, footwear and clothing, and 49 per cent by the Japanese advertising agency, Dentsu. (It has never, although it is frequently reported otherwise, been a subsidiary of Adidas).

ISL produced a marketing programme, which became known as 'TOP', (for 'The Olympic Programme'), whereby forty-four categories of product were identified and worldwide rights to use the Olympic 'marks' (as the Olympic emblems are called) to promote products in one or more of those categories would be sold to a single company, to the exclusion of all competitor companies. The fact that the list of categories, which has not been published, contained forty-four items gave rise to the mistaken impression that ISL intended to recruit forty-four companies. In fact no marketing company would expect to sell the whole of its inventory, and some of the categories (such as pretzels) were not important enough to be worthy of worldwide promotion by themselves. Companies have tended to buy rights in groups of products, defining their fields of interest in such a way as to exclude as many potential rivals as possible. For example, in the second TOP programme ('TOP-2') Mars purchased rights to such snack foods as nuts and crisps, as well as confectionery.

At first sight it is surprising that USOC was a separate party to the agreement. The explanation must be seen against the background of USOC's great economic power and of its perennially uneasy relations with the IOC, which will be discussed later in this chapter. At the last ditch the IOC could resolve this unhappy state of affairs by withdrawing its recognition of USOC, but the victory would be pointless. The Olympic movement, and with it the worldwide market offered by the Games, would be irretrievably split, and once the market had lost its uniquely worldwide character the international companies, many of which are American, would be likely to pull out of TOP. On the other hand, the IOC can present its success in persuading USOC into TOP as something of a triumph, while USOC may have seen joining the scheme as a sop which it could afford to throw to the IOC while protecting its own interests by obtaining a high proportion of the programme's proceeds.

ISL had sold worldwide rights in the past, for example, for FIFA (the international football federation), but in such cases the practical arrangements were relatively simply, since FIFA is in a position to sell worldwide rights without obtaining the approval of individual national federations. The unique feature of Olympic marketing is that each NOC has control over its own marketing programme, and will only join a universal programme if it is its own interest to do so. Therefore, once the IOC had accepted the principle of TOP, ISL's first task was to persuade the autonomous NOCs to take part, which it did with such success that 153 of the 156 NOCs which existed at that time, including all the main Olympic nations, had agreed to the new arrangements in time for the Seoul Games of 1988. These included the Soviet Union, which having 'signed with ISL in November 1986, even organized a seminar in Moscow at which ISL were able to explain the project to twenty-six other countries, including all those from the socialist bloc'.[9] By October 1991 167 out of the by then 170 NOCs (including the newly recognised ones of the three Baltic states) had joined the programme.

In some cases NOCs already had very satisfactory arrangements with companies, which they had to give up because the essence of TOP is that only one company in any given product category (for example Coca-Cola in soft drinks) is given exclusive worldwide rights. In those cases the NOCs in question were able to negotiate substantial compensation in return for loss of income. A good example is the British Olympic Association, which had a thriving link with American Express, but had to jettison it when Visa entered TOP. Usually NOCs accept a percentage of the proceeds of the categories that they give up to ISL, although many strong-minded national Treasurers insisted on an absolute figure being guaranteed in TOP-1. However, now that the programme's success has reassured NOCs that their income is not in jeopardy, the practice of demanding such guarantees has become much less prevalent.

There is considerable commercial secrecy within TOP, for each NOC negotiates with ISL the share of total TOP income that it is to receive and no NOC is told what percentage goes to any other. The exception is USOC, which is known to receive a top slice of 20 per cent of the total proceeds.

TOP is limited by politics in that some product categories, like cars and airlines, are deemed to be too bound up with national sensibilities for any one company to be chosen to receive worldwide rights. Such categories are also excluded by practical considerations, since many NOCs have successful local arrangements which they would not give up.

The companies which do participate in TOP obtain extensive rights. For example, at Seoul they were permitted to use the Olympic marks on products and packaging, and in advertisements, whether printed, on television, or on billboards (but not inside the stadia, where no advertising is allowed), on letterheads, point of sale material, posters, corporate communications, etc. They could also use the designation 'worldwide sponsor/supplier/product of the 1988 'Olympic Games', use Olympic archive material and advertise in official Olympic publications. In addition, the organising committees at Seoul and Calgary offered the right to use their emblems and mascots, preferential advertising in their publications, and the opportunity to buy the best tickets and accommodation.[10]

As products become more similar companies increasingly look for points of differentiation which are exclusive and therefore cannot be copied. Thus, the Olympics provide one of the best imaginable vehicles for worldwide advertising. They also provide a unique opportunity to promote feelings of security in potential customers and to entertain important associates. Olympic entertaining is corporate hospitality *par excellence*, something like a worldwide Derby or Grand National. In consequence it is not surprising to learn that Visa put $14m into the Calgary/Seoul sponsorship programme and spent $25m to advertise its involvement. Similarly, 3M, one of America's largest companies, attempting to raise its image outside the United States, put $15m into the Olympic package, with a further $50m in worldwide back-up.[11]

As well as building on ISL's experience, the IOC had also learned from the 'private enterprise Games' at Los Angeles in 1984. However, an IOC publication does not praise the Los Angeles marketing strategy unreservedly. The organising committee had obtained some important contracts, 'but neglected to seek authorization from the NOCs for any action planned in their territory'. It goes on that there is more to be gained from a few high-level firms than from a host of small sponsors whom it is impossible to satisfy or understand. Its author believes that TOP will strengthen the NOCs and boost the credibility of the Olympic movement as a whole – no bad thing after successive boycotts. But he is not wholly optimistic, because company entertaining could get out of hand. TOP firms had invited 6,000-plus guests to Calgary and 10,000-plus to Seoul and it was 'hoped or feared' that these figures could double in 1992.[12] It may, however, be worth remembering that the Olympic world is prone to exaggeration, and that these figures may be overestimates.

Top-1 did not live up to ISL's expectations in all respects. For one thing, it attracted only nine companies, which between them paid a little over $100m.[13] The nine were Coca-Cola (which has been associated with the Olympics since 1928; it was the first respondent and got the franchise for all cold drinks, including 'sports drinks', as well as its main product); Visa; 3M; Brother; Philips; Federal Express; Kodak; Time Inc. and Panasonic. Evidently some companies which might have participated did not relish having to buy rights in such minor territories as Chad (although, of course, they would not be very expensive). Aris quotes American Express (in the *Wall Street Journal*): 'We didn't want to waste our money buying rights to countries where we don't even have a presence.'[14] Nor would a company

necessarily wish to undertake an Olympic promotion in all its major
territories at once. In commercial terms it is said that an Olympic
promotion is always right in the United States, because of that
country's obsessive patriotism, which in the Olympic context shows
itself in a frantic interest in the number of medals won by Americans.
That does not mean that a simultaneous promotion in, for example,
Germany, would necessarily be judged a correct strategy by a multi-
national company's marketing experts.

Another difficulty was that some of the lesser international sports
federations felt that TOP made it less easy for them to sell the rights in
their own championships, which of course do not form part of the
Olympic marketing programme. This consideration does not affect
the more powerful federations, which are well able to market their
championships. As David Miller has put it: 'ASOIF [the Association
of Summer Olympic Federations] members would like to see . . .
more consultation with the IOC's sponsorship marketing agents, ISL,
who clean up the major sponsorship to the disadvantage of lesser
Olympic sports trying to market their own world championships . . '[15]

Michael Payne, formerly of ISL and now the IOC's marketing
director, underlines the message that sponsorship has become a
highly technical activity and demands a professional approach from
those who are trying to sell it. 'The sponsor', he writes, 'was more
often based on a Chairman's personal sporting preference than on any
professional marketing evaluation. Today sports sponsorship
competes for the marketing dollar against all other forms of advertising and promotional activities.'[16]

TOP-2

Olympic rules do not permit the commercial negotiations to start
again for the next Games until the current ones are over. After Seoul
similar arrangements were made for the Barcelona Games in a new
programme, TOP-2, which attracted twelve companies. To establish
TOP-2, ISL had to complete new deals for various product categories
with each NOC. The companies recruited included all the Seoul nine,
save Federal Express, plus EMS (courier service replacing Federal
Express), Ricoh, Mars and Bausch and Lomb and it was hoped that
between them the twelve would produce as much as $150m.[17] More
recent estimates range as high as $180m.

The variety of commercial contracts is extremely complex and will be illustrated primarily by reference to COOB, the organising committee of the Barcelona Games. There are three types of salesman selling different kinds of 'mark', as the Olympic emblems are called. The salesmen are: the IOC itself; the host cities, in 1992 Albertville and Barcelona; and each NOC, selling the right to use the Olympic emblem in its own territory. The marks on sale are the five rings, which are the exclusive property of the IOC; the local emblems devised by organising committees (for example, Barcelona's mascot, 'Cobi'); and the derivatives of the five rings which individual NOCs embellish with local variations.

As we have seen, TOP allows a small number of companies to use the unembellished five rings worldwide and to use the marks of any NOC which belongs to the programme. These companies may also make worldwide use of the organising committees' marks, though in the case of Seoul they were probably worth very little outside Korea.

Each host city must, by Olympic rule, form a joint marketing body with its NOC, though the precise form of the association may vary. Normally an NOC would expect to benefit from the Games being held in its territory – otherwise it would not allow a candidature to go forward – but in the Spanish case, where the NOC was in an exceptionally weak position, it seems unlikely to have been able to make a good bargain with COOB.

The IOC receives 3 per cent of all sponsorship revenue raised by the host cities (to be increased to 5 per cent after 1992) and reserves the right to vet all their contracts. In addition to receiving a percentage of TOP and marketing their own emblems and mascots in their own territories, organising committees generally enter into bilateral deals with other marketing territories. In general organising committees are enthusiastic to make bilateral arrangements, because they mistakenly believe that the association with their own Games is the most attractive right on the market, whereas what appeals most potently to buyers is the association with the Olympic movement as a whole. Some rather odd deals result: for example COOB agreed with USOC in 1988 that for all product categories except those bought by companies participating in TOP, the purchaser of United States rights from USOC would also be obliged to buy, as part of the package, the right to use the Spanish marks in the USA, whether or not these rights were of any use to the company in that territory.

COOB established various grades of local sponsor. First, all TOP sponsors are automatically local sponsors (in both winter and summer host cities), though not necessarily in the highest grade, Joint Partner. Joint Partners pay a minimum contribution of P2,500m and, like TOP companies, receive a package which includes hotel rooms and tickets to Olympic events.

Next come Sponsors, a grade which includes Coca-Cola and Kodak, both members of TOP; they were required to subscribe at least P600m. Sponsors have similar rights to hotel rooms and so on as do Joint Partners, but fewer of them. Lesser grades are Suppliers (P150m) and Licensees, of whom there were to be 120. This title is granted to companies with a catalogue of at least five hundred products in such sectors as toys and writing materials. Finally comes Official Sports Material, a designation given to a single product, which might not be extended to other products manufactured by the same company. The maximum number expected was 100, and payment was to be made in kind.

However, it is important to remember that TOP is only part of selling the Games. By January 1989 the TOP programme was expected to yield $150–160m (about P18,000m). Of this total Barcelona might expect to receive $60m or about P5,000m net, after COOB had paid commissions to its agents. This would be less than 4 per cent of the total cost of staging the Games.[18] In an interview with *La Vanguardia* in June 1990 Antoni Rossich, Commercial Director of COOB, said that two-thirds of their commercial programme, amounting to P40,717m had already been completed. They had eight companies, with the possibility of a few more, in the Joint Partner category. In the second category, Sponsors, forty companies had been planned, paying an average of P900m and a minimum of P600m. They had so far recruited eighteen companies, ten of which were also members of the TOP-2 programme, which itself would earn P6,000 for Barcelona.

In the third category, Supplier, a maximum of seventy-five companies, paying at least P150m, had been envisaged, but so far only eleven had been recruited. In the final category, Licensees, there were so far forty-nine companies, and 387 different products, ranging in value from P45 to P26,000 for a large aluminium model of the Games' mascot, 'Cobi'. COOB expected to limit this category to seventy companies, selling six to seven hundred products, with sales of P30,000m of which P2,300m would come to COOB. For each successful company it was necessary to disappoint many others, in order to ensure that in each category of product the Olympic mark was only given to one company.[19]

Rossich sounded confident in this interview, but the impression given was that the final third of the total envisaged might be difficult to achieve. The bulk will probably come from a few very large backers, yet at the same time the large number of licensed products, producing relatively little for COOB, may flood the market (or intoxicate it, as Rossich put it) with a vast number of products bearing the Olympic symbol.

Some reports suggest that the IOC is anxious dramatically to extend its commercial control by establishing something like TOP in such commercially active Olympic countries as Britain, France, Japan, Australia, and perhaps Germany (the last has not been very active in the past).

Such reports must be treated with some care, since to extend the IOC's control in this way would require an alteration to the Charter, not to mention considerable persuasion of NOCs which would wish to continue to be responsible for marketing their own marks. However, what is beyond doubt is that the IOC hopes to extend its licensing arrangements, despite the obvious problems of conflict of interest with NOCs and of flooding ('intoxicating', in Rossich's phrase quoted above) the market with a proliferation of licensed goods, and thereby devaluing the Olympic association. The IOC would not seek to impose its will on the NOCs, but if it proceeds with its current intention some hard negotiations lie ahead, if the general interest of the Olympic movement is to be served.

(Average January 1989 exchange rate, $1 = 115 pesetas).

The United States Olympic Committee and the IOC

As has already been suggested, the USOC has long been a thorn in the flesh of the IOC.

USOC was established by a federal statute of 1948. The act protects USOC's exclusive right to use the Olympic rings in the United States, and even the right to use the word 'Olympic'. To seek to protect the use of a word in this way is, of course, very ambitious. USOC does not succeed completely in protecting its copyright, and hence its ability to raise funds, but it does have an attorney on its staff who spends virtually all his time on trying to ensure that the legislation is adhered to.

In 1978 there followed the Amateur Sports Act, which settled the long-running feud between two rival athletic organisations, the National Collegiate Athletic Association and the Amateur Athletic Union, and established the right of athletes to 'due process'. This meant that for an athlete in any discipline who had a grievance against his association or federation the ultimate authority became USOC. The Act also established the autonomy of different sports, each of which became an individual member of USOC. Previously groups of sports had combined under the umbrella of, for example, the AAU and joined USOC as a single member.

USOC is entitled to receive 10 per cent of the fees received for American television rights. This arrangement was made after the IOC had allowed the American television companies, ABC and NBC, to permit sponsors of broadcasts to use their (ABC's and NBC's) logos combined with the Olympic emblem. Thus the use of an Olympic mark was being sub-contracted to companies which had not paid for it directly.

USOC argued that compensation was due to it for this practice, which reduced the pool of companies to which it could sell its own mark, and, further, that the IOC had exceeded its powers in allowing the television companies to sub-contract. USOC is no longer satisfied with its 10 per cent and hard negotiations have taken place with the IOC.

USOC's case rests on two facts about broadcasting in the United States. First, to receive broadcasts is held to be part of the general constitutional right of communication, so that no one would tolerate having to pay to receive radio, and few to receive television. (However, the point is somewhat weakened by the fact that NBC, once it had acquired the North American television rights in the Barcelona Games of 1992, decided to put out some of its coverage over pay television. The decision provoked public protests, to the effect that no one had previously had to pay to watch the Olympic Games, to which NBC replied that the public had never before been offered such extensive coverage.) Secondly, radio and television are sustained by revenue from advertisements, revenue which can be likened to a form of sponsorship.

The argument goes on that the television rights for the Barcelona Games, plus the winter Games of Albertville and Lillehammer, raised over a billion dollars, which is money taken out of the total pool available for sports sponsorship, and so puts non-Olympic sports at a disadvantage. USOC claims to be the only NOC to receive no government funding, and that over 90 per cent of its revenue comes from commercial sponsorship. (The claim is over-stated, since USOC rents its headquarters, an old Air Force base, from the federal government for a dollar a year. Furthermore, donors to USOC receive tax credits on their gifts.) Since it receives only 10 per cent of the Olympic television revenue, the remaining 90 per cent represents a dramatic loss of the advertising and corporate space potentially available to it as a source of funds. The consequential questions, therefore, concern the extent to which USOC should be involved in the negotiations over television rights, with a view to retrieving some part of what it calls 'lost revenues'.

USOC argues that all parties would benefit if it were involved. At present the whole Olympic scene is complicated by the fact that, under the law of 1978 governing USOC, any American citizen has the right to compete in trials for all Olympic events. Thus the rights to the Olympic trials are an asset saleable separately from those to the Olympic Games themselves: for example, in 1988 NBC had the rights to the Games, but USOC sold the rights to the trials to ABC for about $3 million. These trials rights, it is argued, would be more valuable if tied to the Games, and it would also be possible to market packages tying them to rights in other competitions.

There is, therefore a case, USOC believes, for the sale of television rights to be negotiated in North America in partnership with USOC, whereas the Barcelona rights were negotiated by the IOC and COOB (the Barcelona organising committee) without any reference to USOC. So strong is the case thought to be that there have been stirrings in Congress. In 1990 there were hearings before various Congressional Committees, including the Commerce Committee, and there are Congressmen who have been willing to press for legislation to prevent the seepage of what is seen as American money into the Olympic movement at large.

USOC does not demand a specific enhanced percentage, but believes that the united intention of all parties should be to maximise return from the television rights. A starting point would be to establish the needs of the organising committee, and thereafter to establish a formula for sharing.

One obvious counter-argument is to ask why, if USOC takes a hand in the negotiations for its local television rights, should not every NOC do the same? To this USOC replies that most NOCs are much better off receiving a share from the IOC than they would be on their own, but that there can be no objection to any NOC that has anything substantial to sell being similarly involved. Thus, the British Olympic Association might well benefit from being involved in the sale of its own television rights.

A further point made by USOC is that any city that bids for the Games ought to be able to make a surplus from them, with nil risk of making a loss, and that if a city looks unlikely to do so the IOC should think of awarding the Games elsewhere. Thus, USOC contends, the decision to hold the Games in a certain place is similar to the decision to start a new company.

Although the dispute with USOC has not been settled, a drastic change has occurred in the way in which the television rights are handled (which does not give any greater say to USOC, though it also does not exclude the possiblity of USOC's role being made more central). Following the experience of Seoul and Barcelona, where the relationship between the IOC's team and the local organising committees were often extremely difficult, the IOC has decided that in future it will handle the negotiations itself.

The new formula leaves USOC with its accustomed 10 per cent, but the new arrangements represent a significant shift of power. They indicate the IOC's continuing anxiety both to preserve its own supremacy and to avoid clashes between the local organising committees' short-term interest and the longer-term interest of the Olympic movement as a whole. The IOC holds that the belief that television revenue has no upward limit, a view taken by, for example, Pasqual Maragall, the Mayor of Barcelona, may eventually cause the death of the goose that lays the golden eggs. There are, indeed, signs in 1991 of diminishing interest among the major companies, which perhaps may be offset by increased use of cable television. On the other hand, paying huge sums for the rights to the Olympics has always been seen by the companies as a loss leader, and the sums paid have not always been rationally determined. Instead 'the networks have allowed the Olympics to become so emotional an issue, so much a matter of pride and self-importance, that they no longer measure it by any reasonable business standard normally applied to programming decisions'.[20]

The power of business: the role of Adidas

The growing commercialisation of the Games has inevitably bred close relationships between the Olympic movement and certain companies and none has been closer than the one with Adidas. The story of its formal connection with the Olympic movement starts in 1983, when, as we have seen, the IOC was by no means rich.

The IOC had anxiously discussed the problems of long-term finance as long ago as 1974.[21] In 1983 it set up a committee (New Sources of Finance Commission), consisting of Adrien Vanden Eede, Colonel Don Miller and Richard Palmer, the Secretaries-General of the Belgian and United States NOCs and of the British Olympic Association, to look at ways of diversifying revenue sources, because Samaranch's great fear (an exaggerated one, in view of American anti-trust laws) was that the television companies could collude to keep the price down or that a future boycott could destroy the United States television market. The committee decided that the IOC needed outside help and fixed on Horst Dassler, the chairman of Adidas, to market the 1988 Games through ISL. When ISL made its presentation to the IOC in New Delhi in 1983 it had a staff of only five, but Samaranch and the Commission were never in any doubt that Dassler was the man to whom they should turn.

Dassler was already well known in international sports circles. According to Aris, he had started in the late 1950s by spending millions in cash and equipment to induce athletes to wear Adidas kit. The frantic drive for sales had originated in a row between Adolf Dassler, Horst's father, and Adolf's brother Rudolph, shortly after Rudolph had completed a year in prison for having been a member of the Nazi party. (This, however, can hardly be the whole reason for his imprisonment.) The reason for the brothers' quarrel is unknown, but after it Rudolph sold out to Adolf and started a rival sports gear firm, Puma, in 1948. The story of their cut-throat rivalry appeared in an article entitled 'The Shoe Wars' in *Sports Illustrated* in 1969, which revealed, against the background of the 1968 Games, the extent of the under cover payments to athletes (which would have been pointless without television).

After these revelations Dassler was rebuked by Brundage (until then the authorities had been turning a blind eye) – but 83 per cent of winners at the 1968 Games had used his shoes and equipment, and criticism meant nothing to him. Instead he turned his attention from the athletes to influencing federations with cash or by underwriting their programmes and helping his friends to rise within them. Thus he acquired influence and contracts, becoming official supplier to the

Russians, the East Germans and much of the Third World.

The contract made between ISL and the IOC at New Delhi made an already powerful man much more so, and brought to the IOC Dassler's network of friends in the IFs, without whom it would have been hard to put into effect the IOC's plans to sell worldwide advertising rights to a limited number of companies. According to Aris, Monique Berlioux told the *Wall Street Journal* in 1986 that Dassler was the real boss of sport, and had struggled for that position not merely in order to sell more shoes, but because he loved the power. Aris thinks that when Dassler died on 10 April 1987 at the early age of 51 he was the most powerful man in 'Sportsbiz', more so even than Samaranch or Mark McCormack, the leading agent for athletes and arranger of athletic fixtures. But, unlike them, he operated behind the scenes.[22] It appears, too, that Berlioux's reluctance to have ISL associated with the IOC in any role other than that of consultant was an important cause of her sudden downfall.[23]

It will, of course, probably never be known for certain how much influence Dassler had on the choice of Olympic cities, but the rumours were persistent during his lifetime. For example, in October 1986 David Miller repeated a story which had appeared in *La Vanguardia* that Adidas could guarantee 30 votes for Barcelona: Miller did not disagree with the basic idea, but thought fifteen votes would be nearer the mark. He recalled, too, that Dassler had supported Seoul in the last forty-eight hours before the vote. He added that it was a pity that Denis Howell had condemned Adidas's influence a few months before the beginning of Birmingham's campaign.[24] Neil Macfarlane, formerly Britain's Minister for Sport, agrees that Dassler swung the IOC from Nagoya to Seoul.[25] However, David Miller appears later to have changed his mind, and to put the swing down to environmental protesters who lined the streets at Baden-Baden.[26]

In May 1987 Miller reported from Istanbul, where the IOC was holding its 92nd Session, that 'the usual platoon of Adidas representatives can be seen rubbing the genie's lamp of business'. Horst Dassler had died very recently, and not even his family knew who would replace him. Dassler had built up his network over thirty years, ever since his father had given him his first responsibility at the age of 20, at the Melbourne Olympics. For the moment the firm was to be looked after by Dr Albert Henkel, the family lawyer, with Brigitte Baenkler, the sister who had been closest to Dassler, and Professor

Gunther Essing.[27]

Usually Samaranch is respectfully treated by the press, but he faced a tough session with *L'Equipe* after Barcelona had been awarded the Games, in which the interviewer asked why the IOC had not reacted to *La Vanguardia*'s allegations about Adidas. This was not much better than being asked when he had stopped beating his wife, and Samaranch naturally said that any suggestions of impropriety were totally false; that the IOC's contract had only been given to ISL because Dassler had done so much for sport, especially in the Third World, and that in any case it would not necessarily be renewed after 1988.[28]

Since Dassler's death Adidas has maintained a much lower profile. Rumours quickly started that the family might sell out, and *The Times*, quoting *L'Economie du Sport*, reported in October 1989 that it wished to sell its 51 per cent of ISL.[29] The appeal of sports shoes depends to a considerable extent on fashion, and the products are very liable to cheap imitation, as well as legitimate competition. In August 1990 the *Financial Times* reported that the firm had lost DM130m ($86.7m) worldwide in 1989, but had forecast better results for 1990, because of restructuring and slightly higher turnover, which had risen by 7 per cent to DM4.6bn. This figure included licensing revenues and DM3.2bn, slightly more than in 1988, from other activities, including goods sold under the 'Pony' and 'Le Coq Sportif' trade names. Adidas's German operation, including exports, had lost DM112m, against DM9m in 1988: like other similar companies, it had been hit by competition, especially in the United States. The company's AGM earlier in the week had approved the transfer of 80 per cent of the shares from the four daughters of Adi Dassler to Bernard Tapie Finance, which was paying DM440m for them and would inject a further DM300m into the company. The goal was a small profit in 1990 and turnover of DM5bn in 1992, including United States sales of $500m and of $340m in Japan.[30] In August 1991 Bernard Tapie sold 20 per cent of the German holding company of Adidas (which had made a net profit of DM30m in 1990) to a British company, Pentland, which, despite a recent large disposal, still holds 13 per cent of 'Reebok', one of Adidas's main rivals.[31]

It looked in 1990 as if Adidas were a spent force and unlikely to re-emerge as a major player on the field of sports politics, but with the company's return to profit that verdict now seems premature.

Perhaps it is fitting to end this chapter on Olympic finance on a note of doubt. The ambiguity of Dassler's relationship with the world of sport must strengthen the misgivings of people who disapprove of the Games' conversion to a commercial spectacular. But for those who do not disapprove, and who see the Olympic marketing programme as similar to that of any other commercial organisation, Dassler was a natural ally. Without him the Olympics' present prosperity might have been long delayed.

Thus in a single relationship the arguments both ways are symbolised and summed up. On the one hand a purity of intention which does not readily accommodate itself to the world of commerce. On the other hand, enterprising capitalism which sees the fears and doubts of the purists as merely anachronistic.

Notes

1   46th Session, Oslo, 12–13 February 1952, *Minutes*.

2   50th Session, Paris, 13–18 June 1955, *Minutes*.

3   51st Session, Cortina d'Ampezzo, January 24–5 1956, *Minutes*.

4   Neil Wilson, *The Sports Business*, London, 1988, pp. 17–18. However, there is a remarkable conflict of evidence between Wilson and Aris, who states that 'in 1980 the official record shows that the IOC's reserves had dwindled to no more than $241,000'. A possible explanation is that Wilson is taking into account sums held by the IOC on behalf of IFs and NOCs. Stephen Aris, *Sportsbiz: Inside the Sports Business*, London, 1990, p. 160.

5   Monique Berlioux, 'The History of the International Olympic Committee' in Lord Killanin and John Rodda (eds.), *The Olympic Games 1984*, London, 1983, p. 43.

6   75th Session, Vienna, 21–4 October 1974, *Minutes*.

7   David A. Klatell and Norman Marcus, *Sports for Sale: Television, Money, and the Fans*, New York, 1988, pp. 164 and 165. According to Geoffrey Miller, *Behind the Olympic Rings*, Lynn, Massachussetts, 1979, p. 150, the IOC's share of the 1975 television rights was $7.05m.

8   Peter Ueberroth, *Made in America*, London, 1986, p. 54.

9   Wilson, p. 25.

10   I have drawn extensively in this section on a pamphlet published in 1988 by the IOC: *TOP – The Olympic Programme: The National Olympic Committees' Manual of the Olympic Marketing Programme*.

11   David Miller, *The Times*, 16 September 1988.

12   Adrian vanden Eede – 'The National Olympic Committees and Marketing', in *Olympic Message – Marketing and Olympism*, 24 July 1989, pp. 28 and 30–1.

13   Wilson, p. 27.

14   Aris, pp. 171–82

15   David Miller *The Times*, 30 August 1989.

16   Michael Payne 'Sport and Industry' in *Olympic Message – Marketing and Olympism*, July 1989, pp. 37–43.

17 *Sport Intern*, 23, 2, 6 February 1991, p. 5. It should again be noted that reliable figures are hard to find. For example, *Sport Intern* differs from other sources quoted in the text, putting the average price of the sponsor package at less than $10m in 1988, which would give total TOP proceeds in that year of less than $90m.

18 *La Vanguardia*, 27 January 1989.

19 *La Vanguardia*, 4 June 1990.

20 Klatell and Marcus, p. 186.

21 International Olympic Committee, 75th Session, Vienna, 21–4 October 1974, *Minutes*.

22 Aris, pp. 162–8. I have drawn heavily on Aris's valuable chapter on the Olympic Games. The article which he cites on the payments made to athletes was 'Shoe Wars' by John Underwood in *Sports Illustrated*, 10 March 1969.

23 Wilson, p. 16. However, Berlioux would have fallen anyway. The disagreement over ISL's role was a symptom of the deeper question 'Who runs the IOC?'

24 David Miller, *The Times*, 15 October 1986 and *La Vanguardia*, 6 October 1986.

25 N. Macfarlane, *Sport and Politics*, London, 1986, p. 70.

26 *The Times*, 16 September 1988.

27 *ibid.*, 8 May 1987, David Miller, Istanbul. Henkel's involvement was to be short-lived.

28 *L'Equipe*, 20 October 1986. (At the IOC's Executive Board meeting at Berlin in September 1991, ISL's contract was renewed until 1996, to cover TOP-3.)

29 *The Times*, 10 October 1989.

30 *Financial Times*, 25/26 August 1990.

31 *The Times*, 14 August 1991. Horst Dassler's sisters, who still hold 20 per cent of Adidas, also retain their interest in ISL through Christopher P. Malms, the husband of one of them, who in January 1991 was elected president of the supervisory board of Sporis AG, which owns 51 per cent of ISL. The result was that in January 1991 both the President of ISL, Klaus Hempel, and his principal lieutenant, Juergen Lenz, resigned. *Sports Intern*, 23, 1 & 2, 15 January and 6 February 1991.

V

Bidding for the Games: the British experience

This chapter goes into the bidding process, with particular reference to the failed bids by Birmingham and Manchester to host the Games of 1992 and 1996 respectively. Manchester's hat remains in the ring as the British candidate for the year 2000.

There follow four chapters on particular Games, those at Moscow 1980, Los Angeles 1984, Seoul 1988 and Barcelona 1992. It will be seen that the bidding process does not differ greatly from year to year, though attempts are periodically made to cut down its complexity and expense. What does vary is the number of candidates. There were six for the Games of 1992, but only two for 1988, and for 1984 only Los Angeles. A paucity of candidates shifts the balance of power between the IOC and the host city, so that the IOC is now determined that there shall in future always be a good choice of aspiring host cities.

The bidding process

The Olympic Games have until lately been awarded by the IOC six years before the year in which they are to be held. The 1992 Games were awarded to Barcelona in 1986, and the decision between the six contenders for 1996 was made at the IOC's Session in Tokyo in September 1990, when it chose Atlanta. The timetable has now changed: so great an event have the Games become that host cities are chosen seven years ahead. At the Birmingham Session in 1991 Nagano, Japan, was given the winter Games of 1998 and the decision over the summer Games of 2000 will be made in September 1993.

Until 1992 the winter and summer Games will have been held in the same year, ever since the first winter Games were held at Chamonix in 1924, and the choice from both sets of candidates has been made at the same Session of the IOC. However, at the 91st IOC Session in Lausanne in 1986 it was decided to stagger them. The next summer and winter Games will be in 1992 at Barcelona and Albertville respectively. Thereafter the winter Games move into their new cycle and will be held at Lillehammer, Norway, in 1994. The new procedure carries with it the disadvantage that the Olympic movement will be more continuously than ever in a turmoil of campaigning and lobbying, but it is thought that it will be possible to maximise revenue by separating the two sets of Games.

In 1986 there were eighty-nine members of the IOC, of whom eighty-five voted at the crucial meeting in Lausanne, the IOC's headquarters, when it was decided that Barcelona would hold the Games of 1992. Samaranch abstained (as the President normally does) because his home town of Barcelona was a candidate, and he wished to preserve the impartiality associated with his office; one member was in prison (for a political 'crime') and two were ill.

The purpose of a city's campaign is to gain as many as possible of these members' votes. It is necessary to pay heed to a member's second and third preferences, as well as his or her first, since if no city gains a majority on the first round of voting the one with the fewest votes is eliminated, and a second vote is taken. It may be necessary to hold numerous rounds before a decision is reached and once members have seen their first choice eliminated they will feel free to give their vote on subsequent rounds to another candidate, or to different ones as the voting proceeds. There is also some anecdotal evidence that some members change their allegiance even if the city for which they first voted is still in the race. It is therefore desirable for every member to have a first-hand opinion of every bidding city and each city does all it can to persuade each member to pay it a personal visit. This is not necessarily done in the hope of capturing his or her first preference, but in order that he or she will have a clear impression of the city's strengths, in case his second or even lower preference becomes relevant. (It should be noted that evidence is difficult to gather, as the voting takes place in private. The figures for each round are published, but nobody knows how any individual member voted. Nor are members' own accounts of how they voted necessarily reliable, since there is a natural propensity to claim afterwards to have voted for the winner.)

To lobby ninety or so IOC members does not sound an especially demanding task, but there is far more to an Olympic bid than that.

Each international federation (IF) must be satisfied that the facilities for its sport are adequate; National Olympic Committees (NOCs) must be assured that their interests are covered, as must the numerous associations of IFs and NOCs. There must be national and local support for the bid; the technical aspects must be satisfactory, as must security, transport and accommodation for the athletes and the 'Olympic family' and the facilities for the press and television need to be sufficient for world wide coverage. (The 'Olympic family' commonly refers to the IOC and its entourage and to the great number of representatives of international federations, NOCs and so on who always surround the Games.)

Although no one but the IOC members can make the final decision, they are in touch with other sections of the sporting world; some have been athletes themselves; many hold, or have held, office in a federation or NOC, and most of them are political animals. Thus their decisions will be influenced by a multitude of considerations, ranging from the opinions of contacts in the NOC and IFs to their notions of where it would be agreeable to spend two weeks in summer, and most of them will have a lively awareness of the wider political considerations. A few members may also be willing to accept gifts of more than nominal value, though of course there can be no guarantee that they will then deliver their votes.[1]

The politics of choosing the host city

To take an example, now that Beijing has announced its candidature for the Games of 2000, there are no doubt IOC members who would be horrified at the thought of giving the Olympic movement's seal of approval to the Chinese regime; others would be optimistic about the changes that may take place in China over the next ten years; others would come from countries which have political debts to China, and some would believe that to welcome a Chinese bid, even if China did not change at all over the intervening period, would tie that country more securely to the West, and contribute to the decline of socialism and the triumph of capitalism.

To take another example, some members would see a bid from a reunited Berlin as the culmination or symbol of the reunification of Europe, and therefore as something deeply to be desired; others would fear the uncertainties injected into international affairs by the Soviet empire's decline, or be terrified of a united Germany, and therefore would be intellectually and emotionally inclined to vote against a bid from a united Berlin.

Financing the games

Even to bid for the Games may cost as much as $10m. The bill may be met from governmental funds, as at Moscow, where the 1980 Games were held, or from privately raised money, as at Los Angeles (1984), or from a mixture of the two, as at Barcelona.

Once the Games have been awarded, a city has to move into an immensely higher gear and develop an organisation capable of spending billions of dollars on the plans which have been presented to the IOC in outline in the bidding document. The question then arises of what is to happen if the Games make a loss.

In a state-directed economy, where the costs have been borne by government to start with, there is no particular problem: the state merely continues to pay the bills. However, in a capitalist economy, there arise at least two problems. First, there is no rule of thumb by which it can be decided what is to count as a cost specific to the Games. Secondly, after Los Angeles had shown that it was possible to make an enormous profit on the Games ($215m) it has become a matter of pride to outdo Los Angeles, so that there may be a temptation to overstate the figures for public consumption.

Montreal, by including in the profit and loss account capital items, such as a new airport, managed to make a loss on the 1976 Games and has left taxpayers with huge bills to pay off. South Korea, an authoritarian capitalist state, was anxious to outdo Los Angeles and declared a profit of $497m, but this figure included $347m cash donations and advance premiums for apartments built in the Olympic village, and sold after the Games to private owners. However, when it came to calculating the profit for the purpose of dividing it between the various branches of the Olympic movement, Seoul asked that the $347m be excluded, and Samaranch agreed.[2]

The risks

The question naturally poses itself of what risks are involved in bidding for the Olympic Games. It is possible for them to be risk-free in the financial sense, but (as with almost any human enterprise) there must always be risks of a less tangible kind, associated with individuals' reputations.

The types of actor who have something at stake in bidding for the Olympic Games are numerous. They include the charismatic individual, like Bob Scott of Manchester or Pasqual Maragall of Barcelona, who takes the lead in stimulating local enthusiasm to the point where a bid will carry conviction; the local or national businessmen (and in Manchester's case one individual, the Duke of Westminster) who decided to fund the bid; the members of the organising committee recruited by the charismatic leader; the IOC, IFs and NOCs; the government of the country concerned; local or national politicians who may risk losing office if voters are dissatisfied (this of course only applies in countries which are to some degree democratic) and, in countries where all or part of the cost is met from public funds, the taxpayer.

However, it seems sensible to exclude the taxpayer from the list of those at risk, because a risk can only be so called if the risk taker knows that he or she is taking it, and has the possibility of choosing not to do so. This is not to say, however, that the taxpayer has no influence on the decision. In recent years there have been occasions when voters have made their views felt. In California, worried about damage to the environment which they believed would result from holding the Games at Los Angeles, the financial costs (especially in view of the losses incurred by Montreal in 1976) and disruption to their daily lives, they ensured that State and local government funds would not be spent. (See chapter VII.)

A group of citizens from Amsterdam went further in 1986, when their city was a candidate for 1988. They paraded outside the IOC's headquarters in Lausanne, where the vote was to be taken, and demonstrated to such effect (some accounts say that they even spat at the IOC members as they went into the hotel where the votes were to be cast) that Amsterdam was eliminated on the first round of voting. Nor had they confined their opposition to the last lap of the race, as Denis Howell's account of demonstrations in 1985 shows.[3]

As for companies which subscribe to the bidding fund, it must be doubted whether they are taking on increased risks, beyond those normally associated with business. If the money spent comes out of an advertising or sponsorship budget then the outlay is more in the nature of a 'sunk cost' and the company is not in a riskier position than it would have been had there been no bid. Nor is it likely that any commercial concern would base its future prospects and solvency on the chance of a bid succeeding. On the other hand, a company will probably calculate that the exposure given to its name, plus the increased business which may be expected even after an unsuccessful bid (because the city's international profile will have been raised whether or not it succeeds) is worth the subscription. Furthermore, if the city does win, the physical development of the area, not to mention the constant series of high level delegations during the bidding period, the large number of employees taken on by the organising committee, and the great throng of visitors during the Olympic Games themselves, will all generate commercial activity and worldwide publicity. Nor does it seem appropriate to identify as risk money the subscription paid by the Duke of Westminster, who would no doubt prefer to see it as a charitable donation, designed to promote the wellbeing of the region in which he lives and plays a leading part as a major landowner and patron of innumerable organisations.

The charismatic leader indubitably runs risks, but they are personal, rather than financial. The constant travel during the campaign may take its toll of job (if he or she has one outside the organising committee), health and family life, but whether he or she is working solely for expenses, or is paid a salary by backers, these will either be paid, or the bid will have to be abandoned. The same may be said about the salaries paid to employees of the organising committee. As in any enterprise, there is always the possibility of losing one's job, though some employees are cushioned by being on loan from parent companies which continue to pay their normal salaries while they are seconded to the committee.

Support given to the bidding committee by local and central government during the bidding campaign will amount to a letter from the Prime Minister (in the British case), without which the IOC will not contemplate the bid; diplomatic assistance in making contact with IOC members and generally raising the bid's profile, and some kind of assurance that the government will meet a proportion of the loss which may be made, if the city wins the contest to stage the Games. Many countries will involve their Prime Ministers or major Royal figures in their bids, but not Britain, although, of course the Princess Royal is heavily involved in her capacity as a member of the IOC.

The letter of support and the diplomatic back-up are risk-free, though not cost-free in terms of civil servants' and Ministers' time. To withhold them would appear churlish and unsporting, even if the government were not, in its heart of hearts, keen on holding the Olympic Games at all. Even the financial guarantee, which only comes into effect if the bidding city wins, is unlikely to be called upon in these post-Los Angeles days of private enterprise Games. Ninety per cent of the expense of holding the Games occurs in the last six months, and if at that stage the organising committee were not reasonably certain to cover costs from television rights, licensing, ticket sales and so on, it could call off the Games, and might be compelled to do so.

The IOC, IFs and NOCs do incur some risks in their choice of host city for the Olympic Games. If a city is chosen which proves incapable of organising the Games effectively, as has been so widely feared over Barcelona, the Games will still be held, and will probably be successful as a television event, but they will not be counted a success by the athletes and the hordes of officials who accompany them.

The financial risk for all these bodies relates largely to the sale of the United States television rights, since these are the foundation of the IOC's current prosperity and a main source of the grants made to the IFs and NOCs by the IOC. However, if the television fees fell below expectation the Olympic bodies would not die: they would merely have to economise. The IOC would also survive if the Games had to be called off altogether, though perhaps not if this happened twice running.

In concluding the list of individuals at risk, one must not forget the IOC members themselves. They give their services, but since, as we have already seen, each bidding city finds it essential to persuade as many members as possible to visit it, those who enjoy luxury and being made to feel important can make some agreeable expeditions. The down-side is that if they make a foolish choice of city the IOC's reputation suffers, and it becomes correspondingly more difficult to hold the Olympic movement together and to maintain the IOC's position at its head.

It is not outlandish to imagine the IOC losing that position. The possibility of other, commercial, interests 'hijacking' a recognised (though not Olympic) sport has been seen before with Kerry Packer and the alternative cricket test series. The Olympic movement is heavily dependent on television revenue, and television companies would, as commercial animals, quickly desert the IOC if there were a more competent alternative.

Why host the Games?

It is not so much the potential profit that makes a city believe that the award of the Games confers a great benefit as that the winner immediately becomes known worldwide and is given a kick-start into development. Very often the improvements would have happened in any case, but are accelerated, just as when the Queen of England travels by train the station at which she alights may expect to get a coat of paint. Bidding committees may over-estimate the advantages of holding the Games, but they all believe them to be tremendous. Nor, if one compares the cost of bidding with that of prime-time television advertising, is it very great. This is particularly true of 'cities' (some of them are little more than villages) which bid for the winter Games. Nothing has been said here about the latter, but it is worth noting that to bid for these Games is an effective and cheap way of promoting a little-known ski resort.

Bidding for the Games is expensive in terms of a family budget, but not by comparison with other expenditures undertaken by major cities or companies. Now that the age of boycotts appears to be over, there is little risk of television fees being drastically reduced after they have been agreed. The Olympic movement does however rely excessively on these fees, which is why the IOC has in recent years turned its attention to alternative sources of income.

The only people who might be said to be financially at risk are taxpayers in the host country if the Games themselves make a loss, but they cannot properly be said to take a risk, because the decision is out of their hands. As for the cost of bidding, no charge may fall on public funds and even when it does the local taxpayers may gain from the higher profile achieved by their city in the bidding process, even if the bid is unsuccessful.

It appears, therefore, that the individuals involved in that process are the only ones who may be said to be risk-takers, and that the risks they run relate to health, reputation, private ambition and other aspects of personal life, but not to money.

Birmingham's bid

The IOC insists that bids be made by cities, rather than countries, but that no country may have more than one candidate for any particular Games. If a country has more than one city anxious to bid, its National

Olympic Committee must decide between them. This happened in
the British case. In 1986 Birmingham was Britain's candidate for the
1992 Games, but it had first had to beat London and Manchester in
the vote of the thirty-two British Olympic Association (BOA) members. (The BOA is the British equivalent of an NOC).

When a British bid for 1992 was first discussed both Sir Denis
Follows, the chairman of the BOA, and Denis Howell (the former
Minister for Sport who later was to lead Birmingham's bid) believed
London to be the only runner. James Callaghan, the Prime Minister,
agreed early in 1979 that Howell should include a commitment that
the government would assist the bid financially in the sports programme which he was to draw up for the Labour Party's election
manifesto. However, Labour lost the election, so nothing came of it.
When Manchester announced its candidature most of the leaders of
the Birmingham Council decided that Manchester could not be
allowed to bid without a challenge from Birmingham, and were able to
persuade the BOA to extend the deadline for the acceptance of nominations.

At first Birmingham wanted a Midlands-based Olympics, about
which Howell was privately sceptical, partly because the diffusion of
events at the Los Angeles Games over a large area had been much
criticised, and partly because the Olympic Charter required the
Games (with the exception of rowing and yachting) to be awarded to a
single city. Richard Palmer, General Secretary of the BOA, agreed
with Birmingham and the team proceeded to draw up purely Birming-
ham-based proposals, which included a plan for several small
Olympic villages to be placed alongside the National Exhibition
Centre, so that for most of the events the athletes would be competing
within walking distance from their villages. This had obviously good
security implications.

At this stage all Birmingham was trying to do was to sell itself to the
BOA as Britain's candidate: bidding for the Games themselves would
come later – if the BOA were convinced. Howell took on the presidency of the Birmingham Olympic Committee and identified four key
areas: security; financial viability; the village, which had to capture
the imagination; and selling the project to the BOA. Birmingham
knew that it could only get government support if it could demonstrate that a profit could be made and expected to make at least £200m.

As with any bidding city, the key to getting votes was to show the
BOA members the site well before the vote, which was to be taken at

the Café Royal in London on 12 July 1985. The Birmingham team also had to win over the national officers of participating sports. The two most influential British Olympic journalists, David Miller of *The Times* and John Rodda of *The Guardian*, were unenthusiastic, yet Birmingham's bid was technically so good and its team lobbied so well that it gained 25 votes, against Manchester's 5 and only 2 for London. (A bid which is 'technically' good provides excellent sports facilities, secure accommodation, good communications, etc.)

Financial support for the bid came from industry, but the appeal to the City of London produced only £35,000 'which was quite disgraceful – one more sign that the City cares little for life north of London'.[4] For the purpose of convincing the government Birmingham worked on a profit figure of £50m, (although earlier they had been thinking of as much as £200m), which was accepted by the Treasury and by the Birmingham City Treasurer. At that point the new Prime Minister Margaret Thatcher, authorised Kenneth Baker, the Secretary of State for the Environment, to sign the letter to the IOC guaranteeing the Birmingham bid, and guaranteeing the entrance into Britain of the members of the Olympic 'family'. (It was a great disappointment to Birmingham that the Prime Minister did not sign the letter herself.) The government also agreed to cover any loss over £100m, should there be a catastrophe against which insurance could not be obtained, like boycott or war. Some government money came through the Sports Council: £250,000 towards the bid, with the promise of a grant towards a new swimming pool and velodrome if the bid were successful.

The Birmingham team then embarked on the exhausting business of lobbying the Olympic movement, against the formidable competition of Amsterdam, Barcelona, Belgrade, Brisbane and Paris. Birmingham, like any bidding city, had to send representatives to all the main Olympic events, starting with the IOC Session, and continuing through the regional and continental assemblies. At all these a stand would be erected and receptions were given for IOC members and representatives of IFs. The team also took advice on the delicate matter of gifts, and found that it was the invariable practice to give them to IOC members, not only when they visited bidding cities, but also at other gatherings of the Olympic movement. Birmingham decided to follow the custom, but 'modestly, expressing our friendship and respect'.[5]

One of Birmingham's rivals was Amsterdam, but a vociferous body of citizens was opposed to its candidature. Howell recounts that at a meeting of the General Association of International Sports Federations (GAISF) in Amsterdam in 1985 there were hundreds of demonstrators outside the hotel, protesting against the possibility of the Games being held in their city. When the Mayor took the delegates on the canals, the protesters stood on the bridges and dropped flour bombs on them.[6] However, sources in Amsterdam were not above seeking crime statistics for the West Midlands, in an effort to capitalise on the Handsworth troubles.[7]

At the IOC's Session in Seoul in 1985 the Dutch were more co-operative and asked Howell if he would support their proposal that there should be no more exhibitions or receptions until the final presentation of the bids in Lausanne, Howell was acutely aware that Birmingham was trying to do in one year what had taken its opponents three or four, but readily agreed, on condition that the other cities agreed. Unhappily they did not, so the circus continued. However, a delightful camaraderie developed between the bidding cities, with the leaders becoming friends and the technical people helping each other to put up their stands.[8]

The Birmingham team had their first discussion about tactical voting at a meeting with the Soviet Olympic Committee in Moscow in January 1986. They had a similar discussion with the flamboyant Ivan Slavkov (who was to become an IOC member in 1987) in February at Sofia, which was bidding for the winter Games, and for whose candidature there was some solid support. Howell's visit to the 94-year-old IOC member General Vladimir Stoytchev convinced him that no one would be able to instruct the General how to vote, although Slavkov had assured him that the Bulgarian NOC would make its wishes very clear. However his conversations with Slavkov did lead to a deal, of considerable complexity to the reader, though perhaps not to the participants, involving mutual support in certain circumstances: unfortunately Birmingham did not do well enough for the deal ever to be put into effect.

In March the Birmingham team was in Peru to lobby the IOC member, Ivan Dibos. He liked their bid, but told them of the growing pressure among Latin American members to support Barcelona.[9] By late September IOC members had visited Birmingham and the team had talked to most of the others, though they never succeeded in meeting the completely elusive Shagdarjan Magvan of Mongolia. Pasqual Maragall, the Mayor of Barcelona, who was leading his city's bid and was therefore an arch-rival of Birmingham, also came on a visit, and said that he had come to see for himself because he was worried about the impact Birmingham was making. His parting shot was 'Birmingham is indeed an Olympic city, but not for 1992'.

With one exception the visiting IOC members all said how much they approved of the Birmingham slogan 'Give the Games back to the athletes'. However, in the end this perfectly unexceptionable slogan seems to have done Birmingham damage because certain members of the IOC could not stomach the suggestion that the Games might have ever been taken away from the athletes, and because Birmingham overdid the use of the slogan in its final presentation. Howell himself was smooth and ambassadorial, but the homespun genuineness of certain of his colleagues jarred on some IOC members, who were unaccustomed to such cheerfully informal invitations as 'Brothers, come and sit down'. Another great difficulty faced by Birmingham was the British government's attitude to South Africa. Its stand against sanctions caused the Commonwealth Games of 1986, which Birmingham had hoped to use as a shop window, to be widely boycotted. Only twenty-six of the forty-seven members of the Commonwealth took part, and they were overwhelmingly white. Of course, IOC members were not impressed to be told about Birmingham's multi-racial character.[10]

A few days before the crucial vote in Lausanne on 17 October 1986 David Miller wrote a rather gloomy piece in *The Times* about Birmingham's chances. He had seen a meaningful undercurrent of truth in a discouraging remark made on his way up to bed by the aged Lord Luke (the senior of Britain's IOC members, who retired in favour of the Princess Royal in 1988): 'Try not to foul it up too much.' The team's provincial inexperience had been well illustrated, Miller wrote, when each city had been asked to send half a dozen members to dine with the IOC. Instead of including Jimmy Munn, the foremost leisure administrator in Britain, who had built the bid's technically brilliant foundations, Birmingham had included 'a couple of wives' and omitted Munn. The Birmingham team had an unfortunate tendency to introduce old friends to each other, and their cause could not have been helped by the visible rivalry between Charles Palmer (who had succeeded Sir Denis Follows as chairman of the BOA in 1983) and Howell, both of whom were hoping for IOC membership (though Miller shrewdly guessed that both of them might be bypassed by the Princess Royal or Sebastian Coe). Birmingham would have done

better, he thought, to bring Richard Palmer with them than Bobby
Charlton, the footballer, who would not know one IOC member,
other than João Havelange, the President of FIFA.[11]

When it came to the vote Birmingham did very poorly, despite its
technically superb bid, as the table of voting shows.

Round	1	2	3
Barcelona	29	37	47
Paris	19	20	23
Brisbane	11	9	10
Belgrade	13	11	5
Birmingham	8	8	
Amsterdam	5		

Birmingham is thought to have done badly because most of its team
were unused to the corridors of international power, though an
exception must be made for the team leader, Denis Howell. Birmingham had also to contend with the city's rather dull provincial image; it
was, so Howell says in his memoirs, let down by some IOC members
who had promised to vote for it; the bid was not endorsed with any
great enthusiasm by the British government (although bids must be
made by cities, they must also have governmental endorsement), and
at the final vote the government was represented only by the low-
ranking Minister for Sport, Richard Tracey, who in any case arrived
too late to have much time for last-minute lobbying. By contrast
France and Spain sent their Prime Ministers, Jacques Chirac and
Felipe Gonzalez.

It is not clear whether Mrs Thatcher did not come to Lausanne in
October 1986 because she chose not to, or because she was not
specifically invited. Nor is it clear whether Birmingham would have
gained by her presence. Howell had merely asked for the government
to be represented, perhaps because he feared the result of her stand
against sanctions against South Africa, or the permission that she had
given to the Americans to bomb Libyan targets from bases in Britain
in April 1988 or of the attempt to boycott the Moscow Games of
1980.[12] A political row broke out in Lausanne as soon as the decision
went in favour of Barcelona. Howell attacked the British government
and the City of London for not making a greater impression on the

IOC. He blamed the government's monetarist policies, its failure to support sport in general, and for having sent to Lausanne so junior a representative as the Minister for Sport. In Birmingham the resilient Chief Executive, Tom Caulcott, said they would try again for the Games of 2000 and the leader of the city council, Dick Knowles, bemoaned the fact that the bid had not been seen in Britain as a national endeavour. He said £2.3m had been quite enough to spend, but that Birmingham would have benefited from more interest from south of Milton Keynes.[13]

There were naturally many post-mortems. The distinguished journalist John Rodda commented that Birmingham's team had found that the campaign was giving their city such marvellous publicity that they had drifted from the target, and sent people to championships where there would be few or no IOC members. They should, he thought, have made more use of Sebastian Coe. He went on that during the evening after Chirac's powerful speech commending Paris's candidature Barcelona's supporters had panicked and shifted their votes for the winter Games from Falun (Sweden) to Albertville (France), which Rodda thought in some ways the worst candidate of all.[14] Their reasoning was that if the winter Games were awarded to a French contender it would be unthinkable also to give France the even greater prize of the summer Games. According to David Miller, Chirac's presentation had been applauded for two minutes; afterwards Guy Drut, the Paris campaigner and a former hurdles gold medallist, had admitted that Paris's bid had been killed by the support given to Albertville.[15]

Rodda's considered view was that Birmingham had fought a crudely naive campaign around a solid technical base. 'Their bid showed signs of leaning leftwards and carried exaggerated claims more usually found in a general election campaign. The extent of the hype was illustrated when on the morning of the voting so much money was placed on Birmingham with a London bookmaker that they had to make them 2–1 second favourite.'[16] (For further discussion of the politicking over the choice of Barcelona see Chapter IX.)

A post-mortem of another kind was initiated by Samaranch, who had become seriously concerned about the growth of campaign expenditure and wrote to all the bidding cities asking for their views. Howell says that nothing like it had ever been seen before, and that the trouble was that there were no rules governing the campaign. His reply to Samaranch, with which one can have a great deal of sympathy, drew comparisons between the campaign and an election campaign. In most countries there was a limit on expenditure: why not in the Olympics? There should also be regulations relating to gifts and expenses, the number of visits an IOC member might pay to a city, entertainments, the limitation of promotional activity at regional conferences and very heavy limitation of promotional activity at the Session when the vote was taken. By that time members had had plenty of opportunity to make up their minds. Howell had also heard, but could not be sure, that some offers of employment for themselves or members of their families had been made to IOC members. This, and no doubt other, representations, did have some limited effect and restrictions were promulgated by a committee set up under the chairmanship of Mark Hodler, a senior member of the IOC.[17] However, in the campaign for 1996 it appears that the rules were flouted, and that the only person to be worried about it was Hodler, who was especially upset by Athens's conduct.

After Barcelona had won, thoughts immediately turned to the Games of 1996. Manchester was waiting in the wings to compete against Birmingham for the honour of representing Britain and Bob Scott, Manchester's team leader, was anxious to learn from Birmingham's misfortunes. He recognised that the main difference between Birmingham's campaign and those of Paris and Barcelona had been the extent of government involvement. 'You can hardly', he said 'compare Jacques Chirac with Richard Tracey.'[18] Howell sourly records that he and the rest of the Birmingham team got little congratulation from the BOA for their efforts to attract the 1992 Games. He goes on that the BOA was slow to invite bids for 1996, but eventually fixed the submission date for December 1987. Then Manchester asked for a two-month extension, and the BOA wanted to know if any other candidates objected. Birmingham most certainly did, though Howell seems not to remember that he himself had asked for an extension the previous time. Howell is bitter that he got no support against Manchester from leading BOA members, like Mary Glen-Haig, Lord Luke and Charles Palmer. He thought the IOC would find it incomprehensible if the BOA deserted Birmingham.[19]

In his campaign against Manchester Howell set much store by his achievement at the IOC's Session in Istanbul in 1987 of having beaten off great opposition to persuade the IOC to hold its 1991 Session in Birmingham. He was quoted as having seen that victory as a step towards a second candidature to hold the Games, and had said that it would be madness to sacrifice the relationships that he had built up in his first campaign for Birmingham, and that no city was ever awarded the Games on its first bid.[20]

Unfortunately for Howell, the BOA was not greatly impressed by his having secured the 1991 Session for Birmingham. Nor, indeed, was David Miller. It was true, he wrote, that Britain had not hosted an IOC Session since before the war, and the rivals this time had included Budapest, Monaco, Moscow, Nairobi and Riyadh but, he went on, 'A session carries no special significance, other than emphasise a nation's international sporting presence.'[21] Nor had Howell had as much help as he had hoped for from his own side. Lord Luke had not even stayed to the end of the Istanbul meeting to vote for Birmingham and in the end it won by only one vote over Budapest. It may even be that the decision was a matter of chance, since Howell says that he had heard that the elusive Magvan, having left the room temporarily, had not realised that Moscow had been eliminated, and went on voting for it, thus spoiling his paper.[22]

Despite Howell's determined lobbying, the result of Birmingham's failure at Lausanne in 1986 to be awarded the Games of 1992 by the IOC was that when on 19 May 1988 the British Olympic Association had once again to decide between Birmingham and Manchester (this time as its candidate for 1996), it switched to Manchester by 20 votes to 11. The change was received with ill grace by Birmingham, whose leaders still continue their campaign to get it recognised as Britain's second city, and as a city of world stature. On the other hand, it is easy to follow the BOA's reasoning. There was no real difference between the plans Birmingham prepared in outline for 1996 and those it had drawn up in detail for 1992. Unkind gibes had been made that the National Exhibition Centre at Birmingham, in which many of the sports were to be held, was not much more than an enormous shed which would leave no legacy to Birmingham in the shape of new sports facilities once the Games was over. In short, the Committee could see little reason to expect Birmingham to do any better in the voting for 1996 than it had four years earlier.

Manchester's bid

Manchester, after Birmingham's debacle, provided new blood. Its bid was led by the charismatic Bob Scott, a theatrical entrepreneur in

Manchester, and the son of a distinguished diplomat, Sir David Scott. Perhaps the most important factor in its favour was that, unlike Birmingham's bid, Manchester's had no involvement with the city council, though of course it had its backing. Nor were any costs expected to fall on the local or national exchequer, although considerable sums would be required from the Urban Development Corporations (UDCs). Manchester intended, like Los Angeles, to present a 'private enterprise Games', but first, as we have seen, it was necessary to persuade the Birmingham Olympic Association to abandon Birmingham and choose Manchester as the British candidate for 1996.

The competition between the two cities was sometimes acrimonious. For example, when David Miller wrote in *The Times* that, because the UDCs were supporting the bid, it was likely to receive indirect support from the Ministers responsible for the UDCs, Denis Howell, who was again leading the Birmingham team, immediately demanded, and received, assurances from the Ministers concerned that this was not the case![23] He also dismissed the Manchester bid as 'Bob's Scott's theatrical productions. Scott has hyped his production before he has got his act together'.[24] Before the vital meeting of the BOA to decide which city was to be the British candidate another row broke out, with Howell saying that funds would not be available for some of Manchester's sports infrastructure, and Scott replying that Howell was talking malicious nonsense.[25]

The presence of Peter Hadfield (Trafford Park UDC) and James Grigor (Central Manchester UDC), on the bidding committee, plus the promise of huge private sector finance, were indeed major factors in the BOA's decision in favour of Manchester. To enlist such support was a triumph for the entrepreneurial approach pioneered successfully by Los Angeles in 1984. Birmingham's committee was full of city dignitaries and councillors, whereas Manchester's, as Bob Scott put it, contained 'players who feel easy with million dollar games, achievers not talkers'.[26] By having such people in Manchester's team, he had intended to avoid the mistake made by Birmingham in their bid for the 1992 Games, when, in Scott's words, Birmingham had been 'annihilated by the sophisticated juggernauts of Barcelona and Paris'.

According to the *Daily Telegraph*, the meeting at Lausanne at which Birmingham had done so notably badly had offered a nightmare vision of sport being consumed by its own commercial potential. Nor, the paper said, had Birmingham's team behaved with the expected decorum when it came to the decision between Birmingham and Manchester: 'At Lausanne Birmingham had been penalised for lack of sophistication in their efforts. Judging by yesterday afternoon's cameo – a group of councillors chanted "'Ere we go, 'ere we go" – that had not changed.' However, the reporter was scarcely better-tempered about Manchester's presentation, which he had thought dull.[27]

Bob Scott's victory speech was delightfully magnanimous. 'Denis would be a hard act to follow. Denis has been a credit to British sport, a trail-blazer.'[28] David Miller summed it up by saying that Birmingham had failed on the personal record in the international negotiating arena last time. Sir Arthur Gold, the new chairman of the BOA (who had not unexpectedly defeated Charles Palmer for that office), had said that the manner of presenting a bid was decisive and Hadfield had offered the prospect of Development Corporations being able to unlock the £2bn development of the north-western region over the next eight years.[29] John Rodda, in his own post-mortem, said that 'Manchester offered a glossy vision, and there's a harsher view that the BOA did not want another dose of Howell and his buddies.'[30]

After the excitement of winning had died down, Bob Scott said that he would be asking the former Minister for Sport to help Manchester in the run-up to the IOC meeting in Tokyo in 1990 when the venue for 1996 would be decided. Scott commented: 'We still have a lot to learn, but we are hoping that Birmingham will give us the benefit of their advice to strengthen our efforts.' Denis Howell, in return, took defeat well, and stated: 'Our warmest congratulations to Manchester. They will carry our best wishes. Obviously we are disappointed because we thought we had a superb bid. But now we have to give Manchester every help we can.'[31] However, he did not stick to these good intentions and by the time of the Seoul Games it had become clear that Manchester would have to go to the Session without any advice or support from Denis Howell, despite his former promises of both. Howell had publicly expressed his doubts about Manchester's financial capability to launch a successful bid. Bob Scott was terribly offended by Howell's attitude and commented: 'I am sorry, but in spite of Denis Howell's previous expressions of public support, he is in fact disparaging our campaign.'[32]

Howell himself went to Seoul to see how they were handling the 94th Session, in preparation for Birmingham having the 97th in 1991. Members of the Olympic 'family' gathered in Seoul were naturally disconcerted that Howell was being, to put it mildly, grudging about Manchester.[33] Despite all these difficulties, the Manchester team contacted seventy-seven IOC members in Seoul.[34]

Scott always understood that a city could not expect to win with its first bid, but as he told a local paper in 1988, (when he was 44), he would still be a good deal younger in sixteen years than Howell, who was already 65.[35] From the start Scott had a clear idea of what Manchester was trying to do. The first task was to set the bid's overall direction and philosophy. It was to be private-sector-led, 'laid-back' in style, and was to gain national support, especially in London. Its theme was to be urban regeneration and revitalisation of the whole north-western region with the Games as the catalyst of renewal, though it would also be rooted in the region's industrial history, celebrating the centenary of the Manchester Ship Canal. Above all, it would leave a legacy of venues placed to meet the needs of the population for the next thirty years. To get these venues built would entail persuading Local Authorities and Development Corporations of their long-term desirability, whilst making it clear to the IOC that they were being built especially for the Olympic Games. In persuading Local Authorities to invest now rather than at some unspecified future time the catch phrase was to be that the Games of 1996 were the dreams of today's children.

The process of gaining national support started at the Mansion House in the City of London. It was also necessary to keep in intimate touch with the British Olympic Association and the Sports Council, and in due course to gain the Prime Minister's backing. The support of the Foreign and Commonwealth Office was necessary, and readily given, so that Ambassadors and High Commissioners helped the team to meet IOC members, and whenever possible made them receptive to Manchester's ambitions. Similarly, the Home Office was enlisted, so that visa requirements for visiting IOC members were made as painless as possible.

When working out the team's programme, Scott learned from the mistake Birmingham had made in diffusing its effort. His sole objective was to gain a majority of votes in September 1990, so that the prime targets must be Olympic gatherings where IOC members were likely to be present. (One of the most important turned out to be the IOC's Session at Puerto Rico in August 1989.) It would also be possible to go to endless cups and championships, but they would be of little value if none of the IOC members were to be there.

The team had three clearly defined sets of activities. First came preparing the technical bid. From the beginning Manchester realised that the technical bid does not win votes, but it can lose them: in other words, members will use a real or perceived deficiency to eliminate a city from the running. Secondly, there was the international task: this was the most important and difficult activity. It was essential to keep the team small (aided by a broader panel of helpers and Olympic celebrities like Daley Thompson and Sebastian Coe), so that its members could become personally known to and trusted by the IOC members, and it was vital to know the latter as individuals and to study their individual needs. In displaying the bid's virtues, it was thought wise to show the IOC members the benefits of Britain as a whole. Thus, they were to be invited to great sporting occasions, including Henley, Wimbledon or Ascot, as well as visiting Manchester itself and being entertained in such great Cheshire houses as the Duke of Westminster's Eaton Hall.[36]

Thirdly, the slogan 'Driving the Dream' was not merely a slogan but the name of a set of activities, designed to generate local and national enthusiasm, and to establish Manchester firmly in the popular mind as a venue for the year 2000, should it fail in 1996. (Scott was always realistic about the possibility of failure, though he heeded the one piece of advice Samaranch gave him, which was not to advertise the fact that he was prepared to try more than once, because that would only encourage IOC members to vote for other candidates).

The campaign fell naturally into three phases. First, in 1988, the team had to come to terms with the Olympic environment, learn its language and make initial contacts; then came the phase of getting to know the members; finally it was necessary to persuade them to visit Manchester, preferably as late in the campaign as possible – ideally in the spring or summer of 1990. Great attention was paid, as by every bidding city, to the detail of their visits. For example, a send-off would be arranged in their countries of origin; there would be a VIP reception at Heathrow; use would be made of private aeroplanes, helicopters, Rolls Royces; there would be a police escort; carefully thought-out entertainment, inexpensive but pleasant presents and in general the creation of an atmosphere of luxury and respect, without subservience. Later Scott summed it up: 'The secret is to seem like an old friend while not appearing a nuisance.' So birthday cards and enquiries about golf handicaps were legitimate, but Manchester would not follow the example of one team bidding for the 1994 winter

Games, whose members had all turned up in stifling Seoul dressed as Eskimos.[37]

Bob Scott was able to obtain major contributions to Manchester's campaign fund from companies (plus one private individual, the Duke of Westminster) and financed the remainder of the cost of the bid from gifts in kind. As early as October 1988 he was able to report to his committee that major contributions to the campaign fund had been confirmed by the Duke and by Bass, Coats Viyella, Granada, ICL, the Manchester Ship Canal Company, and NatWest Bank, and discussions with other possible backers were well advanced. Donations in kind had also been promised by several companies, including British Airways and British Rail. The Chamber of Commerce was to launch an appeal to businesses, asking for mininum donations of £10,000. By October 1989 the number of companies giving £100,000 had risen to sixteen, and the total sum raised was £2,160,000. Members of the team had already met seventy-seven out of ninety-three members of the IOC; a successful presentation had been made to the Executive Board, and a dinner party, attended by Princess Anne, had been given in Seoul on the first night of the Games.

There were hopes of holding two important events in London in 1989. These were, first, a reception at the Mansion House, to be hosted by the Princess Royal and the Lord Mayor of London, for fifty or so key figures in finance and commerce. Secondly, the idea had been born of seeking to hold the 1996 Session of the IOC in London immediately before the Olympic Games, whether or not Manchester proved successful. (This was perhaps not a very realistic idea, since it had already been decided at Istanbul in 1987 that the 1991 Session would be held at Birmingham, and the IOC would hardly have held two Sessions in the same country within a few years.)

Relations with the Sports Council, vital to broadening support for the bid, developed well. In July Manchester had asked for £500,000, on the grounds that Birmingham had received £250,000 for a one-year campaign, and Manchester's was to last two years. However, in October the Minister for Sport announced plans for a radically reshaped Council. In November Bob Scott and his colleague Rick Parry had met its new Director-General, David Pickup, when it had become clear that the Council would prefer to spend its money on specific projects rather than a contribution to campaign expenses. It had therefore been agreed that its support should take the form of giving help with the preparation of the technical bid and of under-writing some of the international sporting events which were to be attracted to Manchester during the run-up to the Games, as part of the 'Driving the Dream' programme. Pickup had pointed out that it was difficult for his Council to make a long-term commitment to the development of sports facilities in one city, if the BOA persisted in changing its nominee every four years.

The international task had taken Manchester's team far and wide, notably to the Annual Congress of Pan-American NOCs in Puerto Rico, where the most important event from Manchester's point of view had been a private 'audience' with Samaranch, who had stressed that a north-western bid, to include Manchester and Liverpool, would not be viewed as a weakness, even to the extent of there being two Olympic villages. Armed with that assurance, it was possible to get on with preparing the bid on a regional basis.

Samaranch had also said that holding a spectacular centenary birthday party in London before the 1996 Games could be a very attractive proposition, and that the Princess Royal's leadership was crucial if the bid were to succeed.

The international federations are naturally of great importance to the success of any bid. The team picked up the feeling among them that the IOC would probably vote for Athens on sentimental grounds, but that the IFs were not happy about the Greeks' ability to organise the Olympics. However, one difficulty which faces all organising cities is that the IFs are slow to work out details of what they want. As Samaranch plaintively asked: 'What can I do when there is uncertainty in some minds, for instance, as to what it a canoe and what is a kayak.'[38]

Scott later developed an extremely subtle (albeit risky) line in public references to Athens's candidature: his policy was to be deferential and even to say that they had a moral right to the Games, but that if the IOC decided against them, Manchester was the best of the rest. It was not, in other words, up to Manchester to point out the political instability, environmental pollution or administrative incompetence of the Greeks, although Nicholas Winterton, the MP for Macclesfield was to say, rather pungently: 'Any athlete who wants to go to Athens instead of Manchester will need a respirator.[39]

It was also already becoming clear that the doubts about Barcelona's organising ability were likely to have some adverse effect on how IOC members viewed Athens's candidature. Two important

developments were the announcements that Melbourne would be the
Australian candidate and that NBC was to pay $401m for the United
States television rights at Barcelona. The former was received
with almost universal disbelief, because Melbourne had hosted the
Games as recently as 1956 and Brisbane had made an impressive
showing in the campaign for those of 1992. The latter caused
optimism in Manchester, because Barcelona's figure was comfortably
above Manchester's target figure of $365m (£250m) after payments to
the United States Olympic Committee and to the IOC, and by going
against recent market trends showed that the Olympics had a value all
of their own. It also helped to destroy the 'myth' that the Games
needed to be held in North America in order to keep television
revenue up.

Scott was much encouraged by a visit, on which he reported in
February 1989, which he had paid to Lillehammer, the victor in the
competition for the winter Games of 1994. It was two and a half hours
from the nearest airport; it had fewer inhabitants than there were
members of the Olympic 'family', and on the day before the vote
experts has considered it a rank outsider. However, Lillehammer's
lobbying strategy fitted very well with that being developed by Manchester: their team had confirmed that it was necessary to have a
different marketing message for each IOC member and that the main
objective must be to gain their trust and friendship, and they were
convinced that the bidding team must be very small to avoid confusing the members.

On the home front Scott and Professor John Ashworth, a former
member of the Cabinet Office who was about to become Director of
the London School of Economics, had paid their first call on Sir Robin
Butler, the Secretary to the Cabinet, the first of what would
undoubtedly be a series of meetings with senior civil servants. Sir
Robin had confirmed what Scott already knew, that there would be no
government money for the bid, but he had also said that there was no
reason why support from the highest level should not be forthcoming.
In June Scott reported to his committee that it would now be appropriate to seek from the Department of the Environment (DoE) the
assurances required in the Olympic Charter. An appointment had
been made with Bernard Ingham, the Prime Minister's Press Secretary, to discuss the support that might be given by Mrs Thatcher, and
its timing. Manchester was not anxious to elicit such expressions of
support too soon, and too loud support from Mrs Thatcher might lead

to trouble with Third World countries, but at a similar stage of Barcelona's campaign it had been getting far more governmental support than Manchester was yet receiving. Meanwhile the first indication of the government's stance had been obtained in a letter from the Minister for Sport, Colin Moynihan, himself a junior Minister in the DoE. A successful meeting had been held with north-western Conservative MPs, and Mrs Lynda Chalker, Minister of State at the Foreign Office, had been enthusiastic, but puzzled about how she should form a view about the desirability of Britain's holding the Games. Thus, relations with government were proceeding satisfactorily, though they would presumably have gone even better if Britain's Minister for Sport had not been so junior in the hierarchy. A more senior Minister would have been in a far better position to guide the government's thinking on the Olympic Games, and on sporting issues in general.

In the end Mrs Thatcher wrote an excellent letter to Samaranch on 10 November 1989. It read:

Dear President Samaranch

I was very pleased to hear that your recent visit to Manchester had served to underline that the people of Manchester would welcome and support an application to host the 1996 Olympic Games. It is certainly the case that the athletes of all nations would receive the warmest welcome and take part in a superbly staged Games if Manchester were chosen as the host city.

I have been impressed by the enthusiasm being shown by Robert Scott, Chairman of the Manchester Olympic Bid team, and his colleagues in their efforts to bring the Games to Manchester. You may be aware that they have adopted the message 'Driving the Dream' for a special programme of sports events to promote their bid both locally and nationally. There is expertise and enthusiasm aplenty to ensure that the dream can become a reality.

The Government wishes Manchester every success in its efforts to bring the Games back to this country and will offer whatever promotional help it can. Colin Moyniham, the Minister for Sport, has written to Mr Scott confirming that the Government would pay full regard to the Olympic rules and byelaws and would do all within its power to facilitate entry and unrestricted movement to members of the Olympic family. Manchester and the North West of England has a long and illustrious sporting tradition and is well versed in providing the very best in sport. The region has an excellent road, rail and air communications network and the Government has recently announced approval of the development of the Metrolink Project which will provide a light rapid transit system through the city centre. This is but one example of our commitment to the economic regeneration of the region.

Britain is justifiably proud of its heritage and sporting tradition and I am

E

confident that holding the Games in Manchester would be a fitting tribute to the Centenary of the modern Olympic movement.

yours sincerely
Margaret Thatcher

Apparently, when the letter was first drafted for her, the Prime Minister asked her officials to rewrite it more robustly, and even after the draft was changed she added a few words of her own to strengthen it further. It seems unlikely that she would have written such a letter on behalf of Birmingham.

Relations with the BOA also continued to deepen. Sir Arthur Gold was very keen to play an active part in the bid, and all the BOA members had been invited to the reception at the Mansion House on 20 February. This may have reduced its value as a means of consolidating support in the City, but must have veen invaluable in unifying the sporting establishment. Indeed, the reception was a success and the Lord Mayor of London became enthusiastic to help entertain IOC members. By April 1989 Richard Palmer, whose experience as a former member of the ANOC's inspection team was expected to be invaluable, had been appointed Technical Commissioner to the bid. The BOA's press officer was to take over the bid's press relations, and the BOA decided to hold its Annual General Meeting in Manchester in October 1989, the first time it had been held outside London.

The Princess Royal did indeed turn out to be a tremendous help, just as Samaranch had advised. For example, at the IOC's Puerto Rico Session in 1989 she had given a dinner party for twenty-three IOC members, all of whom had sent written acceptances and had turned up. Somehow the message had got through that the normal Olympic protocol, or lack of it, whereby givers of parties never know whom to expect, would not be acceptable.

One of the principal objectives of any bidding city is to attract important visitors. So far as Manchester was concerned, the visit to end all visits was paid by Samaranch on 10 July 1989, rather early for Scott, as he told the *Manchester Evening News*.[40] He combined the visit with Wimbledon, and had modified an extremely important trip to North Korea in order to accept an invitation to dinner at Buckingham Palace with the Princess Royal, who knew exactly how to treat him with the friendly deference due to his age and importance in the Olympic movement. He arrived at Manchester by helicopter (perhaps not a good touch, as he does not like helicopters). The police provided a band at the airport, an escort for his motorcade, a visit to their headquarters (it became clear as the campaign progressed that a visit to the police command centre was a strong selling point with IOC members), and the present of a policeman's helmet. Fifteen mayors in robes and chains turned out to greet him (emphasising the regional unity behind the bid), and at lunch he met industrial barons, all of them supporters of the bid. The formality was balanced by a mass display of children's sports at the G-Mex centre, and tea at Henbury Hall, the home of the businessman Sebastian de Ferranti. Samaranch pronounced it a perfect visit. The facilities were important, he said, but the people were even more so. He had come to see the people and 'You have obviously got the right people.'

Only Ian Wooldridge in the *Daily Mail* spoilt the tone of the press comment by pointing to strikes, trouble in the National Health Service, the disaster at Hillsborough football stadium: so unlikely did he think a Mancunian victory that he offered odds of 66–1 against, compared with even money for Athens. As he pithily put it: 'Moscow in 1980 staged a magnificent Games because anyone opposing the concept could be arrested or shot.'[41]

A bidding committee naturally needs to be able to answer questions about the likely effects on the city's economy if the bid is successful, and to that end the committee commissioned an independent report from Sir Douglas Hague, one of Mrs Thatcher's favourite economists, and a team from the Manchester Business School. In a special supplement *The Times* noted that elaborate plans had been drawn up to create facilities which would leave a permanent legacy for the people of Manchester and the wider region beyond. The cost of staging the Games was put at £750m (£350m on building the facilities and £400m running costs). The expected revenue was £600m and the bidding Committee was optimistic that the gap could be bridged with private sector investment.[42]

On 30 June 1989 the chairman of the each city's bidding committee was sent a vast pile of questionnaires and related documents, including the contract to be signed between the IOC and the winning city. Twenty copies of the answers, ten in English and ten in French, had to be presented to the IOC not later than 1 February 1990. The IOC's decision would be made on 18 February and the contract signed with the winner immediately after the announcement.

The candidature file was duly presented at Lausanne by Rick Parry on 1 February 1990, with a message of support from the Princess Royal, as President of the British Olympic Association. However the campaign still had over seven months to run and there remained much to be done. The main business was to persuade as many IOC members as possible to visit Manchester, but there was also a great deal of political and administrative activity. For example, the city had to make clear its anti-apartheid stance, which it did by means of an announcement, of which copies were sent to every British Embassy, as well as to NOCs, IFs, and other interested bodies.[43] How much this counteracted the damage done by the African boycott of the Commonwealth Games at Edinburgh in 1986, and by the government's opposition to sanctions against South Africa, it is, of course, not possible to say.

The detailed bid was published on 14 March 1990. There were to be twenty-four venues in thirteen towns and cities from Chester to Accrington around the hub of the thousand-acre Olympic centre on the Ship Canal at Dumplington, now renamed Barton Cross. The estimate of expenditure on new arenas and housing had risen to £500m, of which £325m would be spent at Barton Cross, and £59m on upgrading existing facilities. It was envisaged that the new facilities would be rented from the private developers and Local Authorities which had funded them, and that donations would be made from the Games' expected £125m surplus to defray subsequent running costs. By this time only fifteen IOC members had visited Manchester (but it must of course be remembered that it had always been Scott's intention to ask them in the spring and summer, when there would be a chance of good weather).[44] The IOC's Evaluation Commission visited Manchester on 21 March 1990, and on that very day Howell dropped his bombshell. Manchester's bid, he was reported to have said (he subsequently denied the reports) was fundamentally flawed and no British city would win while Samaranch wielded influence in the Olympic movement. The flaws were that not all the sports were to be held in Manchester, although the Charter insisted on one-city bids, and that there could be no guarantee of planning permission for the new facilities which would have to be built. As for Samaranch, since Birmingham had made its bid eighteen new members had been elected to the IOC, all of them protégés of Samaranch.[45] All this caused a considerable political furore in London, but the members of the Evaluation Commission said that they would not be influenced by

Howell's views.[46]

Manchester continued to campaign through the summer, and right up to the decision in Tokyo in September, but in the end gained only eleven votes in the first round of a hard-fought contest between Athens and Atlanta, of which Atlanta emerged the victor. Yet it would be a mistake to see the defeat as a disaster. For the relatively small sum of not more than £3m Manchester has been placed on the world map. Although many of the facilities for an Olympic Games have still to be built, the bid has given impetus to projects of modernisation and improvement which were necessary if Manchester was ever to be transformed from a run-down post-industrial city, with its roots in the Victorian age, into a modern city able to face the twenty-first century with confidence, and to vie with Birmingham for the title of Britain's second city.

Attention has now turned to the Games of the year 2000. Immediately the results of the voting in Tokyo were known Sebastian Coe announced that he would put forward London as the British candidate for 2000. Unfortunately a rival group also put itself forward as London's standard bearer, and it was only at the last minute, after the BOA had extended the deadline, that the two groups agreed on 8 February 1991 to coalesce as a single board. On 24 April the BOA decided unanimously in favour of Manchester, their main reasons having been that London's bid was under-prepared; its details were hazy; there was a lack of leadership, since Coe's first priority was to pursue his political career and the City and boroughs of London were lukewarm in their support. Manchester was well supported, largely by its existing sponsors, who saw a bid as being good for business and did not attach very great importance to winning.[47]

Notes

1   Stephen Aris records a conversation with Lord Killanin, in which the latter remembers a representative of Mexico City having tried to buy his vote by leaving behind him a valuable gold coin, which was discovered after he had left the house. *Sportsbiz: Inside the Sports Business*, London, 1990, p. 156.

2   Dr Kim un-yong, a prominent member of the IOC, gives these and other financial details, which are unfortunately incomplete and rather confusingly presented, in his *The Greatest Olympics: from Baden-Baden to Seoul*, Seoul, 1990, pp. 285–8.

3   Howell, *Made in Birmingham: the Memoirs of Denis Howell*, London, 1990, p. 319.

4   Howell, p. 314.
5   *ibid.*, p. 318.
6   *ibid.*, p. 319.
7   *Daily Mail*, 20 October 1985.
8   Howell, p. 320.
9   *ibid.*, pp. 323–4 and 335.
10 *ibid.*, pp. 327–30.
11 *The Times*, 14 October 1986, David Miller, Lausanne.
12 *ibid.*, 15 October 1986.
13 *The Guardian*, 18 October 1986: John Rodda in Lausanne and Paul Hoyland in Birmingham.
14 *The Guardian*, 21 October 1986.
15 David Miller, *The Times*, 18 October 1986. Monique Berlioux wrote Chirac's speech (*The Guardian*, 21 October 1986) but because of her unpopularity with some of the Olympic high command she was kept out of the way (*The Guardian*, 17 October 1986).
16 *Running Magazine*, December 1986.
17 Howell, pp. 330–4.
18 *The Guardian*, 18 October 1986: John Rodda in Lausanne and Paul Hoyland in Birmingham.
19 Howell, pp. 337–40.
20 *The Standard*, 6 May 1987, Michael Hart, Istanbul.
21 *The Times*, 8 May 1987, David Miller, Istanbul.
22 Howell, p. 342.
23 *The Times*, 29 April 1988.
24 *The Independent*, 18 May 1988.
25 *The Guardian*, John Rodda, 19 May 1988.
26 *The Independent* 20 May 1988.
27 *Daily Telegraph*, 20 May 1988.
28 John Goodbody, *The Times*, 20 May 1988.
29 David Miller, *ibid.*
30 *The Guardian*, 20 May 1988.
31 *Daily Mail*, 20 May 1988.
32 *The Times*, DATE September 1988.
33 David Miller, *The Times*, DATE September 1988.
34 *Manchester Evening News*, 12 October 1988.
35 *Manchester Evening News*, 28 April 1988.
36 I am greatly indebted to Bob Scott and Rick Parry for generously giving me their time, and for allowing me to read press cuttings and other documents held in their offices in Manchester.
37 *Manchester Evening News*, 14 November 1988.
38 *Sunday Times*, 11 December 1988, Muriel Bowen.
39 *Manchester Evening News*, 21 February 1989.
40 *ibid.*, 10 July 1989.
41 *Daily Mail*, 11 July 1989. The *Manchester Evening News* diary of 19 July noted that Wooldridge's piece has been gleefully picked up by the *Melbourne Herald*.
42 *The Times*, Supplement, 2 October 1989.

43 *The Times*, David Miller, Auckland, 22 January 1990.
44 *The Independent*, Neil Wilson, 15 March 1990.
45 *Daily Mail*, Ian Wooldridge, 22 March 1990.
46 *Mail on Sunday*, 25 March 1990.
47 *Financial Times*, 27/28 April 1991, Ian Hamilton Fazey.

VI

The Moscow Games of 1980

Everything in our lives is governed by political decisions. We have varying degrees of freedom, but that freedom is obtained by political decision. What we in sport and the Olympic movement need is the interest and support of politicians, not their interference. – Lord Killanin[1]

Late in December 1979 the Soviet Union invaded Afghanistan, nominally on the invitation of its government. In January President Jimmy Carter warned that the United States would boycott the Moscow Olympic Games, due to begin at the end of July, as a retaliation for the Soviet action. Although not well informed on Olympic procedures, he did understand that only the United States Olympic Committee could decide not to send a team to the Games, and in February he informed USOC that he expected it to withdraw the United States team. After extreme pressure had been put upon it by the government USOC duly agreed to withdraw by a substantial majority. It did so, not only because of the pressure, but also because of the traditional respect in which Americans hold Presidential policy in international affairs, and because many delegates to the meeting at which the decision was taken agreed with the government that it would be improper to take part in the Games.

The American boycott (a word which was never officially used) was almost certainly the direct cause of the Soviet counter-boycott of the Los Angeles Games in 1984 (when 'boycott' was avoided in favour of 'non-participation'), and threatened to split the Olympic movement. The choice of Seoul as host for the 1988 Games made a split even more likely, and it was largely thanks to the skill and determination of Samaranch that the Soviets took part in the 1988 Games. Since then it has become customary to say that the age of boycotts is past.

How the Games were awarded to Moscow

It may seem surprising that the International Olympic Committee should have awarded the Games to Moscow in the first place, since the choice must have been seen as likely to provoke the anti-communist West, even if no boycott could have been foreseen. The best clues to this puzzle may be found in the explanations offered by Lord Killanin, who was President of the IOC at the time. He asserts that the voting for Moscow was purely on sporting grounds, in recognition of its facilities and professional ability. If, he says, the vote has been taken on political grounds it might well have gone differently, since the IOC is basically a conservative body. (At the same time he admits that the vote was at the height of east-west detente and that some IOC members may have cast their votes with that in mind.)[2]

The Games, he says elsewhere, 'surpass all political and ideological barriers' and 'To-day, thanks to the Olympic Movement, countries which have very different political, religious and social views are able to come together in peace to compete in sport . . . it is not the duty of the Olympic Movement to encourage revolution or effect changes in a government's policies.' He also says that 'Provided he or she is eligible, it is up to the individual to put him or herself forward for selection to take part in the Games', a puzzling remark, which accords with Killanin's view of how the Games ought to be, but not with the real state of affairs.[3]

Killanin's assessment of the supra-political value of the Games deserves respect, although it is difficult to see it as having much connection with the real world. It may be true that Olympic competitors compete in peace, but since the murders in Munich in 1972 they do so only because the most extraordinary security precautions are taken, including United States warships at Seoul. Nor does the Olympic movement refrain from congratulating itself when it does bring about change in a country's political system, even if to promote such change is not part of its duty. Killanin himself passionately defends the Berlin Games of 1936 on the (dubious) ground that for every spectator who closed his or her eyes to events in Germany there was another who went home and disseminated the truth[4] and Samaranch believed that the Seoul Olympics were a major factor behind the rapid democratization of the Republic of Korea'.[5]

As for the contention that it is up to an individual to put himself or herself forward as a competitor, this is true if Killanin means that

competitors can only attract the attention of the leaders of sport by
their own efforts. But it is misleading if he means that individuals may
be accepted directly by the IOC as participants in the Games. This is
the old view of the Olympics, and one which traditionalists like
Killanin and Monique Berlioux would dearly love to believe is still
alive today. But in fact teams are national and sent to the Games by
national Olympic Committees; they are chosen by the various sports
federations and it is not possible for an individual to offer him or
herself as a competitor without a federation's blessing. The irony is
made more intense by the fact that Killanin was given an opportunity
to evade the United States boycott by allowing athletes who wished to
defy USOC's decision to take part as individuals, but refused to take
it.

Although Killanin's account has weaknesses it also contains the
kernel of the truth. The Olympic movement sees itself as universal.
To extend it is to be more successful; to cover the whole world is to be
supremely so. If the IOC had not decided to give the Games to a
socialist country it would have been open to the accusation of keeping
them as the private plaything of the capitalist world. Even if the IOC's
members do not vote with international political considerations in
mind, the symbolism is inescapable. Tokyo was welcomed back into
the family of nations by being given the Games of 1964; Moscow was
welcomed in 1980.

Those who see the Olympics as a sophisticated kind of capitalist
enterprise, and not much more, will also remark that the 1980 Games
were a successful piece of capitalist expansion which brought the
Soviet bloc overtly into the new world of commercialised Olympic
sport. (So successful has it been that the first Olympic marketing
seminar was held in Budapest in November 1990 for the NOCs of the
USSR and of the other seven countries of the former Soviet bloc.)[6] It
has even been suggested that 'the Games were awarded to Moscow
through a political deal between Leonid Brezhnev and Richard Nixon
in June 1974 in the course of a visit paid by the American President to
the Soviet Union shortly before his resignation in the wake of
Watergate'.[7]

The story, which Killanin mentions only in order to ridicule it, is
enjoyably implausible. What is clear from Killanin's remarks is that
the Olympic movement sees itself not only as universal but as a force
for peace. Even within its own 'non-political' terms, therefore, it is
possible to justify the award of the Games to Moscow, especially if the

IOC judged that detente was a reality and deserved to be encouraged. But the movement is open to the accusation that in taking such grandiose steps towards peace it was overestimating its own importance, and running risks which would better have been left to the professionals.

The award of the Games to Moscow in 1974 symbolised the USSR's complete integration into the Olympic movement. Tsarist Russia had taken part in the Games of 1908 and 1912, but after the revolution the USSR eschewed bourgeois competitive sport. However, in the post-war flush of victory the Soviets were ready to take on the world; they sent officials as observers to the 1948 Games, formed an NOC in 1951 and first took part in 1952.[8]

After the war Olympic officials feared that the Soviet Union would take the Olympic movement over and bring politics into what they saw as a hitherto politics-free club. It was agreed at Vienna in 1951 that the Soviets should return to the movement at Helsinki the following year, though there it was clear that the Soviet athletes could not properly be described as amateurs.

When they returned they did indeed bring the Cold War into the Games by setting up their own encampment. The result was that for the western athletes the Soviets became the enemy and, to the IOC's chagrin, the press began to keep a competitive medal score between the Soviets and the United States.[9] According to Guttmann the Soviets succeeded in ignoring the usual Olympic practice and insisted that they, rather than the IOC, should nominate the Soviet members of the IOC. Once their members had been elected they politicised the Games, in the sense that there were now disagreements along established political lines. In 1956 they proposed that the IOC be expanded to include representatives of all the NOCs and IFs, and by 1970 they had thoroughly politicised elections to the Executive Board.[10]

Killanin sees the decision to hold the IOC's 1962 Session in Moscow as a halfway house, ten years after the Soviets had come back into the Olympic movement, and says that once the Session was over they began to work towards being awarded the Games. Their first attempt was at Amsterdam in 1970, where they were bidding against Montreal and Los Angeles for the 1976 Games. Los Angeles had been over-flamboyant, and was eliminated on the first round, after which its 17 votes went to Montreal. The senior Soviet IOC member, Constantin Andrianov, was deeply upset by Moscow's failure. However, he was reassured when the Executive Board, from which he was about to retire, invited him to stay for another term, as a mark of confidence in him personally and in Soviet sport. At Vienna in 1974 Los Angeles bid again, this time for the Games of 1980, but realised that Moscow was likely to be favourite, and gave a very low-key bid.

After Moscow had won Killanin made the unprecedented ruling that the votes should not be made known but that the choice should be announced as having been unanimous, because he feared that if Los Angeles had realised how few votes it had got it would not have tried again. According to Killanin, only he and two tellers knew how many had voted for Los Angeles, and he was not at liberty to reveal the figures, but he does reveal that the IOC was nearly unanimous for Moscow.[11] Elsewhere he describes Los Angeles's bid as showing signs of inexperience. According to Hazan, *Sovietski Sport* identified the tellers as the Marquess of Exeter and Prince Franz Josef II of Liechtenstein. He adds that the envelope containing the ballot papers was torn up and thrown in the Danube.[12] Tyler and Soar give a different picture of the voting (but without identifying a source) and assert that only 39 out of the 61 IOC members who voted chose Moscow.[13]

Genesis of the United States boycott

Several speakers in Congress and in the House of Commons made the same point, that there had been opposition to Moscow from the start, both outside and within the Soviet Union. Kanin, a CIA man rather surprisingly writing in the *Journal of Sport and Social Issues*, believes that the Soviets timed the arrests of some of their dissidents well in advance of the Games, in order to allow any protest to die down before the West might have considered boycott as a policy option. Kanin, who must have had some inside knowledge, although he only used unclassified sources for his article, goes on that Carter ruled out a boycott in relation to the treatment of dissidents in 1978 but that after Afhanistan 'Sport, that most peripheral and most publicized form of international relations, provided the perfect answer'. He thinks Carter was reluctant to boycott, perhaps because the President wanted to be consistent with his earlier decision, or perhaps because he thought most Americans would prefer the United States team to compete.

The idea of a boycott may not have been Carter's own and perhaps, as Kanin suggests, he would have preferred to send a team to the

Games, had not polls and statements from public figures and such powerful bodies as the AFL–CIO (American Federation of Labour – Congress of Industrial Organizations) made it clear that boycott was a popular option – perhaps as an outlet for frustration over America's impotence in Iran.[14] Be that as it may, the Soviet Union invaded Afghanistan on 27 December 1979, and in the first two weeks of January the boycott campaign began to roll. On 28 January Killanin was asked to see Lloyd Cutler, the President's Counsel, and Cutler called on him at his home in Dublin on 2 February.[15]

There had been bad feeling between the IOC and Carter even before his boycott. On 20 October 1978 Tom Bradley, the Mayor of Los Angeles, had arranged that the ceremony of signing the contract between Los Angeles and the IOC for the 1984 Games should be held at the White House, expecting Carter to attend – but he did not, because his wife had been on television that morning, and he did not want to upstage her. Carter was only a few yards away and Killanin, used to being greeted by Presidents, was furious.[16] It is, therefore, hardly surprising that his hackles rose when he found that Cutler had come to Dublin not to discuss the crisis, but to demand that the IOC should either postpone or cancel the Games. Killanin found Cutler ignorant about the Olympic movement and, once he had read the President's memoirs, passed the same verdict on Carter, whom he describes as 'scrambling for his political life'.[17]

Denis Howell describes the campaign for the 1980 Olympics as 'the most epic political battle in which I have ever been engaged'. Like many other commentators, he shows that the Americans had no understanding of the Olympic movement. For example, Cyrus Vance, the Secretary of State, said the administration hoped there would be no American citizens in Moscow during the Games, a position he had to abandon when it was pointed out to him that, if all western countries followed suit, the control of all the federations could fall into non-western hands. Later in the American campaign Howard Cutler came to London, where he met a small group including Howell and Roger Bannister, and seems to have come off worst. Among other *bon mots*, Howell told Cutler 'In this country Magna Carta rules, not Jimmy Carter'.[18]

In January 1980, after the Americans had begun their moves against the Moscow Games, the Greek President, Constantin Karamanlis, took the opportunity to announce his intention to revive the proposal that Athens should provide a permanent home for the

Games, and the *New York Times* supported the idea in a number of editorials, in one of which it criticised President Carter for not supporting it himself.[19] Karamanlis presented the proposal to the IOC in February. In April the IOC sent Louis Guirandou N'Diaye, the IOC's member in the Ivory Coast and a member of the Executive Board, to inspect sites at Olympia. Greece delivered detailed proposals in May, and Maurice Dryon, head of the committee set up by the Council of Europe to study the proposal, said it ought to be put into effect by 1984. Although the 1984 summer Games were booked for Los Angeles, the Republican Presidential aspirant Ronald Reagan supported the idea, but when it was discussed at the Congress of the Olympic movement at Baden-Baden in 1981 it made little headway.[20]

NBC and the television rights

The position of the media, especially television, was not easy. NBC had paid $85m for the United States television rights to the Games, and was in great uncertainty over whether to proceed with the expensive and complicated preparations. They were covered at Lloyds of London and elsewhere for 90 per cent of their expenditure, but industry spokesmen estimated that the company stood to lose over $20m if there were a boycott and there was speculation in advertising circles that if there were no Games the advertisers who had been prepared to spend $170m with NBC might not be able to find alternative slots. At first the company announced that it would proceed normally: once the Senate had passed its pro-boycott resolution, it said that it had not changed its posture, which was 'to be guided by the policies and regulations of the US Government'. At the end of March it was still going ahead with the preparations, in order to be sure of being able to collect the insurance, but finally NBC announced that it would not cover the Games. This cancellation would cost them at least $22m, and perhaps more than $40m, in lost advertising and expenses already incurred and not covered by insurance.[21]

Killanin records that, when he went to call on Carter on 16 May, Cutler said, in response to a question by Madame Berlioux, that NBC would be allowed to cover the Games on a news basis. This remark, though it may well be accurate, does seem to exaggerate the extent to which Cutler thought the American government was in a position to give orders to NBC. It would have been fantastic to seek to prevent the company from giving the Games some coverage, and it did so in the same way as any other broadcaster, by buying clips.[22]

The international federations

It was not only NBC and the IOC which were worried about television coverage. As we have seen, a proportion of the television fees is shared among the international federations, and the outcome would have a strong influence on their prosperity over the coming years. For example, the IAAF's Council had learned at its Montreal Congress in August 1979 that the 1980 TV rights would yield double the amount achieved in 1976, though the IAAF's share had not yet been determined; at Rome in June 1980 they heard that some TV companies; including the Japanese and the European Broadcasting Union (EBU), were reneging on their contracts to cover the Moscow Games, but that NBC, fortunately for the Olympic movement, had no let-out clause allowing it to break the contract if the USA did not take part in the Games.

The IAAF's first Council meeting after the threat of boycott became definite was held in Paris in March 1980, when it played its part in scotching Carter's notion of alternative Games by announcing that it would not contravene the Olympic Charter by sanctioning athletics meetings during the Olympic Games. However, the American government had been pressurising members of federations as well as the USOC, and at the next IAAF Council meeting, held in Rome in June 1980, an American Council member, Mr Cassell, sought to persuade his colleagues that to hold two invitation meetings (not needing IAAF permits) during the period of the Olympic Games would be within the spirit of the IAAF's earlier decision. The point at issue was whether 'during the Games' meant the whole period of the Games, and not just the days when athletic events were being held. Although the Council sympathised with the athletes who were not being allowed to go to Moscow, it confirmed by 14 to 2 that the words did indeed refer to the whole period of the Games. The Council urged Cassell to help to preserve the Olympic spirit, and to stage the invitation meetings at some other time.[23]

The battle with USOC

Nor was life easy for the USOC, which alone could take the decision not to send a team to the Games. President Carter professed that his boycott was motivated partly by a concern for human rights, but his treatment of USOC suggests that he was not always interested in what went on in his own backyard.

USOC's President and Secretary-General, Robert J. Kane and Colonel Donald Miller, expressed shock, sadness and disappointment and feared that Carter's warning that a boycott of the Games was in his mind might reduce USOC's fund-raising capacity. USOC said, as Killanin had done, that it would not be physically possible to transfer the Games from Moscow and warned of possible repercussions on the Lake Placid and Los Angeles Games. It continued to reject boycott, relocation or the 'Free World Games' proposed by President Carter, but welcomed the opportunity to discuss the crisis with White House officials on 18 January 1980. After the meeting they were still brave enough to say that they would not necessarily comply with a decision by the US government to withdraw from the Games.[24]

The government recognised that under Olympic rules the decision would ultimately be made by USOC, but that the athletes, working through their federations, would have some influence. It therefore put great pressure on them to decide in the right way. Some brave athletes resisted, like the oarswoman Anita DeFrantz, who simply went ahead with her training and later, when USOC had decided to withdraw, sought with eighteen other athletes, to overthrow the decision, contending that the Committee was blocking the athletes' constitutional right to take part in the Games.[25] She had presumably been waiting to announce the suit until the IOC had decided whether it could accept individual entries, instead of teams chosen by federations and authorised by NOCs, since a day earlier Killanin had said that individual entries would be impracticable.

As well as pressure from the administration, there was enormous pressure from both political parties and both Houses of Congress. The Republican National Committee approved a resolution urging USOC to boycott. The Senate Majority Leader, Robert C. Byrd, was in favour of moving the Games, or boycotting if moving them were not possible. The House of Representatives' Foreign Affairs Committee overwhelmingly backed Carter, having spent a day hearing Kane, who again warned that Carter's boycott could produce counter-boycott of Los Angeles in 1984. The House itself approved by 386 to 12 a motion urging USOC to press for the Games' transfer or cancellation. The House of Representatives' pronouncement was followed closely by the Foreign Relations Committee of the Senate,

which unanimously approved relocation, postponement or cancellation, while the full Senate went further and overwhelmingly
approved the boycott, whether or not the Soviets withdrew from
Afghanistan.[26] Such opposition as there was came from a coalition of
dyed-in-the-wool Republican Democrats to the left of Carter.

By mid-January Carter was saying that if there were no Soviet
withdrawal within a month he wanted USOC to vote to transfer or
cancel the Games; if that failed he would suggest USOC formally
withdraw the American athletes. Senator Kennedy, his main oppo-
nent for the Democratic nomination, reluctantly supported him.
Killanin saw Carter's decision as a tragedy and reiterated that it would
be legally and technically impossible to move the Games, but it is not
surprising that Kane and Miller began to cave in, and agreed to try to
obtain other nations' agreement to moving them.[27]

Killanin was thought to have chided USOC privately for having
begun to give way to pressure from its government, in contravention
of the Olympic ideal, which enjoins upon all the 'Olympic family'
complete independence from political pressure. At the same time
Carter sent a personal letter to more than a hundred heads of government asking support for a boycott, but gained no immediate new
support, as most countries were anxious to defer a final decision for as
long as possible, and many were not at all anxious to be seen to exert
pressure on their NOCs.[28] USOC's collapse gathered momentum
when its Executive Board agreed to explore the possiblity of a national
sport festival to replace the Games.[29]

According to evidence to a Congressional sub-committee, a public
opinion poll carried out for the *San Francisco Chronicle* had shown
that 75 per cent of respondents favoured the boycott.[30] These sub-
committee hearings, under the chairmanship of a Mr Madigan, were
unimportant in themselves, but interestingly demonstrate how the
high purposes of politics may degenerate into time-wasting farce.
This was particularly apparent in some contributions by the chairman, whose geo-political thinking and knowledge of African geo-
graphy cannot have inspired confidence. He said that Nigeria was a
principal supplier of light crude oil to the United States. The Soviet
Union had surrogate forces in Angola and Ethiopia, which he stated
were countries 'in close proximity' to Nigeria. He then posited a
hostile move against Nigeria by these surrogate forces in 1984, when it
would, he said, obviously be in the United States' national interest to
send troops to Nigeria. He asked Colonel Miller whether, in this

hypothetical set of circumstances, he thought the USA would have voluntarily to retire from hosting the 1984 Olympics. Miller no doubt drew a deep breath, but was able to answer that his first feeling was that Los Angeles should nevertheless go ahead and host the Games. He added 'If the games are to be disrupted every time there are human rights violations or aggressions in the world, the games would never have been conducted for the last twenty-five or thirty years.'[31]

Another example of ignorant misjudgement can be found in a tour, apparently arranged by the State Department, undertaken by Muhammad Ali, formerly Cassius Clay, the Olympic boxer. He was asked to visit a number of African states to present the American position. When he arrived in Tanzania he stated that the USA was looking for an alternative place for the Olympics; the USA would support the alternative games financially and would not allow South Africa to take part. However, he was shaken to discover that his hosts were favourably inclined towards the USSR because it funded some African liberation movements, and was unable to answer when pressed to explain why the Africans should join the US boycott. A State Department unclassified telegram, containing the transcript of his press conference on arrival at Dar Es Salaam, shows that his briefing had been woefully inadequate. He was reduced to saying 'I can't answer the question of what America did or didn't do or what Africa did because I don't know. But I can box. I can tell you about boxing.' This naturally provoked the response 'But you think President Carter was correct then in sending you, a boxer, here rather than a diplomat to discuss this very sensitive issue?'.[32] Muhammad Ali went on to Kenya, where he said that his real object was to head off war between the US and the USSR. Then he visited Nigeria, where he got a cool reception, and finally Liberia. Despite the apparent chaos, the State Department had said during his tour that it was 'useful' and when he got home Muhammad Ali said he thought it had been a success.[33]

USOC's collapse

Meanwhile at USOC's headquarters in Colorado Springs its Executive Board unanimously agreed to ask the IOC to postpone, cancel or transfer the Games, which was exactly what the President had asked for. However, Julian K. Roosevelt, an American IOC member, remained loyal and attacked Carter's warning that he expected USOC to withdraw from the Games if the Soviet Union had made no significant move over Afghanistan by mid-February.[34]

The next big encounter was at the IOC's Session, just before the winter Games at Lake Placid, which was opened by the Secretary of State, Cyrus Vance. He considerably irritated Killanin by allowing the world press to see his speech, under embargo, before Killanin saw it. When he did, he found it grossly political, and bound to offend the Soviets. So he warned them that they had better stay away from the ceremony, at which Vance's speech was received in complete silence. In response to Killanin's urgent summons, Kane also went to Lake Placid, where he duly urged the IOC's Executive Board to transfer the Games, although, according to Killanin, he did so with obvious lack of enthusiasm.

As Killanin emphasises, Vance's speech did have the good side-effect of drawing the IOC together; they were, after all, a conservative body of men (no women in those days), and it would have been surprising if none of them had been impressed by the American arguments. But their sense of propriety and dislike of being bullied were strong, and all seventy-three who were present at Lake Placid backed a document in Killanin's name, which stated that the Games must be held at Moscow as planned.

Not all members stuck to their resolution: for example an Australian member, Kevin Gosper, twice voted in his NOC for Australia to join the boycott, which in the end it did not, despite very heavy pressure from the Prime Minister, Malcolm Frazer. Killanin suspects some other IOC members of having been less honest than Gosper, and having clandestinely opposed the IOC's resolution. He even believes that Samaranch should have caused investigation to be made and expelled from the IOC those members who had worked against its unanimous decision at Lake Placid.[35]

When the USA won a gold medal for ice hockey at the Lake Placid Games, having beaten the Soviet Union in the semi-final, Carter again displayed crass insensitivity by immediately inviting the team to a party at the White House, when he called them 'modern day American heroes.'[36] This move is said by Killanin to have antagonised the USOC and most of the athletes (though the latter did use the occasion to make one of several unsuccessful appeals to the President to change his position), and Killanin thinks the invitation added to the politicisation of an already highly-charged situation, and was a response to popular chauvinism rather than a party to celebrate a gold medal. However, this was not Carter's worst exhibition of insensitivity. That accolade must be reserved for the occasion in 1982, well after he had retired, when he was photographed jogging in an Olympic tracksuit, which had been designed for the sole use of Olympic athletes in the US team.[37]

The administration regretted the IOC's reaffirmation that the Games must be held at Moscow and stated that it now had no choice but to proceed with its plans. It therefore told USOC that it must reach a prompt decision. Kane and Miller said that they would accept any decision that Carter might make, but were against alternative Games being held. It was announced that USOC's final decision would be taken at the meeting of its House of Delegates at Colorado Springs on 11–13 April.[38] Carter's deadline of 'mid-February' had become more precise over the preceding weeks, and he had fixed on 20 February as the date by which the Soviet Union must make a move which would persuade him that the Games could after all be held in Moscow. Once that date had passed without any response from the USSR he announced that his decision was firm and irreversible, and urged USOC not to send a team to the Games.[39] Killanin points out that twelve days after the IOC's decision at its Lake Placid Session America suffered the humiliation of the bungled attempt to rescue hostages from Iran, and thinks that disaster may have stiffened Carter's resolve to prevent American athletes going to Moscow.[40]

In April the administration began a drive to ensure that the House of Delegates' meeting would comply with its wishes. Vance, plus the chairman of the joint chiefs of staff, General David C. Jones, told USOC that the boycott was essential to national security. It was further reported that Carter was considering emergency economic powers to stop athletes going to Moscow and it was confirmed that there had been discussions with House Speaker Thomas P. O'Neill Jr and Senate Majority Leader Robert Byrd about stopping them with amendments to the Amateur Sports Act of 1978, which authorises USOC to field a team at Olympic events. USOC officials then had little choice but to say that the President's threats of legal actions seemed to have closed the door on American participation.[41]

At the meeting at Colorado Springs a vast congregation of sportsmen and women and sports administrators was addressed by Vice-President Walter Mondale, after which the boycotters, by now including USOC's President, Robert Kane, won comfortably, by 1,604 to 797.[42] Macfarlane, soon to become Britain's Minister for Sport, watched the meeting on television (as did Killanin) and wrote:

'It was almost embarrassing to watch the emotional nationalism that charged the meeting. It reminded me of an American political convention and there was no doubt about how a vote would go'.[43] As the months went by at least one former athlete changed his mind towards favouring the boycott for a bizarre reason: this was Bruce Jenner, a former decathlon gold medal winner, who received letters from members of the patriotic public, threatening not to eat Wheaties, which he promoted.[44]

USOC did also reject the idea of holding alternative Games. It was of course suggested that the major decision, to boycott the Games, had been influenced by promises of more government money to assist USOC's flagging fund-raising, and of a suitable honour for athletes. Later the Senate approved striking gold-plated medals for them and in May Carter told USOC officials that he had asked Congress for $10m and promised to help raise $20m more from private sources.[45] On the other hand, although the IOC had much to complain of in USOC's conduct, it is difficult not to agree with Ueberroth that the Committee had no choice. Ueberroth's close associate Harry Usher had gone to the meeting on his behalf and reported that the government was considering not backing legislation whereby people would be able to give USOC $1 by ticking a box on their tax return (such a Bill came before the Senate in 1984, but made no progress). Furthermore the government had privately threatened to renegotiate the 'sweetheart lease' of USOC's headquarters and training ground in Colorado Springs, both of them government-owned.[46] It is even said that the government was ruthless enough to threaten Miller, who was a retired army colonel, with the loss of his pension.

A few USOC members had earlier voted against the boycott, because they had been so mandated by the athletes. These dissidents were sent for to Washington to be rebuked for their lack of co-operation, since Lloyd Cutler thought that a better impression would have been made on the public if USOC had been unanimous.

Once USOC had decided for boycott Killanin needed to talk to its officials and to Ueberroth and to gauge the feeling of the IFs and the European NOCs. In advance of Killanin's meeting with Kane and Miller, Carter sent a message reiterating that the United States' opposition to sending a team to Moscow rested solely on international law, human rights and the national security of the USA and many other free world nations. He added that this stand did not detract in any way from the United States' devotion to the Olympic movement.

He continued to believe that sports should be run by private bodies and not by governments; the USA would continue to oppose the efforts of other governments to establish UNESCO Games, and would welcome athletes of all eligible nations at Los Angeles, as they had at Lake Placid.[47] The first part of this message may sound like claptrap, but the second was shrewd, since it appealed to the fear of interference by UNESCO which Killanin justifiably entertained and pre-empted threats to remove the 1984 Games from Los Angeles.

The IOC's response

When Kane and Miller appeared before the Executive in Lausanne on 23 April the Board took a tough line. There were some who wished to take immediate action against USOC, since by succumbing to its government's pressure it could be held in breach of the Olympic Charter, as the IOC's lawyer advised. However, they were told that no decision would be taken until after the Games.[48]

Although the federal government had won its battle to prevent athletes from attending the Games, it took heed of the warnings it had had that, if representatives did not attend the various Congresses the USA would have no say in elections to the ruling bodies of the various federations. (The Soviets readily grasped the same point when they boycotted Los Angeles in 1984, but sent officials and judges.) Carter would not allow the United States' flag to be run up at the end of the Games, but Ueberroth managed to obtain a Los Angeles flag, which was used in its place.

The Soviet reaction

Once the prospect of a boycott became something to be reckoned with, the Soviet press began a counter-campaign. The Soviet campaign did not accept that the invasion of Afghanistan was the reason for the boycott. The 'real' reasons were that the USSR was a socialist country; that President Carter wished to undermine detente and that he needed to salvage his failing popularity. The campaign's main lines appeared in an article in *Sovietski Sport* on 20 January 1980:

We understand clearly why all real friends of sports and Olympism decisively oppose the provocative manoeuvres of supporters of cold war in the United States, England and some other imperialist states, who are striving to utilise sport as an instrument of their policy and hinder the forthcoming meeting of world youth on the arenas of the Moscow Olympic Games . . . The foreign policy of the USSR which is clear to the peoples of the world, corresponds with their basic interests . . . and serves as a reliable support of all forces struggling for peace and detente. Supporting the cause of preserving the unity of the Olympic movement, striving to prevent interference of politicians in sport and participating in Moscow's holiday of youth – despite threats, slanderous tricks and political pressure – this is the attitude of the sports world and the public of the countries participating in the Olympic movement toward the Olympiade in the first country of socialism.[49]

Kanin thinks that by the middle of March Moscow had probably decided that the Americans would definitely not take part in the Games, because from then on their reaction to the boycott included extremely harsh attacks on Carter and hints that a boycott could harm overall East/West relations.[50]

Hazan sees two stages in the campaign: up to 25 May the possible negative consequences were stressed; after that date had passed, and there was little prospect of further acceptances being received from NOCs, the line was that nothing serious had happened. There were vague threats of boycotting Los Angeles and the defeat of United States athletes by their own politicians was stressed. Afghanistan was seldom mentioned; when it was it was presented as Carter's excuse for something that he had long been planning. Some further Soviet arguments were that the boycott violated international law as well as the Helsinki agreement and the Charters of the United Nations and of UNESCO. By denying athletes the right to compete it violated the fifth amendment to the American constitution, and it was rumoured that the CIA and FBI were to use the Games for subversive purposes.[51] Thus the Soviet press fought back with a will, no doubt aided by the Soviet Union's long experience of using sport as a propaganda weapon.

As the Games approached, the Soviet authorities began to acknowledge that there would be fewer foreign visitors than had been expected (perhaps a blessing to the KGB) and lowered their guess from 300,000 or more to 70,000. As the final preparations for the Games began they closed Moscow to all Soviet citizens, except those who could prove that they lived and worked there.[52]

The Games and after

In the end 81 countries participated, compared with 88 at Montreal (1976), 122 at Munich (1972) and 113 at Mexico City (1968). The

Games were attended by 5,326 competitors compared with 6,085 in 1972. The most important boycotters in terms of ability to win medals were the USA, West Germany and Japan. As Macfarlane puts it: 'In some ways the Games were devalued but, had the boycott succeeded, there would have been a real danger that the Olympic movement would have been destroyed.'[53]

For Killanin the Games were joyless. But he still believed that without the boycott, and with the presence of the three to four hundred thousand foreign visitors who had originally been expected, the Games might have played a part in breaking down the barriers between East and West, despite the difficulties of visitors meeting Soviet citizens. But so politicised had the Games become that the political journalists, according to Killanin, nearly outnumbered the sports writers, and many papers carried two accounts of the same events, though from two very different points of view.[54]

After the Games were over, Samaranch told a press conference on 31 October 1980 that the Executive Board was happy with the Moscow Organising Committee's preliminary report on their Games. He asserted that the Moscow Games had won the Olympic movement new strength and respect and that the Executive Board had been keenly aware that it could save the Games from fiasco only by collaborating closely with the Moscow organising committee.

The Executive Board asked the sixty-six Olympic Committees which had stayed away to explain why they had done so.[55] However, it seems that the enquiries were not very energetically pursued and that some quite feeble excuses were allowed to pass.

Looking ahead to Los Angeles

Peter Ueberroth, the organiser of the Los Angeles Games, was, to put it mildly, keenly interested in the boycott, though not himself at the eye of the storm. In the absence of any public money Ueberroth was running the first 'private enterprise Games' and the boycott immediately raised the possibility of all his sponsors defecting. However, although a boycott was very much against Ueberroth's interest, he seems to have understood at least part of the President's case for it. The season of primary elections was just beginning; Carter's nomination as the Democratic candidate was being contested and the negotiations over the Iran hostages were stalled. In Ueberroth's judgement Carter desperately needed a bold public relations stroke. Ueberroth himself was torn between supporting the government or supporting the athletes, and chose the latter (though he does not seem to have been his usual outspoken self). All his Board, save David Wolper, the film producer, voted for the government, and Ueberroth would have gone with Wolper, if he had had a vote.[56]

The Los Angeles Olympic Organising Committee (LAOOC) was not ignored by the administration. Ueberroth and Wolper went to a meeting at the White House War Room, attended by Cutler; the National Security Adviser, Zbigniew Breszinski; the CIA Director, Admiral Stansfield Turner; Cyrus Vance, the Secretary of State, and other senior officials. At this meeting the officials must have been heartened to find that Wolper's concern for the athletes had caused him to change his mind and had gained them his support for the alternative Games, which Carter had proposed, and which Ueberroth had told Cutler were doomed to failure because they could not be held without the active involvement of the international federations. The State Department officials further demonstrated their ignorance, by producing a list of countries to which they had cabled for support: this included South Africa, which had been expelled from the movement in 1970.[57]

Just before the Moscow Games Ueberroth took a small delegation to Moscow, in order to inform the IOC of LAOOC's progress with the preparations for the 1984 Games. According to Ueberroth, most of the Olympic family treated them like pariahs, partly because they were tainted with their President's policy, but also because there were some IOC members who disapproved of the strong line taken by Ueberroth in negotiating the city's contract with the IOC. Madame Berlioux and Killanin were supportive, but Reginald Alexander (the IOC member in Kenya) called Ueberroth the ugly face of capitalism.

Although upset by the boycott, Ueberroth could not bring himself to defy Carter outright during this visit to Moscow, and would not be photographed drinking champagne with V. V. Kuznetsov (first Vice-President of the Soviet Union) 'which would have been an insult to the athletes and government of my country'.[58] No doubt he had also realised that his relations with the administration could be complex during the years leading up to the Games, and that he must do his best to stay on good terms.

He had been allowed to go to Moscow to report to the IOC just before the Moscow Games, but not to stay for the Games themselves: 'Because of this farcical ruling the Los Angeles Organising Committee lost an opportunity to learn at first hand about the running of the games'.[59] So Ueberroth was back in the United States during the Moscow Games and went to a 'showcase meeting' of American swimmers, held to compare their times with those achieved in Moscow, and to meet Ronald Reagan. He briefed Reagan on how important the 1984 Games were to the USA and was disconcerted to find that he appeared to have taken nothing in. But a littler later Reagan played it all back in a speech to the crowd, as if the ideas had been his own.[60] It must be added that Reagan had chopped and changed over the boycott. He at first supported it, then said the decision should be left to the athletes, then supported participation in the Games, but finally returned to supporting the boycott, while denying that he had changed his position.[61]

As for the verdict of American history, Tip O'Neill, one-time Speaker of the House of Representatives, may be typical. He approved of Carter's stand: 'People criticized him for that decision, arguing that sport should not be confused with politics, but Carter knew that to the Soviets, the two were already deeply entangled. Our withdrawal from the Moscow games signified the true extent of our anger and came as a resounding thud to Soviet prestige.'[62] In his own memoirs Carter sounds less sure: 'I was determined to lead the rest of the world in making it as costly as possible. There was a balancing act to perform – America being the leader, but at the same time consulting and working closely with the other nations. To be effective, punitive action had to be broadly supported and clearly defined.' But he goes on: 'I knew the decision was controversial, but I had no idea at the time how difficult it would be for me to implement it or to convince other nations to join us', and 'we had a struggle all the way; the outcome was always in doubt. Most Olympic committees were wholly independent bodies, whose members deeply resented any government involvement in their decisions.'[63]

Perhaps if he had his time over again he would not have embarked on a crusade which was indeed costly in political credit and energy, and whose results were negligible.

International repercussions of the Moscow boycott

At its meeting in Lausanne on 23 April the Executive Board addressed the questions, which arouse so much passion, relating to the use of national flags. For example, the Italian government had made it clear that the Italian flag was its property, and that it could prevent its use outside Italy, though it would not seek to prevent athletes making their own decisions as to whether or not to attend the Games. It was agreed that they could use their NOCs' flags, or the Olympic flag, and that they could use the names of their NOCs rather than of their countries if necessary. This fitted with Killanin's long-term ambition to 'denationalise' the Games (an ambition which Samaranch has done nothing to promote). However, President Carter did not have his own way in every particular, for as the politburo filed in to the opening ceremony, performed by President Leonid Brezhnev, two Americans defied Carter's wishes, and unfurled the American flag in protest against their country's absence. But the IOC had to give way to Carter's pressure, and not raise the American flag or play its anthem at the closing ceremony.[64]

Killanin went to Moscow to see Brezhnev on 7 May. Brezhnev, like Killanin, believed that western Europe would follow whatever line West Germany decided to take – though in the end there was more diversity than they had expected. There was some attempt at bargaining, although the two men's requests were disproportionate: Brezhnev asked that the West German government should not put pressure on its NOC, while Killanin asked if Brezhnev could do something regarding the Afghanistan position to avoid the political destruction of the Olympic movement.

Once Killanin was back in Dublin, Lloyd Cutler paid him another visit, this time to arrange for Killanin to call on Carter. He said West Germany was about to withdraw, which turned out to be correct, and thought, as Killanin and Brezhnev had done, that the rest of western Europe would follow, which turned out to be wrong. Cutler had by now given up the idea of alternative Games, which he had been trying to organise during a visit to London only a fortnight earlier. He now showed some anxiety that the IOC might accept individual entries for the games, a possiblity which the IOC had examined and found too difficult, as we have seen in connection with Anita DeFrantz. It is a pity that Killanin does not explain why this was so, since to move back to individual entries, rather than teams under the auspices of NOCs, can at least be argued to be in the original spirit of the Games and would have given Killanin the opportunity to deliver a tremendous snub to Carter.

Killanin saw Carter on 16 May 1980 and immediately realised that Cutler was a strong man behind a weak President. Carter said that steps were being taken to improve USOC's financial support and Killanin notes that it had of course been suggested that this prospect was what swayed the USOC. (This, however, must be an incomplete statement of the case: what seems to have swayed the USOC as much as the promise of improved funding was the patriotism of Americans and the government's threats, of which Killanin says nothing, to reduce their funding, or at least to increase their costs.) Carter went on to ask Killanin about the possiblity of a permanent home in Greece for the Olympics and, while having the grace to recognise that the decision was the IOC's, said that his government would support such an innovation, especially as it had a very large number of ethnic Greek citizens.[65]

The western European response to Washington's pressure was marked by vacillation, because many countries (France was a notable exception) hoped to present a united front, and because governments' responses were linked to other issues in foreign and domestic politics. For instance, West Germany desired to preserve its good relationship with the United States, yet did not wish to jeopardise its Ostpolitik (at whose heart lay the intention to normalise relations with East Germany) by joining in the boycott. Nor were most western European governments willing to be seen to bring great pressure to bear upon their NOCs. West Germany was an exception, but the Italian government (to take an example) did not have any hard feelings when the NOC decided to participate, although the government had been in favour of the boycott. Among governments of developed nations the most important to follow the American were those of West Germany, Japan and Great Britain. The last was a special case, (which will be considered at length below), in that the British Olympic Association decided to defy the government and to send its team to Moscow.

In the Third World the satellite or 'client' states of both superpowers followed their leaders: for example in Africa (where the American cause had not been helped by Muhammad Ali's tour) Zaire, Libya and Kenya embraced the boycott, whereas Nigeria did not, while in the Muslim world Pakistan and Saudi Arabia boycotted and Iran did not. Smaller states which had no particular relation of clientship with either party were divided, and most of Latin America took part in the Games.[66]

The British response

Britain would no doubt not relish being described as a client state, but its government, under the enthusiastic guidance of the then Prime Minister, Mrs Margaret Thatcher, made a major effort to follow American policy, although in the end without success. The issue sharply divided Parliament, the country and the media. Neil Macfarlane, who was later to be Minister for Sport, was not involved at the time, but writing four years later he refers rather acidly to Carter having chosen to plunge the Olympic movement into the greatest crisis in its history. His verdict on the Prime Minister was 'that Mrs Thatcher was wrong not only in the way in which the Government handled the affair but in principle too'.[67]

In the early days the government focused on the questions of moving the Olympics to another city or holding alternative games. No one wished simply to cancel the Games, since even politicians who were not involved in sport were concerned about the disappointment which would be suffered by athletes who had for years had the Olympics in their sights.

The Commons Select Committee on Foreign Affairs met on 16 March and reported in a great hurry. Its recommendings were very much in accordance with the government's view that the boycott should be joined, although its chairman (Anthony Kershaw) said in the full-scale House of Commons debate on 17 March that its members had disagreed about whether a boycott would be effective and a Committee member (Kevin McNamara) revealed that the chairman had used his casting vote on half-a-dozen occasions.[68]

Outside the House considerable pressure was put on the British Olympic Association and the athletes, though to nothing like the same extent as in the USA. Macfarlane records that the BOA received no fewer than three letters from the Prime Minister. Sir Denis Follows (Chairman of the BOA) and Richard Palmer (its General Secretary) met Hector Monro (whose responsibilities as a junior minister at the Department of the Environment included sport) once and Lord Carrington (the Foreign Secretary) on four occasions, on one of which Carrington was supported by another cabinet minister (Michael Heseltine, Secretary of State for the Environment) as well as by one of his own junior ministers, Douglas Hurd.

Follows had appeared before the Select Committee on Foreign Affairs and had said that he was sure that if the House took a particular decision the BOA would give great consideration to it. However, a few days after the debate, the BOA decided to go to Moscow. Macfarlane believes that their decision and Follows's later efforts did much to convince the majority of countries in western Europe that they should go too. When the whole affair was over there was, Macfarlane says, a particularly strong feeling that Follows, whom he describes as 'a charming and adept leader' had been shabbily treated.[69]

The American line did have some success in Britain. For example, the Chairman of the British appeal, who was also chairman of Barclay's Bank, Sir Anthony Tuke 'stood down' taking all but one or two members of the Council of the appeal with him. The Council acted en bloc, because it had no wish to scupper the appeal, although a high proportion of its members were privately sympathetic to the Conservative government's position. They could hardly have approached other company chairmen for donations, yet did not wish to create unfortunate publicity by resigning one by one. Thus they remained loyal to the British Olympic Association, while remaining true to their convictions.

The BOA's marketing programme took off in 1980 and it was fortunate that 90 per cent of the contracts had been signed by the end of 1979, without any escape clause in respect of the British team attending the Games against the government's wishes. The trade unions in part filled such gap as there was, as did local authorities, overwhelmingly Labour. Denis Howell had a hand in finding these funds and even got some backing from the Soviet Union. This occurred because he had refused repeated personal invitations from the Soviet government, but did suggest that the Soviets could help by giving the British team free transport to and from Moscow, which they did.[70]

Parliamentary proceedings

In Parliament responsibility for the Games was constantly shunted from Department to Department. The first Parliamentary Questions had come in January and been dealt with by the Prime Minister in the Commons and a junior minister from the Department of the Environment in the Lords. In answer to a question on 6 March, this time asking what support the government had received from NATO allies and from sporting bodies in the United Kingdom for their policy on a boycott, the government spokesman, because of the NATO context within which the questions had been put, was Lord Trefgarne, a junior minister at the Ministry of Defence. He said that the governments of the United States and the Netherlands had publicly supported a boycott (not surprisingly in the case of the USA, since the policy had originated there!), that an increasing number of sporting bodies seemed to be having doubts and that the BOA had agreed to defer its acceptance of the invitation to the Games.

In response to further questions he said that the government had strongly advised both athletes and spectators not to go to the Games, and the media not to cover them. Trefgarne could make no commitment on the financial implications: nor would he admit that there was any contradiction between having for years tolerated the international misdeeds of the Soviet Union, and seeking now to remove the Games because of Afghanistan. The enormity of the Soviets' latest action lay in their having invaded a neighbouring, unaligned and sovereign nation.[71]

On 14 April responsibility passed to the Foreign Office. Lord Carrington linked the Games with recent actions in Moscow, such as the arrest of dissidents and measures to prevent contact between Soviet citizens and foreigners.[72] On 22 May the ball was passed back to the Ministry of Defence, and Lord Trefgarne rejected the suggestion, which had repeatedly been made in the Commons, that it was inappropriate to ask the athletes to make sacrifices by exercising sanctions which the government itself was not prepared to operate: 'we do not think it is wrong to ask them to do their public duty.' Nor would he accept that the Soviet NOC had not been at fault, because he found it difficult to distinguish between the Soviet Olympic Committee and the Soviet Government. Perhaps the most important commitment was made in answer to Lord Paget's question about whether the government could ensure that the athletes did not go to Moscow. 'My Lords, I still live in a free country, as does the noble Lord. We will not take away their passports.'[73]

Very often Lords debates are more thorough, reflective and serious than those in the Commons, but in the case of the Games the main Parliamentay action occurred in the Commons. Nevertheless, it took some years for the Peers who have been on opposite sides over the Games to make their differences up.

The Commons debate

The main debate took place in the Commons on 17 March, and was the longest the House had ever had on a sporting subject. It was of course ironic that the debate was held because the Olympics had become an issue in national and international politics, and not because the House was especially interested in sport for its own sake. Indeed, the unfortunate Minister for Sport, Hector Monro, was not even allowed to take part in the debate. (Monro, according to his successor, Neil Macfarlane, was on the point of resignation from the government, because of the humiliating treatment meted out to him, and because he fundamentally disagreed with the government's line. However, he decided not to resign at once, and was sacked in the following year.)[74] Denis Howell, who described Monro as a relaxed man and easy to talk to, regretted that he had not survived the fiaso of 1980.[75]

The motion before the House was proposed by Sir Ian Gilmour, the Lord Privy Seal. It read 'I beg to move that this House condemns the Soviet invasion of Afghanistan and believes that Great Britain should not take part in the Olympic games in Moscow.' As Gilmour rightly said, the first part of the motion was relatively uncontroversial, although there were a few members, of whom the most notable was Tam Dalyell, who, while not exactly congratulating the Soviet Union on the invasion, nevertheless wanted the Commons to understand why it had judged the invasion to be necessary.

Sir Ian got off to a bad, indeed farcical, start when it was pointed out that the motion ought to refer to the United Kingdom, if it were meant to include Northern Ireland, and the Minister was obliged to put down a last minute amendment to this effect. The gist of Sir Ian's speech was that the invasion had 'underlined the selective and self-interested nature of the Soviet attitude to détente and the underlying expansionist aims of Soviet imperialism'.[76] It was therefore more than ever necessary to maintain western military preparedness and to show the Soviet Union that it could not enjoy western technology, credits and food while flouting the other areas of détente. So enmeshed did the Minister become in answering members who were dissatisfied with the extent to which credits and the supply of food were being reduced that it took him a long while to get on to the Olympic Games, but his argument was that, just as many other sections of the public were being involved in the various measures that were being taken, so it was reasonable to ask the sportsmen and women to play their part.

The government was no longer asking for the Games' relocation, but for their boycott and Douglas Hurd was in Geneva examining the possibility of other games, similar to the Olympics, being held. However, the government did by now understand the practical difficulties:

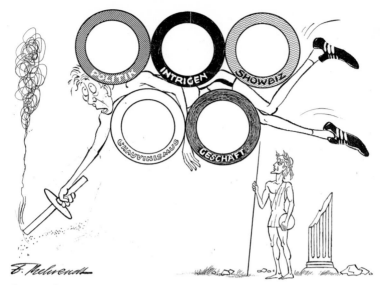

1 Cartoon from *Frankfurter Allgemeine Zeitung*, 15 May 1984

2 First page of the Financial Report of the Committee of the Wenlock Olympian Society, year ending 1 March 1871

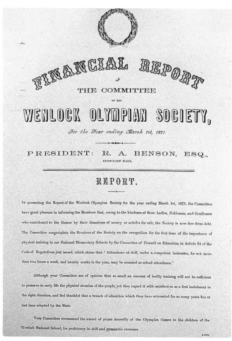

3 (*left to right*) President Samaranch, Yomi Mambu (Lord Mayor of Manchester), and Bob Scott (Manchester Olympic Bid Chairman), in front of Manchester Town Hall, 10 July 1989

4 Arab terrorist on the balcony of the Israeli building in the Olympic Village, where Israeli athletes were being held hostage, prior to the events which led to the Munich Olympic massacre at the 20th Olympic Games, 7 September 1972

5 An 'Under Protest' placard being carried by the leader of the Nationalist Chinese team at the opening ceremony of the 17th Olympic Games in Rome, 26 August 1960. They were protesting against the IOC's decision that they should march as Formosa and not China (Communist China was not competing in the Games)

6 M. Song Zhong (*right*), Secretary-General of the Chinese Olympic Committee, meets Lord Killanin, President of the International Olympic Committee to include China in the IOC, Lausanne, Switzerland, 14 March 1979

7   The first Olympic Village – a primitive barracks in a poor position built as a shelter for those competing in the 8th Olympic Games, Paris, 1924

8 King George VI opening the 14th Olympic Games at Wembley Stadium, Middlesex, 29th July 1948

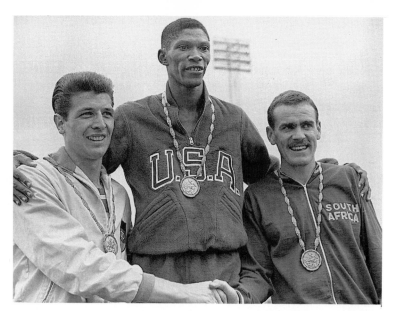

9 (*left to right*) C. Kaufmann (Germany), Otis Davis (USA) and Malcolm Spence (South Africa) after receiving their medals in the 400 metres final, 17th Olympic Games, Rome, 7 September 1960

10 British supporters showing their opinion of Mrs Thatcher's Olympic stand and pride in the achievements of the British team, 22nd Olympic Games, Moscow, 6 August 1980

'governments in the free world cannot organise sporting events. They can encourage and facilitate the holding of games, but the organisation rightly and properly is a matter for the sporting bodies themselves.'[77] On the other hand, special paid leave for civil servants and members of the armed forces to take part in the Games would not be granted, though consideration would be given to the grant of unpaid leave, subject to the requirements of the public service. This reasonable-seeming decision was greeted with great distrust on the other side of the House, and with anxiety by some Conservatives because some members believed that anyone who ventured to ask for unpaid leave would be marked down as not worthy of promotion.

Much play was made by the government with a Soviet 'Handbook for Party Activists', part of which read (in translation):

The forces of reaction are trying to exploit the Olympic Movement and games in the interests of the exploiting classes, for the goals of business and commerce, as propaganda for the bourgeois way of life, capitalist construction and its ideology, and for the distraction of youth from the political and class struggle'.[78]

The pamphlet went on that the award of the Games to Moscow was evidence of the historical importance and correct foreign policy of the USSR and of the huge services of the Soviet Union to peace.

Thus, Gilmour continued, there was no question of the USSR keeping sport separate from politics. Clearly, to allow the USSR to keep the Games would not only be to connive at their view of the Games as an exercise in propaganda, but to make their propaganda more effective, by showing that the west could tolerate the invasion of Afghanistan. Not to participate in the Games would be the most effective way for Britain to demonstrate to the Soviet government and people its disapproval of the invasion. Sir Ian was not alone in being shocked by this pamphlet, but it does provide a good example of how widely adherents of different ideologies may vary in their estimation of a document's importance. To Brezhnev, when Killanin read him a rather similar extract, the pamphlet appeared trivial, and he could not understand why it should seem so significant to British or American readers.[79]

Of course, in attacking those who believe that sport and politics can be kept apart Gilmour was attacking a straw man. That naive view has become increasingly discredited in recent years; indeed, some converts against it seem to have been made by the debate. It was certainly not held by Denis Howell. His view was that the two are undeniably connected, but that statesmen must not make use of sport as a cheap means of conducting foreign policy.

Unfortunately Peter Shore, and not Howell, was leading for the Opposition, and he evidently disagreed with Howell or misunderstood him. His amendment, a not very strong one, which the Speaker had chosen from the three available, called upon the Soviet Union to withdraw from Afghanistan; it asserted that an effective response on the Olympics, as in the economic, trading and political fields, could only be achieved by securing substantial agreement among the governments of western Europe, the USA and elsewhere; regretted the government's failure to consult properly with the sporting bodies in Britain and asserted 'the right of individual citizens at the end of the day to make their own decisions'. Thus, the House was not being invited to make a clear-cut decision for or against participation in the Games.

Shore concentrated on the 'almost laughable sense of proportion' which had led the government to give such prominence to the Olympics in its response to the invasion. To Howell's horror, he then alleged that sportsmen were so ignorantly limited in outlook (which, of course, may be true of some sportsmen) that they were 'hardly at all concerned with the political systems under which they and their competitors live, or with the external policies that their Governments pursue'.[80] Shore went on that he understood this view, but did not share it. He had no difficulty about linking politics and sport – there was already the South African example. The questions about whether it was sensible to make the link in the case of Afghanistan was whether enough common agreement could be found for it to be effective.

Shore also had great difficulty about giving any positive guidance, because he thought it wrong to have held the 1936 Games in Berlin, right to have cancelled those of 1940 and doubted whether withdrawing the Games from Moscow would make human rights there any worse. It would be doing Moscow a favour to allow it to keep the Games. He believed the government had been reasonable in considering the possibility of alternative games, provided that the international federations approved. But now the government had switched to a straightforward policy of boycott, which would lay itself open to failure if only a handful of nations stayed away from Moscow. If the IOC and British federations did not agree with the government, there was every chance that large numbers of sportspeople would attend, whatever the government's view.

His complaint was that the government had not consulted widely and intensively enough to give itself a chance of getting general agreement. He believed that, having initially been rebuffed by Sir Denis Follows, the Prime Minister had lost her patience, and was venting her anger on the athletes. 'His recommendation, therefore, was that there should not be a boycott, 'but rather that we concentrate on how our athletes can avoid the more offensive ceremonies which are built into but are not crucial to the Games themselves'.[81]

On both sides of the House there were those who could not support Gilmour's motion because it did not go far enough. For example, the Conservative Nicholas Winterton would have had no difficulty if the government had proposed a total boycott of trade, culture and political activities. What he could not accept was a policy which seemed to place a disproportionate burden on the athletes' shoulders. Thus the issue cut across party, rather as in the United States, where those opposed to Carter had come from Democrats to the left of the party, and Republicans who tended towards the right.

There was debate about whether the absence of athletes from Britain or the USA would ever become known to the Soviet public. Some members thought that the Soviet propaganda machine was capable of anything: others believed that it would be impossible, even in the Soviet Union, to edit out of the news the absence of major teams. There was division, too, about whether dissident opinion would be encouraged or discouraged by a boycott. Some dissidents were reported to have swung one way, some the other, but the best known, and therefore most frequently quoted, like Andrei Sakharov, seem to have wanted the boycott.

There were naturally comparisons with South Africa. Why, members on the left wanted to know, had the government not taken anything like the strong line against athletes who played games against South African teams that it was now taking against potential Olympians? It was not suggested with any conviction that improper pressure was being exerted: more that to expect special sacrifices from the athletes was in itself an improper expectation.

A homely, and therefore effective, intervention came from Mrs Jill Knight, who quoted a recent letter in the press. What, the writer had asked, would you do if, having arranged to play bridge with an acquaintance on Wednesday, you found out that he had spent the previous weekend overpowering and murdering a neighbour's family?[82] Winston Churchill sharpened the point further. Would we, he asked, contemplate taking part in the Olympics if the USSR had invaded Finland instead of Afghanistan?[83]

There were many sub-plots to the Commons debate. Some members recalled that they had been against the award of the Olympics to Moscow from the start; James Lamond pointed out that Mrs Thatcher could not have been one of these original opponents, despite her current stance, as she had become a patron of the fund established to send the British team; some castigated the IOC – Jim Spicer (who believed that the British athletes should not compete) said it had 'become a superannuated, pampered élite, divorced from reality and mainly concerned with preserving an empire which visibly is crumbling around them'.[84] Some members took the opportunity to draw attention to the plight of Soviet Jews. Several recalled that Japan's invasion of Manchuria had cost it the Games of 1940.

Clement Freud, the Liberal, was in favour of the boycott, but only as part of an integrated policy. He thought the Olympic movement was 'dead in its present form. The old art of competing is a thing of the past. It has given way to the hell-bent desire to win in order to cash in. Amateurism is no more.'[85] Terence Higgins, himself a former Olympic runner, took the same line. 'The athletes view the proposals with great cynicism . . . The real concern of athletes is to know what position the Government are adopting. They want to see an overall policy of which they are part.' He ruled out an alternative Olympics, basing himself on his knowledge of the IAAF. He believed that if no further measures were immediately announced against the USSR, the athletes would indeed choose to go to Moscow.[86]

One of the senior Conservatives who had been unimpressed by Sir Ian Gilmour's introductory speech was Eldon Griffiths, a former Minister for Sport. He thought that the athletes could not expect to contract out of the national problem, but that they were entitled not to stand alone. He, like everyone else who declared himself on the issue, believed that it was not for Parliament to tell people what moral decisions they should come to, though he added the rather confusing rider: 'None the less, I believe they should make that decision with the advice, and perhaps the consent, of the House of Commons.'

Griffiths commended Sir Denis Follows for having quite fairly said, when he appeared before the Select Committee, that he would give careful consideration to any resolution of the House. But he had, in Griffiths's view, gone too far when he had stated that in these matters he and the BOA had rather more experience than the Commons. Of course, no remark could commend itself less to the more self-important type of Member, but Sir Denis himself cannot have been pleased by what Griffiths chose to say about him. 'I like Sir Denis Follows. Indeed, I think that I may have appointed him to the Sports Council. He can sometimes be pompous, occasionally unctuous, but he is a man of enormous sincerity. But his sincerity has been misplaced insofar as he judges that he knows better than the House on the wider issue of how Britain should respond to the Soviet invasion of Afghanistan.'[87]

When it came to Denis Howell's turn to speak he agreed with Terence Higgins and the many other speakers who had pointed out that the inextricable connection between sport and politics did not provide any reason for allowing politicians to use sport as a political weapon. He went on that, if countries made a habit of confronting the world's many evils by using sport, the result would be to destroy the good contained in the Olympic Games, and there would soon be no international sport at all. How, he wondered, would the government protest at the Soviet Union's next act of aggression? He complained that from the moment the government had decided on its policy it had not once asked the BOA to discuss the matter and contrasted the rough handling the BOA had received with the mild treatment of the British Lions rugby team when it had announced its intention to tour South Africa.

He desplored the exclusion from the debate of the Minister for Sport, and pointed out that the unfortunate Monro was not even included in the negotiations that were going on in Geneva in the hope of organising an alternative Games. That task had fallen to a Foreign Office Minister. Howell was sure that the alternative Games were a non-starter and the Geneva meeting a ludicrous charade, because he had with him a list of eighteen international federations which had authorised him to say that they had no intention of allowing 'such a jamboree' as an alternative to recognised fixtures.

Howell went on to refer to the discussion in the Council of Europe's committee of Sports Ministers (over which he had presided when in office) which had asserted in a resolution in the previous year the importance of the independence and integrity of the Olympic movement. That had been in the context of a proposal by the Afro-Asian group in UNESCO that UNESCO should take the Olympics over, but the principle was the same, and had been supported by representatives of the American State Department.

Howell referred to the contradictions athletes found in the American government's attitude. How could President Carter have allowed the Russians to go to the winter Olympics at Lake Placid, and why should he not have opposed an American boxing team fighting in Moscow, while he was already advocating a boycott of the summer Games?

Another powerful point made by Howell was that only a week previously a major contract had been signed with the Soviet Union and the Minister for Trade, Cecil Parkinson, had stated that Britain was still prepared to trade on a mutually beneficial basis with the Soviet Union. At this point Parkinson intervened in the debate to confirm what he had said but also to ask 'What is mutually beneficial to this country about taking part in a gigantic propaganda exercise extolling the virtues of Communism, which is what the Russians want to make the Olympic Games into?'[88]

Earlier Howell had said he would advise the athletes to go to Moscow, but when he wound up his long speech he changed his ground by saying that they had every right to go, and should make up their own minds. Thus he brought his speech back to the amendment to which he was speaking, and did not appear to be taking too sharply different a line from that of his colleague, Peter Shore, who had led for the Opposition.

The debate was wound up for the government by Michael Heseltine, Secretary of State for the Environment, under whom sport normally fell, although we have seen that much of the activity had been undertaken by the Foreign Office. He admitted that much was being asked of the athletes, but in the circumstances of the 'unique contrast of the Olympic Games and Afghanistan' the role was one that only they could be asked to accept. Nor would he agree that there had been inadequate consultation with sporting interests. But he did assure the House that reprisals would not be taken against public servants who asked for unpaid leave to attend the Games: ordinary citizens wishing to go as spectators would not be interfered with, and the government would not interfere with decisions over coverage of the Games taken by the BBC and IBA.[89]

It was necessarily rather a weak speech, but the House broke on more or less predictable lines, defeating the Labour amendment by 305 to 188 votes. However, as Macfarlane points out, thirty Conservatives abstained, despite the three line whip on attendance, by which the government ensured a good turn-out.[90]

The subject of the Games continued to come up in Parliament from time to time. On 2 May 1980 William Whitelaw, taking questions as Home Secretary, said that the BBC and IBA, in consultation with the independent programme companies, had jointly confirmed that they would not go ahead with full live coverage, as they had originally intended.[91] On 5 June the broadcasting authorities issued a joint statement that total coverage would be less than a quarter of the 170–180 hours which each service had originally planned.[92] Killanin, however, had his doubts about the degree of pressure exerted on the television companies. He had heard of discreet reminders that the BBC would soon be seeking to increase its licence fee and that the independent television stations' franchises were due for renewal in 1981.[93]

Killanin tells the story, later retold by Denis Howell, of the Duke of Edinburgh, who appeared at Lausanne as President of the International Equestrian Federation. The redoubtable Ian Wooldridge of the London *Daily Mail* had spoken to Prince Philip and obtained his confirmation that he had taken a hand in wording the statement that all the IFs would be present at Moscow. There followed what Killanin (himself a journalist) understandably calls 'one of the most appalling instances of news manipulation I have known'. The story was replaced with a denial from Buckingham Palace, after appearing only in the first edition, and Wooldridge's follow-up, reconfirming what he had written, was not printed at all. Killanin does not believe that the Prince was a party to all this, but does imply that, since the story was against the *Daily Mail's* editorial line, it may not have been difficult for the Palace to have it suppressed.[94] It must however be added that Wooldrige himself, who might well have told this story in his retrospective collection of articles, instead pays tribute to the *Daily Mail's* willingness to print his stories, although he disagreed with its editorial policy. The paper believed that this was an example of the freedom which was not allowed in the Soviet bloc and which America and its allies were seeking to defend.[95]

Killanin comments on the messiness of argument and extent of misinformation in the House of Commons' debate of 17 March 1980, but he exaggerates its poor quality. The impression one gets from reading it today is that of course few of the members who spoke knew much about the minutiae of the Olympic movement (though a few, like Terence Higgins, had direct experience) but many of them did have a perfectly sound understanding of the political issues and deployed the arguments for and against taking part in the Games in a reasonably competent manner.

The British government did not display the same mixture of ruthlessness and stupidity as the American, but what turned public opinion against it was its insistence that the athletes would be behaving irresponsibly if they went to the Games, while it allowed trade and other official links to continue undiminished.

The BOA's decision to send the British Olympic team to Moscow may have marked a turning point in thinking in British sports circles about the relationship between sport and politics. According to Macfarlane, Dickie Jeeps, the chairman of the Sports Council, thought sport would never again have an existence independent of politics. Richard Palmer, General Secretary of the BOA, strongly differed and thought the moral was that sport must form itself into an effective political pressure group, in order to protect itself against undue political pressure.[96] In either case, British sport could never again be politically innocent.

Notes

1   Lord Killanin, *My Olympic Years*, London, 1983, p. 3.
2   *ibid.*, pp. 166–9.
3   Lord Killanin and John Rodda (eds.), *The Olympic Games 1984*, London, 1983, p. 13.
4   Killanin, p. 3.
5   Kim Un-yong, *The Greatest Olympics: from Baden-Baden to Seoul*, Seoul, 1990, p. 14.
6   'Sports Marketing in the East: on your Marks', *Olympic Review*, 278, December 1990, pp. 545–6.
7   Killanin, p. 4.
8   James Riordan, 'Elite Sport Policy in East and West', in Lincoln Allison (ed.), *The Politics of Sport*, Manchester, 1986, pp. 70–3.
9   Richard Espy, *The Politics of the Olympic Games*, Berkeley, 1979, pp. 26, 28, 34 and 38.
10 Allen Guttmann, *The Games Must Go On: Avery Brundage and the Olympic Movement*, New York, 1984, pp. 129, 139, 171, 172.
11 Killanin, *My Olympic Years*, pp. 164–8.
12 Baruch A. Hazan, *Olympic Sports and Propaganda Games: Moscow 1980*, London, 1982, p. 3.
13 Martin Tyler and Phil Soar (eds.), *The History of the Olympic Games*, London, revised ed., 1980, p. 161.
14 David B. Kanin, 'The Olympic Boycott in Diplomatic Context', in *Journal of Sport and Social Issues*, 4, 1, Spring/Summer 1980, pp. 5 and 6.

15 Killanin, p. 172.

16 Kenneth Reich, *Making it Happen: Peter Ueberroth and the 1984 Olympics*, Santa Barbara, 1986, pp. 210–11 and Killanin, pp. 105–6.

17 Killanin, *ibid.*, p. 174. (However, Carter's memoirs say little about the Games!)

18 Denis Howell, *Made in Birmingham: the Memoirs of Denis Howell*, London, 1990, p. 304. His remark is also quoted with admiration by Neil Macfarlane, Conservative Minister for Sport from 1981 to 1985. *Sport and Politics: a World Divided*, London, 1986, p. 225.

19 *New York Times*, 17 January 1980.

20 *Killanin*, p. 231.

21 *New York Times*, 29, 30 January, 29 March, 7 May 1980. Neil Wilson, *The Sports Business: the Men and the Money*, London, 1988, p. 18, puts NBC's uninsured loss at $34m.

22 Killanin, p. 214 and David A. Klatell and Norman Marcus, *Sports for Sale: Television, Money and the Fans*, New York, 1988, p. 170.

23 IAAF Council, Montreal, 22–4 August 1979, *Minutes*.

24 *New York Times*, 8, 16, 17 and 19 January 1980.

25 *New York Times*, 24 April 1980. Although the suit made no progress, DeFrantz has subsequently had a notable career in the Olympic movement. She was active in LAOOC, and was instrumental in persuading all the African NOCs, save Ethiopia's, not to follow the Soviet Union into boycotting the Los Angeles Games. In 1986 she was elected to the IOC, of which she is an atypical member, being female, black and not especially rich. At the IOC's Istanbul Session in 1987 she spoke passionately for the Games being open to all, amateur or professional, and in 1988 and 1989 respectively she became a member of the IOC's Athletes' Commission and Programme Commission.

26 *New York Times*, 20, 24, 25, 29, 30 January 1980.

27 *ibid.*, 9 February 1980.

28 *ibid.*, 22 January 1980. This appears to be the communication, a list of whose addressees Peter Ueberroth was to see in mid-February, and which included South Africa: *Made in America*, London, 1986, p. 66.

29 *New York Times*, 28 January 1980.

30 Evidence before Sub-Committee on Transportation and Commerce of the House of Representatives' Committee on Interstate and Foreign Commerce, pp. 48–9.

31 Sub-Committee proceedings, p. 47.

32 *ibid*. The telegram is at p. 27.

33 There were daily references to the Ali story in the *New York Times*, 3–9 and 11 February 1980.

34 *New York Times*, 7 February 1980.

35 Killanin, pp. 194 and 221–2.

36 *New York Times*, 20 February 1980.

37 Killanin and Rodda (eds.), p. 48.

38 *New York Times*, 13, 15, 21 February 1980.

39 *ibid.*, 21 February 1980.

40 Killanin, p. 192.

41 *New York Times*, 9, 10, 12 April 1980.

42 *ibid*. 12 and 13 April 1980.
43 Macfarlane, p. 221 and Killanin, p. 192.
44 *New York Times*, 28 May 1980.
45 *ibid*., 26 May 1980.
46 Ueberroth, p. 69.
47 Killanin, pp. 193–4.
48 *ibid*., p. 194.
49 Quoted by Hazan, p. 129.
50 Kanin, p. 7.
51 Hazan, pp. 131–45.
52 *New York Times*, 3 and 10 July 1980.
53 Macfarlane, p. 223.
54 Killanin, pp. 217–18.
55 *The Times*, 1 November 1980.
56 Ueberroth, pp. 65–6.
57 *ibid*., p. 68.
58 *ibid*., pp. 71–2 and 74.
59 Killanin, p. 4.
60 Ueberroth, pp. 75–6.
61 *New York Times*, 1, 6 and 11 April 1980.
62 Tip O'Neill, with William Novak, *Man of the House; the Life and Political Memoirs of Speaker Tip O'Neill*, London, 1987, p. 298.
63 Jimmy Carter, *Keeping Faith: Memoirs of a President*, New York, 1982, pp. 472, 482, 526.
64 *New York Times*, 1 August 1980.
65 Killanin, pp. 210–13.
66 Kanin, *passim*.
67 Macfarlane, p. 229.
68 981 *H.C.* Deb., cols. 135 and 138.
69 Macfarlane, p. 230.
70 Howell, pp. 294–5, 305, 306.
71 406 *H.L.* Deb., cols. 389–94, 6 March 1980.
72 408 *H.L.* Deb., cols. 108–9, 14 April 1980.
73 409 *H.L.* Deb., cols. 1033–6. Quotation at c.1036.
74 Macfarlane, p. 225.
75 *The Times*, 24 February 1990, p. 54, where Howell's memoirs were featured as 'Sports Book of the Week'.
76 981 *H.C.* Deb, cols. 33–47, 17 March 1980.
77 *ibid*., cols. 39–41.
78 *ibid*., col. 43.
79 Killanin, pp. 207–8.
80 981 *H.C.* Deb., col. 50, 17 March 1980.
81 *ibid*., cols 48–59. Quotation at col. 59.
82 *ibid*., col. 109.
83 *ibid*., col. 118.
84 *ibid*., col. 127.
85 *ibid*., col. 85.
86 *ibid*., col. 88.

87 *ibid.*, cols. 96–7.
88 *ibid.*, cols. 140–9. Parkinson's interjection is at col. 146.
89 *ibid.*, cols. 149–60. The quotation is at col. 154.
90 Macfarlane, p. 229.
91 983, *H.C.* Deb., col. 707, 2 May 1980.
92 986 *H.C.* Deb., col. 474, 16 June 1980.
93 Killanin, p. 203.
94 *ibid.*, pp. 196–7.
95 Ian Wooldridge, *Sport in the 80s: a Personal View*, London, 1989, p. 9.
96 Macfarlane, p. 228.

VII

The Los Angeles Games of 1984

The Los Angeles Games of 1984 will no doubt be remembered largely as an exercise in super-power politics, but they were also significant for domestic Olympic reasons. They marked a shift in power (which has proved temporary) from the IOC to the host city. Because there was no competition to host the Games the IOC could not have its own way to anything like the normal extent, and once Los Angeles had been awarded the Games it was able to ignore established practice in a manner which would not have been tolerated if any alternative city had been available.

Thus, the Games were sharply political, both for these internal reasons and because of the Soviet boycott. They were also sharply commercial, because the taxpayers of California refused to fund them. The organising committee (LAOOC – the Los Angeles Olympic Organising Committee) responded to the taxpayers by creating the first private enterprise Games, and therein gave a lead to the whole future development of the Olympic movement.

Harry Edwards claims that 'Most commonly, sportspolitics becomes manifest in the tendency of a society's established political authority to characterize athletic achievement as demonstrable proof of the adequacy, if not superiority, of prevailing ideological sentiments.' In other words, American governments see athletic prowess as proof that capitalism and the American way of life are better than any other system. (Very similar notions may be found in Soviet writings: for example, Riordan quotes a publication dating from 1951: 'Each new victory is a victory for the Soviet form of society and the socialist sports system; it provides irrefutable proof of the superiority of socialist culture over the decaying culture of the capitalist states'.)[1]

Edwards's remark contains an element of truth, since it is true that ever since the Soviet Union rejoined the Olympic movement in 1952 American governments have been willing to use the Games as an instrument of political competition. However, in the case of Los Angeles it was not the 'established political authority' that asserted the peculiar value of capitalism, but the businessmen who ran the Games as a commercial enterprise. Nor was it the government that revelled in chauvinism, but the people. Had there been no boycott the Games would have been nothing like as popular as they turned out to be under the stimulus of anti-Soviet sentiment.

Los Angeles had held the games in 1932. They had bid again in 1970 (for 1976) when, according to Killanin, 'their representatives appeared short on experience' and were defeated by Montreal. At their next attempt, in 1974, Killanin thought them 'resigned to a Soviet victory'.[2] Geoffrey Miller puts a rather different gloss on the 1974 attempt. He records that at that time the city's standing could not have been higher; the bid was sensibly cheap (for example, the athletes were to be accommodated in universities, so that no Olympic village would have to be built), and Mayor Tom Bradley made a good impression on the IOC. Nevertheless, despite Los Angeles's good showing, the Committee felt that it had no alternative but to give the Games to Moscow, although Killanin praised Los Angeles's bid and encouraged the city to try again.[3]

Los Angeles's bids were led by John Argue, a prominent lawyer and President, like his father before him, of the Southern California Commission for the Olympic Games, which had been founded in 1939. Argue, Ueberroth says, had a powerful team, 'But it was Argue's drive that got the bid, and it was his ability to work with the mayor that kept it after the voters rejected public funding of the games'.[4]

Public expenditure in California had been much reduced under the Governorship of Ronald Reagan and the taxpayers were worried about damage to the environment, which they believed would result from holding the Games at Los Angeles; the financial costs (especially in view of the losses incurred by Montreal in 1976); and the prospect of disruption to their daily lives. Local antagonism was enough to ensure that State and local governments refused to contribute to the cost of bidding or, once the bid had been successful, to that of holding the Games. Nor would the federal government risk unpopularity by giving any subsidy, although in fact some cost fell on federal security agencies, and a great deal of governmental time was spent trying (half-heartedly and ineffectually, according to Ueberroth), to fend off the Soviet boycott.

The voters' attitude rested on an overwhelming popular referendum of 1978, which resulted in what is known as the Jarvis Amendment, limiting statewide property tax increases to 1 per cent and thereby severely constraining the State's spending power. Ueberroth had voted for it, believing that many other causes were more worthy of public money than a sports event, and not wanting to see money wasted as it had been in Montreal. Nor was it possible for the Games to benefit from a State lottery, since these were illegal in California. LAOOC also decided not to seek donations from the public because it would have been competing against many good causes, including the United States Olympic Committee (USOC).[5] The result of this complete absence of public funds was that in May 1978, when it was the only candidate for the 1984 Games (Tehran having withdrawn), the Los Angeles team was truculent, stated its own terms, and in a dozen places on the application form said 'no' where 'yes' would have been expected. The most glaring example was in respect of television, where the IOC has to approve every contract and, since it owns the proceeds, divides them between the various parties entitled to a share. However, Los Angeles said it would retain the entire proceeds, but would agree only as an act of grace to remit an appropriate portion of the net revenue to the IOC.

John Rodda, the London *Guardian*'s distinguished sports correspondent, was, according to Geoffrey Miller, the first journalist to discover what was happening, because he acquired a copy of the completed questionnaire. At that point the dozen or so IOC members to whom Miller had talked privately wanted to reject the Los Angeles bid out of hand, knowing that Mexico, Munich, or even Montreal would have been able to step into the breach at short notice. Normally, Killanin records, 'there would have been a polite rejection and the show business people behind the application would have been turned aside', but he preferred a flexible response, in the hope of persuading Los Angeles to enter into suitable contracts. So long drawn out were the negotiations that in January 1979 Killanin began to look for other possible host cities. In due course Los Angeles changed most of the offending replies, although the contracts were not ready until March 1979, the biggest delay having been caused by the difficulty of finding a formula which would release USOC from financial responsibility if the Los Angeles organising committee failed.[6]

Miller adds some detail and a rather different emphasis to Killanin's sparse account. He records that Los Angeles insisted on a contract drawn up by its own lawyers rather than by the IOC, as is customary. It required a cast-iron guarantee against losses that would involve its taxpayers and refused to sign a contract to which the USOC would be a party. This, of course, was entirely contrary to the Olympic Charter, but, according to Miller, Kenneth Reich (a journalist who had long specialised in Olympic news, and was to write a book about the 1984 Games) had to explain at an IOC press briefing that USOC was dominated by easterners, with whom the Los Angeles committee could not get on. USOC's partnership in the Games was required by the Olympic Charter, but was a sham.[7]

The negotiations over the contract dragged on. The IOC tried to persuade Los Angeles that the city could hardly make a loss when all it had to build was a new swimming pool and rowing course, and when television income could be expected to continue to rise. As Reich records:

When the IOC met in Athens to award the Games, it had appeared a foregone conclusion that Los Angeles would get them, since it was the only bidder. But the stubborn IOC membership made the grant conditional on the city signing the contract in its original form. Bradley refused and when the IOC persisted, he announced he would ask the City Council to withdraw the bid for the Games.

This caused the IOC to think again and in the end it voted the Games to Los Angeles on condition that it toed the line by signing a satisfactory contract by 1 July 1978. In the event, they missed the deadline by many months, but 'the fact was that the IOC had no place else to take the 1984 Games'.[8]

The IOC found an acceptable formula for funding the Games, although it did not accord with the letter of its own Charter; that is, the Games were to be awarded to Los Angeles, which would hand them over to an independent organising committee. This body would accept final responsibility jointly with the United States Olympic Committee, and its officials, Robert Kane (President) and Colonel Don F. Miller (General Secretary) would seek guarantees from industry to cover losses. Thus, the solution was a form of sponsorship. Los Angeles had won the battle with the IOC and the Charter was changed, so that henceforward the host city and NOC were 'jointly and severally responsible' for the Games, instead of 'jointly and indivisibly', as in the past.[9]

In all but the most legalistic interpretation the language of the contract under which the Games were formally awarded by the IOC represented a clear violation of IOC rules by absolving the city of Los Angeles of all financial liability for them. Killanin comes surprisingly close to admitting that there was a breach of the rules: his justification is the hard-headed one that he believed the agreement reached was in accordance with the Olympic spirit and offered a viable way forward for the movement.[10] Although he justifies his own actions as President, he was not as satisfied with some of the changes made to the contract after he handed over office to Samaranch, and says that they would not in his view have been accepted by the IOC members had they been proposed at the time.[11]

According to Reich, Madame Berlioux and Lord Killanin had committed themselves to allow all the profits of the 1984 Games to stay in the USA. Of course, they had no idea how great the profits would turn out to be and when Ueberroth, after the Games, began to reveal the real figures, he states that Samaranch, according to Berlioux, 'briefly considered trying to abrogate the 1978 agreement but bowed to advice not to do so. Actually, there might have been legal grounds for a challenge. In the view of IOC lawyers the 1978 verbal [sic] agreement on the profits had never been legally formalized'.[12] This extraordinary assertion would be quite unacceptable from a less respected reporter than Reich. As it is, one can only marvel that Madame Berlioux, normally a tigress in support of the IOC's rights, can have allowed Ueberroth to make a fool of her by permitting an oral agreement to govern the destination of the Games' profits.

Private enterprise Games

This, then, was the origin of the 'private enterprise' Games, from which the Olympic movement drew so much of its inspiration for the Games' wholehearted commercialisation under Samaranch. The grandees may not particularly like Peter Ueberroth, and his memoirs show that he did not become excessively attached to them, but they owe him a great deal.

It was possible to organise the Games on a private basis at Los Angeles because they were spread out over a very large geographical area, 250 miles long by 50 miles wide, in order to use existing facilities and so to avoid great capital expenditure. It was necessary to have all twenty-three venues arranged by the time of the Olympic movement's Congress at Baden-Baden in 1981 in order to prove to the Olympic world that it had not been a mistake to award the Games to Los Angeles. As Ueberroth put it 'We weren't going to be the whipping people for the Carter boycott.'[13] This great geographical spread was not, of course, ideal from the spectators' point of view, but it makes little difference how far the events are physically separated from one another if the Olympics are regarded primarily as a television spectacle, on which the medium imposes an illusory sense of place.

Another advantage of the 1984 arrangements, just as of the city's bid for the 1980 Games, was that there was no single Olympic village, but universities were used to provide two villages at the University of California, Los Angeles (UCLA) and the University of Southern California (USC), with a sub-village at Santa Barbara. To fail to provide a single village was not at that time in accordance with Olympic practice, because it undercut one of the principal justifications for the Games, namely that they bring together (albeit at inordinate expense) young people from all over the world, who by being brought together are expected to learn to understand one another. It appears (again according to Reich) that the generality of IOC members was not kept informed of what the Executive Board had agreed with LAOOC, on this and other points.[14]

In his reminiscences Ueberroth says:

From the beginning people said private enterprise would not step forward. But from the beginning I said, doom sayers be damned. The Olympics were the perfect vehicle to join the public and private sectors in a partnership. It had all the right elements: youth, healthy competition, tradition, drama, and a worldwide audience. It was an opportunity for private enterprise to enhance itself and show what is good about mankind.

Ueberroth continues that he knew he would succeed because America was the greatest country in the world: if enough Americans believed in an idea or project, anything was possible; patriotism was alive and well and all the people needed was a rallying point to 'make them share their great spirit with the peoples of the world'.[15]   Ueberroth was a businessman, whose travel company was, he says, the largest in North America after American Express. He had been approached in the autumn of 1978, having played golf some months earlier with John Argue, to allow himself to be considered as President of the committee, and had won by a single vote over Ed Steidle, another businessman, one of whose backers was Mayor Tom Bradley. In his new task he had to start more or less from scratch. Although the city had hosted the Games in 1932 all he received by way of guidance from City Hall when he started work was one cardboard box, marked 'All the records of the Los Angeles Olympic Games'. There were other difficulties too. For example, the owner of LAOOC's first offices reneged on the lease, and had the locks changed, as he disapproved of Los Angeles holding the Games.[16]

Despite these inconveniences Ueberroth swiftly built up a powerful organisation. He was not, however, unequivocally admired. Reich suggests that his management style was authoritarian, erratic and unpredictable. His public utterances were often misleading and contradictory, so that it was not always possible to tell, even in retrospect, when he had been telling the truth. At the end of his long book Reich remains ambivalent about Ueberroth, yet he is able to say 'To me the organizing committee . . . became a kind of totalitarian Utopia.'[17]

Forecasting the profits

In particular, Ueberroth persistently said that the Games were going to make only a small profit, although he must have known some time ahead that the profit was going to be very large. Indeed, he admits as much when he says 'We made a conscious decision to underestimate projected revenues as this was our only protection against unknown cost factors and an unstable international political environment.'[18] So dedicated was Ueberroth to secrecy that, according to Reich, he kept the real position even from people whom one would think would have had the right to be informed. For example, when he visited the IOC ten days after the USSR had declared its boycott on 8 May 1984 he angrily refused to discuss LAOOC's financial state.[19]

The ticketing department offers an interesting example of Ueberroth's methods. Reich comments that it was run, by a certain Ed Smith, with such secrecy that it would have been very difficult for Ueberroth to have sacked him. But he had no wish to do so, because he appreciated Smith's extremely conservative forecasts of receipts, and his wish to charge even higher prices than were eventually decided upon. When others were estimating revenue of $125m–$135m from ticket sales, Smith was still sticking to $90m, which helped Ueberroth to convince his own managers and the world that the Games were hardly going to make a profit.[20]

One advantage of pleading poverty was that Ueberroth was able to drive hard bargains with, for example, Francis Loyola University, over the cost of rooms for the athletes. But Ueberroth's reference to political uncertainties suggests that the possibility of a Soviet boycott was in his mind from very early on. He apparently believed that LAOOC needed a secret cushion, or reserve, in case the Soviets should not take part. If they pulled out and if ABC's viewing figures fell unacceptably (both conditions had to be satisfied), then the television company would have had the right to renegotiate its payment. Reich, who also suggests that announcing the true profit as late as possible improved Ueberroth's chance of being named *Time Magazine*'s 'Man of the Year', does not say how acceptable viewing figures were agreed upon in advance, but does state that ABC was entirely satisfied with the ones actually achieved, despite the Soviet boycott. In any case, their payments were made monthly and only one payment, of $15m, was made after the Games. Ueberroth seems to have threatened that, if ABC made any difficulty about any of the last few payments, he would simply not allow them to televise the Games – even at that late hour![21]

Ueberroth insisted that the winner of the contest for the North American television rights must agree at the same time to act as host broadcaster, which would cost $75m. ABC paid $225m, so that from Ueberroth's point of view the deal was worth $300m, although the figure generally used is $225m. Ueberroth rightly forecast that, in view of the IOC's precarious finances (about which he had, as we have seen, received private information), Madame Berlioux was hardly likely to use her power to veto the contract. He is, however, scathing about the IOC's business acumen in those days and recounts that the IOC counsel carried the first cheque, of $25m, about with him for twenty days, losing bank interest all the while and giving Ueberroth an insight into the IOC's financial carelessness.[22] Again, the assertion seems fantastic, but there is no reason to doubt the accuracy of Ueberroth's memory.

Ueberroth had to make it clear that he intended to be master in his own house. Thus, ABC was left in no doubt that, although it had paid heavily for the Games, it was not going to be allowed to run them, as it had done at Lake Placid.[23] Similarly, Ueberroth had to stand up to the overweening egos of the grandees of the Olympic movement and his frankness about them must surely have made him enemies: perhaps that is why he was not even invited to the Seoul Games.

Relations with the IOC and international federations

Ueberroth shows his talent for settling old scores when he discusses Monique Berlioux. He recalls that he had been warned that she was a stickler for detail and would demonstrate her superiority by testing his knowledge of the Charter and the Olympic movement. Ueberroth had managed to deflect her from her original insistence that the IOC must approve all contracts made by LAOOC (a right that the IOC has retained with subsequent organising committees) but she had insisted on approving the television contract for United States rights, and paid what sounds like a state visit to Los Angeles for the purpose. Ueberroth remembers that her demands were encyclopaedic.

> We had to make sure that a swimming pool was available, that Evian water was supplied, that there were exquisite flower arrangements, that the room service met her French tastes, that restaurant arrangements were made for the finest eateries, that appointments were not scheduled either early in the morning or late at night, and that her travelling staff received equally impeccable treatment.[24]

Likewise he concluded, after a visit to Moscow in July 1979 had shown him how great were the demands made on the Soviets by the IFs, that the Presidents of the IFs and NOCs must be kept in their place.[25]

The IF presidents, Ueberroth writes, are 'accustomed to pomp and circumstance and are extremely status conscious'.[26] In searching for venues LAOOC not only had trouble with city officials and the public but also with the IFs, and had particularly difficult dealings with FIFA, the football federation, and with Tom Keller of rowing. FIFA did succeed in having new stadia built, but when Adriaan Paulen, then President of IAAF, threatened to withdraw from the Games if they did not build him a new stadium, LAOOC called his bluff.[27] Both Reich and Ueberroth have stories to tell about Primo Nebiolo, who succeeded Paulen as President of IAAF. Reich says that at the Los Angeles Games Nebiolo asked for the positions of the IAAF and the Olympic flags to be reversed from what had been intended, so that he could look up from his seat at his own flag. LAOOC did as he asked.[28] For his part, Ueberroth recalls that Nebiolo had been daily pressurising Samaranch for special treatment and extra accreditations at Los Angeles, and that Samaranch asked Ueberroth to help.

Although the latter had always vowed to give no special treatment to anyone, he knew that he would have to relent in this case and agreed that Nebiolo could have what he wanted, but not until nearer the Games, in order to prevent all the other IFs from making similar demands. As he ruefully puts it: 'Not all sports federations, or NOCs for that matter, – so it turns out – are created equal.'[29]

Although Los Angeles had been able to make its own terms with the IOC the committee continued to keep its usual close eye on the preparations for the Games. In February 1981 the IOC's Executive Board met in Los Angeles. Samaranch and Berlioux had separate meetings with Ueberroth and Don Miller, reflecting the lack of working contact between the two bodies. Ueberroth presented his second annual report to the Board, and was congratulated by Samaranch, who declared himself highly satisfied with all that had been achieved. Some decisions of the Board were that all teams, without exception, were to be housed in the Olympic villages in conformity with the 1978 contract; the Greek proposal to provide a permanent home for the Games was to be studied further and remitted to the Baden-Baden Session, and an overall study on obtaining funds from commercialisation was to be made.[30] Ueberroth had also to keep the United States government's support behind the Games. For this reason he was pleased that Samaranch, who had been pressing for a meeting with President Reagan, achieved it on 28 January 1982 and obtained a stronger version of the letter of support that President Carter had signed when Los Angeles was first awarded the Games. 'More important', Ueberroth writes, 'it meant support for the Games had passed from one administration to the next.'[31]

The sponsors

Ueberroth's originality lay in limiting his sponsors (whose contributions came to $126.7m) to relatively few, though not as few as became the IOC's practice in its TOP programme (see Chapter IV). Ueberroth decided that there should be no more than thirty, with a minimum subscription of $4m and an 'exclusivity program': that is, not more than one company from any product category was to be included in the list of sponsors. He always dealt with the chairmen of companies, partly because he might want them to call on President Reagan for support for the Olympic Games. Perhaps not surprisingly, the first company to subscribe was Coca-Cola, which gave $30m to

LAOOC, as well as sponsoring, according to Ueberroth, more than thirty countries' teams. Madame Berlioux, the guardian of Olympic propriety, was displeased by the early announcement of the Coca-Cola and ABC deals, which she saw as stealing Moscow's thunder.

Ueberroth displayed his well-known determination in dealing with another sponsor, Kodak, and the story has passed into Olympic folklore. The company was dragging its feet over signing a contract, which irritated Ueberroth into making alternative arrangements with Kodak's Japanese competitors, Fuji. This strange dilatoriness caused heads to roll at Kodak, as Ueberroth recalls. Another close observer adds that Fuji increased its penetration of the American market from 3 per cent to 9 per cent, while Kodak had to undertake extremely expensive 'ambush advertising' and, as a second best, sponsored the American track and field team at the Games.[32]

The torch relay

One of Ueberroth's most striking innovations, which had connections with international politics which, though serious, also bordered on the farcical, was the torch relay which brought the Olympic flame from Greece to Los Angeles.

The Olympic torch is a modern invention, dating only from 1936. Samaranch and Madame Berlioux were at first worried about Ueberroth's intention to commercialise it by selling off kilometres at $3,000 each as it was carried across America, but withdrew their objections on learning that the proceeds were to go to youth charities. Meanwhile Ueberroth had a willing sponsor in the communications company AT&T, which became even more anxious to back the relay when it needed to reconstruct a national image after a federal judge had ruled that it must deregulate. However the Greek IOC members Nikos Filaretos and Nikolaos Nissiotis, backed by Angelo Lambessis, the President of the Greek NOC, objected to the commercialisation of the flame, which was, of course, already heavily commercialised by the Greeks, as it played a significant part in the economy of Olympia, and the Japanese sports goods manufacturer Mizuno was even allowed to engrave its name on the torch! (Ueberroth trusted Nissiotis, but thought Filaretos's opposition was politically motivated, and even hints that there may have been Soviet inspiration behind the campaign.) In an attempt to appease the Greeks Usher agreed that the sales of kilometres would continue no longer than

April. However, the written agreement, made with the assistance of Alexandru Siperco, the Romanian IOC member and a close associate of Samaranch, was not satisfactory and LAOOC refused to sign. Later Nissiotis was to apologise to Ueberroth and to tell him that the trouble had been caused by the recent dramatic shift to the left in Greek politics.[33]

Ueberroth, as so often allowing his dislike of the IOC high command to show, records that he had to deal with the imbroglio himself because 'Samaranch, always concerned with his power base, never wanted to get his hands dirty'. Although the Papandreou government naturally hoped to stay out of the trouble, Ueberroth thought that he could play upon the Greeks' wish to have their National Theatre included in the Olympic arts festival. This was a pet project of Margaret Papandreou, the Prime Minister's wife, who promised that the flame would be passed to LAOOC in an orderly manner, although as it turned out neither the Greek NOC nor the Communist Mayor of Olympia paid any heed to her wishes. Another plan was to by-pass Olympia altogether, by establishing a permanent flame at the IOC's headquarters in Lausanne.

The problem, of course, was how to abstract the flame from under the eyes of the recalcitrant Mayor of Olympia, who was making considerable political capital from the affair, and Samaranch, despite Ueberroth's complaint that he was unwilling to dirty his hands, solved it in a dramatic manner. Suddenly he telephoned Los Angeles to say that the flame was safely in Lausanne. Two Swiss students working in Greece on an Olympic project had been to Olympia and, armed with an instruction manual, had lit the flame by the sun's rays. The whole operation had been filmed to avoid any possibility of the Mayor claiming that the flame was not truly Olympian. Now that the ground was cut from under the Mayor's feet Ueberroth made one last request for an official lighting of the flame at Olympia, accompanied by a threat that otherwise he would not only make public the manner of its removal, but also oblige the Greek team to march in its alphabetical position at the opening ceremony of the Games, instead of in its customary place of honour at the head of the procession. Filaretos swiftly caved in (though it is not clear how he overcame the Mayor's objections), but despite Filaretos's assurance Ueberroth also made arrangements for the flame to be brought clandestinely from Lausanne to the United States.[34] At this point it appears that Samaranch saw a need to be magnanimous, for he let it be known that the IOC might seek a compromise between LAOOC and the Greek Olympic authorities, and might weaken its hitherto strong endorsement of the scheme to sell kilometres.[35] Indeed, it sounds, from an astringent, even horrified, article written at the time by Ian Wooldridge, as if the Olympic authorities would have done well to act according to their first doubts and that if they had wished the flame to retain any vestige of its mystical dignity they should never have endorsed the event at all.[36]

Security

Security became a major preoccupation: indeed it is a feature of all Games since Munich in 1972 that the conditions are akin to those of an armed camp, though the athletes, preoccupied as they are with winning, may not particularly notice the precautions taken on their behalf. By late June Samaranch was getting edgy about rumours that the Soviets might try to create an incident.[37] Later Samaranch said that the Israeli secret service, Mossad, had told him that their great mistake at Munich had been to have two agencies involved. This led Samaranch to ask which agency would be in ultimate charge at Los Angeles, as well he might, given the proliferation of police and security services in the USA. According to George Schultz, the Secretary of State, to whom the question was referred, the ultimate authority was the FBI. However, rivalry between the FBI and the police threatened security planning, and the Los Angeles police commander would not agree that the FBI was ultimately responsible.[38]

Ueberroth did not simply leave security to government agencies. As LAOOC's head of security he head-hunted Ed Best, 'the FBI's special agent in charge of Los Angeles' and eventually there were no fewer than eighteen sub-committees for different aspects of security. Ueberroth evidently had no difficulty in obtaining cooperation from government intelligence agencies. He states that 'We recognized the importance of intelligence early on and by late 1982 the international intelligence community had begun targeting its networks to potential Olympic threats for analysis and follow-up'. While still with the FBI in 1981 Best had emphasised the need to arouse the CIA's interest in the Games. In addition the Security Planning Committee received federal funds amounting to $50m for equipment. This subvention raised the question of taxpayers' money being spent after all and caused Ueberroth to issue a very strong press statement insisting, perhaps disingenuously, that 'Any government services we request, we will pay for, but we will not pay for any services we do not order'.[39]

There were differences with the police, who wanted enhanced security and its chief went so far as to say of LAOOC 'I don't think I would ever describe their attitude as being cooperative.' He believed that LAOOC was trying to save money, which was true up to a point, but their main concern was to preserve an unoppressive appearance. For example, Ueberroth and Usher were adamant that barbed wire must not be used to repel intruders and the police agreed to use the much less effective smooth taut wire. In the end a compromise was reached, although Ueberroth admits that Rathburn would have been entitled to use his professional judgement and oblige the committee to pay for whatever level of protection he considered essential. Yet the precautions sound thorough. Ueberroth and Usher had bodyguard drivers; they took special precautions at home and in their cars and there was tight security at the committee building, partly, Reich thinks, because Usher had a mania about the security of documents. Police precautions were at their most intense at the Olympic villages, where they required two perimeter fences and had specially trained counter-assault teams, and special protection for such teams as the Turks and the Israelis.[40]

Ueberroth, not surprisingly, shared Samaranch's worry about the great number of police forces in the Los Angeles area. 'Since athletes would be transported through more than forty separate law enforcement jurisdictions during the Games, we needed a system that would work and lessen the prospects of disaster.' The various agencies 'needed a compatible communications system just to talk to one another'. Ueberroth perceived that some forces hoped to make money out of the Games and it became necessary to prevent new equipment being charged to LAOOC, which a force had been unable to obtain by conventional means. But he was firm in scotching such try-ons and successful in promoting co-ordination between rival forces, thanks in large measure to the expertise of Ed Best.[41]

The Soviet boycott of Los Angeles

On 8 May 1984 the USSR announced its intention 'not to participate' in the Los Angeles games which were due to begin on 28 July. The factors involved in the decision were many and complex, but the simple explanation for the boycott is probably the right one – tit for tat.

Had relations between the two governments been happier it would have been possible to overcome the various grievances offered by the USSR as explanations for its action. As things were, the USSR relied on a series of reasons (some of them of concern to governments and others purely domestic issues within the Olympic movement) which in other circumstances would have been no more than excuses, readily to be circumvented. Their reasons included the United States' refusal to accredit the USSR's Olympic attaché; difficulties about Aeroflot flights and the Soviet wish to moor a ship in the harbour at Los Angeles; the fear that Soviet athletes would be mugged, kidnapped or persuaded to defect; the need for the United States to recognise Olympic identity cards instead of visas; and the cost of staying in the Olympic villages.

Many political actors were involved: in the USA the State Department; the CIA; LAOOC; and of course public opinion manifesting itself through such fringe groups as the 'Ban the Soviets' organisation, which gave great offence to the USSR. In the Soviet Union the main actors were the government and the not even nominally independent NOC, and holding the ring between the super-powers stood the IOC and the various other organisations within the Olympic movement.

The lead-up to the boycott

Although the USSR did not announce its intention to boycott the 1984 Games until very shortly before the deadline for acceptance of invitations, there had been doubt about whether they would attend ever since 1980. Samaranch had shown his nervousness and desire to nip in the bud any tendency to boycott at his very first press conference as President of the IOC, given in Moscow on 4 August 1980. On that occasion he promised to make every effort to restore the unity of the Olympic movement, and to work to ensure that the Los Angeles Games were 'even better' than those of Moscow. However Vladimir Popov, chief press officer at the Moscow Games did not exclude the possibility of the Soviet Union's boycotting Los Angeles, although he thought it unlikely to do so unless the USA violated Olympic rules. (He is here referring to the argument frequently used by Soviet officials that the USA had broken the rules by pressing for the Moscow boycott.)[42]

According to Reich, Samaranch and Madame Berlioux had feared the possibility of a boycott from the start, and had always tied it to relations between the governments and to the American boycott in 1980. Over a year before the Games Samaranch had been telling Ueberroth and others that he had received reports that if the United States sent Cruise and Pershing 2 missiles to Europe in the autumn of 1983, the Soviets would boycott.[43] There was an element of whistling in the dark about some of Samaranch's press statements. For example, in the context of his concern about the deployment of new missiles by NATO he said in Moscow in July 1983: 'I know the word boycott does not exist in the Soviet Union. I also know very well that the Soviet Union always maintains that it is essential not to let politics mix with sport.'[44]

On the United States' side of the diplomatic battle, the government and LAOOC did not always agree. Ueberroth, who throughout the crisis over the Soviet boycott seems to have had an exaggerated idea of the importance of the Games to the United States government (he even at one point expressed the opinion that the outcome of the Games could have a profound effect on the Presidential election), records that the boycott forced LAOOC to 'establish our own foreign policy and repair the international damage that the L.A. Games had suffered. At the same time we had to work with our government and make sure it respected and upheld the Olympic Charter.' So convinced was he of his own ability to influence events that he always regretted that he had not been allowed to meet President Konstantin Chernenko and to try to talk him out of the boycott.[45]

The shooting down by the Soviets of a Korean airliner at the end of August 1983 immediately made Ueberroth think the possibility of a boycott more likely, and he turned out to be right, because the incident provoked reactions in the USA which in turn provided one of the excuses for Soviet non-participation. As a result of the attack the California State Legislature passed a resolution condemning the USSR and recommending that the Soviet athletes be banned from Los Angeles. A more significant result was the formation of the 'Ban the Soviets' Coalition, an unimportant body in itself, but one to whose activities the Soviets were able to point as evidence of the United States' hostility. Ueberroth, in order to counter the resolution, wrote to Soviet officials, saying that they and their athletes would be welcome, but that there was little he could do to counter the anti-Soviet campaigners.[46]

In November 1983 Ueberroth learned that the Soviets were to visit Los Angeles. 'Knowing I couldn't count on the Reagan administration (which couldn't differentiate between its policy towards the Soviet Union and its views on the Olympic Games), I'd been working for a year and a half on my own foreign policy of repairing bridges between the national Olympic committees of the countries in the Eastern bloc.' He had started this policy in February 1982, when he had travelled to East Germany and in May had signed a protocol to the effect that the East Germans would be at Los Angeles in strength, 'provided we adhered to the Olympic Charter'.[47] He had made similar agreements in Warsaw and Moscow, where Sergei Pavlov, at that time President of the Soviet NOC, had ranted about the dangers that Soviet athletes would face in Los Angeles, but he realised that none of the officials with whom he had dealt would make the decision. 'That would be done in the Politburo of the USSR.'[48]

The Soviet demands

Having sent one reasonably successful delegation in December 1983, the USSR sent another to the Executive Board's meeting in Los Angeles in January 1984. This time the portents were less good. At the last moment the fourteen-man delegation was reduced to seven and Pavlov was replaced as its leader by Victor Ivonin. Samaranch was not surprised, and said that Pavlov's influence had been steadily diminishing since Yuri Andropov had come to power a year earlier. Most NOCs were satisfied with the arrangements being made at Los Angeles, but at his press conference Ivonin raised four of the issues listed at the beginning of this section: the cost of the athletes' stay in the Olympic villages; the United States government's recognition of Olympic identity cards instead of visas; permission for Aeroflot to take athletes to Los Angeles; and for a Soviet ship to dock in Los Angeles harbour.

A few weeks later came the notification that 'Marat Gramov, a veteran Soviet propagandist from the Ministry of Information, had replaced Pavlov' as President of the Soviet NOC. He complained about LAOOC's plans for transport, security and housing, and, according to the *Los Angeles Times*, alleged that the refusal to pay expenses of foreign officials and judges would increase reliance on local judges, and therefore the possibility of biased decisions. The decision whether or not to participate would not, he said, be taken until 24 April 1984.

Ueberroth soon went to Moscow to see Gramov. The latter, having explained that the word 'boycott' does not exist in Russian, reiterated the familiar requests, which Ueberroth thought could probably be met if the Soviets were willing to give the additional information needed by his government. On this occasion Gramov did not question the quality of judging that might be expected at Los Angeles, since he now realised that judging was the responsibility of the IFs.

The Olympic attaché

Ueberroth asked for an Olympic attaché to be sent to Los Angeles as soon as possible and made it clear that, if he were appointed some months in advance, his application would have to be processed in the normal way. (Usually NOCs appoint someone who lives permanently in the host city, so that the question of entry does not arise.) So began one of the more famous rows of the Los Angeles Olympics.

The affair moved forward when Gramov sent a list of twelve people who would accompany him on his forthcoming visit to Los Angeles. It included a certain Oleg Yermishkin, and within two hours Best, LAOOC'S head of security, was able to say that Yermishkin was a 'known KGB operative', who had served at the Soviet embassy in Washington for several years. (History does not relate whether Best thought it necessary to obtain this information, or whether it was forced upon him.) Despite Yermishkin's KGB membership the State Department allowed him a visa and at their first meeting in Los Angeles Gramov told Ueberroth that Yermishkin was to be their Olympic attaché. An agreement was signed whereby the attaché would take up residence in Los Angeles not later than 1 March 1984, LAOOC would process the Soviet requests for landing rights and docking privileges and the USSR would notify its participation by the new deadline of 2 June 1984.[49]

It seems perfectly clear to the observer, though evidently it was not to Ueberroth, that he had begun to overplay his hand in conducting his own foreign policy, and to promise more than he could deliver. After the meeting with Gramov he tempted fate by telling the White House that the Soviet requests were in accordance with the Olympic Charter, and should be seen as a test of the Reagan administration's willingness to abide by it. It would hardly be surprising if professional diplomats, faced with such self-importance, had formed the opinion that Ueberroth needed taking down a peg. Certainly the diplomats took little notice of him, perhaps foolishly, when one considers what an effective worldwide network the Olympic movement offers. For example, he notes that in his five and a half years' connection with the Olympics an American ambassador never once took the trouble to see him – a systematic discourtesy which can hardly have been accidental.[50] There had also been an agreement to establish Olympic liaison officers at every American embassy and consulate, but the State Department had not followed it up, and when the officers were appointed they rarely took the job seriously.

By early in January Gramov was demanding answers and saying that the United States government was blocking various Soviet requests: for their attaché to be appointed; for charter flights, and for their transport ship, the Grazia, to be allowed to dock in Los Angeles. Gramov, who must have realised that Ueberroth was playing out of his league, asked whether he should go directly to the State Department, instead of working through Ueberroth. To this Ueberroth naturally replied that Gramov should abide by the Olympic Charter and work through LAOOC. He then went to Washington to complain about bureaucratic foot-dragging, but was told by Michael Deaver, the responsible official, that there was nothing to worry about: 'the Russians will be here'. Once back in Los Angeles he learned from his representative in Washington that the Soviet requests had been sitting on another official's desk for a month, and that no one in the State Department had even seen them.

On 19 January Gramov publicly complained that the State Department did not recognise LAOOC's authority. Publicly, Ueberroth played down what he saw as the administration's inefficiency (which may, of course, not have been inefficiency in fact), because he could not afford to antagonise the White House, although he resented its taking him to task for dealing directly with the Soviet NOC. He claims that the procedure had been agreed with Deaver, and that it was for Deaver to tell appropriate agencies that Ueberroth's independent activity had official blessing.[51] Soviet complaints continued about such matters as restrictions on the movements of embassy and consular personnel; their belief that the Americans would encourage their athletes to defect, and anti-Soviet car stickers and demonstrations. In a long statement on 9 April the Soviet NOC introduced a new complication by attacking both the United States government and LAOOC for commercialising the Olympic flame; the statement also predicted that profiteers would charge high prices at Los Angeles, and claimed that LAOOC was charging NOCs for traditionally free services.[52]

Meanwhile the Yermishkin affair lingered on. According to Best, the Soviets were genuinely worried about defections and wanted Yermishkin as a professional shepherd. Best also understood that the appointment of a KGB officer as Olympic attaché would have been popular in the FBI, which would have enjoyed playing at spies with the KGB. Nothing had been heard about Yermishkin's visa, and it was not until 1 March, the very day on which he had been due to arrive, that the State Department refused to issue it. The timing suggests either that the State Department enjoyed the childish non-sense of playing cat and mouse until the last moment, or that an inter-departmental wrangle between FBI men and diplomats had gone on so long that it could only be brought to an end by using as its cut-off point a deadline which there was no real need to respect, since it had been set by LAOOC (which had agreed Yermishkin's arrival date) and not by the government.

Not only did the State Department cause a crisis between LAOOC and the USSR, but it incurred Ueberroth's wrath, and in his view grossly violated the Olympic Charter, by informing the Soviets directly of its decision instead of going through LAOOC. It is possible that the State Department simply wanted to assert diplomatic nor-mality in the face of Olympic pretensions but, if so, it was not consistent, since in mid-March when the State Department approved in principle the Aeroflot charter flights and berthing of the Grazia, LAOOC was allowed to tell the Soviets itself. (The timing may be coincidental, but on 2 March, the day after Yermishkin's visa had been refused, Ueberroth agreed to become United States Commis-sioner of Baseball once the Games were over.)[53]

The Soviet decision

Whatever private games the governments of the United States and the USSR were playing, it was plain that for the Olympic Games the crisis was approaching. On 24 April Samaranch called what he probably saw as a last ditch meeting at Lausanne, at the Soviets' request, attended by the three Vice-Presidents of the IOC, Madame Berlioux and delegations from LAOOC and the Soviet NOC. The press release after the meeting noted the firm Soviet intention to take part in the

Games, provided the Charter were respected. It affirmed that the
Soviet NOC and any other NOC would have free scope to solve
problems relevant to the Olympic Games through the sole agency of
LAOOC, particularly with regard to the Olympic identity cards and
the list of participants. All members of the Olympic family and
accredited journalists would have free access and the rules governing
the ships anchored in the port of Los Angeles would strictly conform
to international regulations and the hospitality usually granted to
Games participants. (This rather obscure formulation means that the
United States authorities would have the normal right to inspect the
Grazia, but that the IOC hoped the right would be exercised with
restraint.)[54]

This communiqué showed that the IOC and the USSR were doing
their best to talk to each other, but of course it was no more than a
statement of Olympic hopes. Its intentions could only be achieved
with the active agreement of the United States Government. Nevertheless, although Samaranch knew full well that the Soviet NOC was
not autonomous, he seems to have seen the meeting as a crucial
demonstration of Soviet willingness to solve the problems that they
and the United States government had created, and to have felt
correspondingly let down when the decision to boycott was announced a fortnight later. As we shall see, the Soviets consistently claimed
afterwards that the decision had been precipitated by a bad meeting at
the State Department on 27 April, three days after the encounter at
Lausanne.

On 5 May Gramov broadened the arena by informing Mario
Vásquez-Raña, the president of ANOC, that he was not sure that
LAOOC was capable of organising the Games according to the
Charter, and inviting him to Moscow to discuss the role of the NOCs
in future Games. This shift to a concern for the power of the NOCs
was a new complication (though not a new concern of the NOCs), and
one with which much play was to be made later. It was a subtle move,
both because Raña, whatever his personal views, could not be seen to
avoid taking seriously any wish to give power to the NOCs, and
because it was a clear signal that the USSR intended to retain influence
in the Olympic movement, whatever happened over Los Angeles.
The new development worried Samaranch, who had already arranged
to meet President Reagan after attending the opening of the torch
relay in New York on 8 May. He now thought that it would be helpful
to have a firmer letter of support from the President than the one

already given and Nicolae Ceauşescu (the dictator of Romania and a rather unfortunate friend of the Olympic movement in the light of the events of 1990) had been of the same opinion.

But it was too late. Just before Samaranch and Ueberroth took off from New York for their meeting with the President in Washington a first report was received that the Soviets were to boycott and on arrival in Washington Samaranch's party received an agency message written by Victor Louis (whom Samaranch identifield as a journalist often used by the Soviets to break news stories in the West), confirming the report.[55]

Reactions to the Soviet boycott

The full text of the Soviet communiqué focused most of the Soviet attack on the United States government, since the USSR plainly did not want to create an irretrievable breach within the Olympic movement. Thus the attack emphasised the government's connivance with the anti-Soviet campaign by reactionary forces in the USA, and the authorities' continuing interference with LAOOC's business. It was well known, the communiqué continued, that from the beginning of the preparations for the Games the American administration had intended to use them for political purposes. Chauvinist sentiments and anti-Soviet hysteria were developing in the United States. Washington had recently given assurances concerning its desire to respect the Charter, but American actions were directed to undermining it and showed that they had no intention of safeguarding the athletes' security, nor of respecting their rights and creating normal conditions for the Games. In these conditions the Soviet NOC was obliged to say that its participation was impossible. To have behaved differently would have been to approve anti-Soviet actions by the American authorities and by the organisers of the Games. It had no wish to influence American public opinion, nor to spoil the good relations between their sports people, and would support the IOC and other Olympic institutions.[56]

Once Tass had announced the Soviet 'non-participation' the Soviet bloc, with the exception of Romania, fell into line quite quickly, but it appears that no advance warning had been given, either to the satellites or to sports bodies within the USSR. This, at least, was what Marian Renke, the President of the Polish NOC, said, and it appears that he may at first have hoped that Poland might not be obliged to

G

follow the Soviet example.[57] On the other hand the East German decision to follow the Soviet lead, unwilling though it was, had been foreshadowed in April in an aggressive statement about the inadequate preparations being made for the Games.[58]

As we have seen, the news reached Samaranch just before his meeting with President Reagan, who readily agreed to write to President Chernenko, in the hope of changing his mind. However, during the meeting Samaranch decided that Olympic protocol would be better served if Reagan were to address his letter to him, Samaranch. The idea that Reagan might invite Chernenko to the Games was mooted, but vetoed by the Secretary of State, George Schultz, as such an invitation would 'complicate other existing issues'. [59] In the United States the 'Ban the Soviets' organisation, the body of Soviet emigrés whose activities had so enraged the Soviets, naturally saw the Soviet withdrawal as a personal victory. Reagan, as well as expressing disappointment, said he wished the modern world were as civilised as the Greeks, referring to their so-called 'sacred truce'.[60] Meanwhile, it appeared that the Soviet decision was not intended to cover all sporting events, or perhaps there had merely been a failure of communication, for it was reported on 9 May that the French basketball federation had received a telex confirming Soviet participation in the men's qualifying Olympic tournament.[61]

Press reactions to the boycott

The boycott naturally attracted considerable coverage in the press. Reagan's letter to Samaranch, published the day after he received it, was supportive but it was made clear that the United States government intended to make no further concessions, nor would it beg the Soviet Union to reconsider. Ueberroth himself did not think Reagan would give any more help, as the boycott would help him electorally.[62] The USSR was correspondingly firm. Its Ambassador in Washington swiftly announced that the decision was irreversible[63], and the fact that Samaranch had received a supportive letter from Reagan would not, specialists thought, make any difference. The decision had been political, and taken at the highest level.[64]

AFP, reporting from Paris, saw the boycott as the culmination of a series of Soviet discontents, going back to 1981. At that time Soviet sports leaders had already been protesting against the excessive commercialisation of the Games, and the Springboks' tour of the United

States while the Olympic Congress was going on at Baden-Baden had caused a dozen Soviet Olympic champions to sign a letter condemning Reagan's policies. The calm induced by Baden-Baden had not lasted long, and there had been numerous gloomy articles about the problems facing the Los Angeles Games in such perodicals as *Sovietski Sport*. These had not only complained about commercialisation, but about such issues as the lodging of the Olympic athletes, the lack of a single Olympic village, poor security, the partiality to be expected from American judges, transport and the great distance between venues, and smog.[65]

Much of the press saw the Soviet decision as part of a general Soviet hardening, both internal and external, of which other symptoms were the internal exile imposed on Madame Elena Bonner, wife of Professor Andrei Sakharov, and the renewal of the army's offensive in Afghanistan.[66] According to Tass, the KGB had foiled a large-scale operation by Sakharov and his wife, who had been operating with the United States Embassy in Moscow. The American intention was said to have been to bring her out of the USSR to become 'one of the Soviet outcasts who work for western special services'.[67]

Le Monde also saw the Olympic decision as just one more in the recent list of Soviet 'niets' to western proposals. The paper considered that the boycott should be seen partly as revenge for 1980, and partly as a signal to the Americans that the USSR still had a variety of shots in the political locker. It might also give some indication of the personal character of Mr Chernenko. On the other hand, the Soviet NOC's tone had been moderate, and the word 'boycott' had been carefully avoided, perhaps in order to play down the comparison with 1980.[68]

At least one columnist gave credence to the Soviet fear of defections as a major reason for the boycott. Something, he said, had been going on in the Soviet hierarchy with regard to the Games for some months. The motive had not been revenge for 1980; the major Soviet interest had been to prevent defections. 'The reason for the Russians' hesitation in taking this step was that, since the death of President Yuri Andropov, no one individual or faction in the Soviet hierarchy has sufficient authority to make a speedy decision.[69] However, many commentators did see the motive as simple revenge.

Of course not all the press was sympathetic. For example, the *Frankfurter Allgemeine Zeitung* of 15 May 1984 published a pungent cartoon, featuring an exhausted flying athlete, brandishing a battered-looking torch, and surrounded by the five Olympic rings, marked Politics, Intrigues, Showbiz, Chauvinism, and Business.[70]

Politicians' responses

The Soviet decision inspired world-wide comment by major figures, many of whom must have seen some political advantage in taking a view, or political disadvantage in not doing so. Mayor Bradley intended a visit to Moscow in order to repeat personally the assurances that he had already given concerning such Soviet preoccupations as their athletes' security.[71] Vice-President George Bush, who was in Tokyo, hoped the USSR would change its mind.[72] Jacques Chirac pronounced himself dismayed but not surprised and said, no doubt with an eye to Paris's candidature for the 1992 Games, 'All this could provide cause for reflection for the International Olympic Committee on organising the Olympic Games in countries too politically committed.'[73]

Chancellor Helmut Kohl said the Soviets' action was inconsistent with their claims to desire dialogue with the West[74] and the West German Foreign Minister, Hans-Dietrich Genscher, said in Washington that he was going to Moscow on 20 May and would try to dissuade the Soviets.[75] The Vatican City appealed to Moscow to change its mind and Constantin Karamanlis, the Greek Prime Minister, repeated the offer made in 1976 to provide a permanent home for the Games.[76] The Revd Jesse Jackson, a candidate for the Democratic presidential nomination, asked the Soviet ambassador for a meeting at which he would seek to persuade him. Jackson and Ueberroth agreed that whoever got to Castro first would carry an Olympic message from the other and in the event it was Ueberroth who took a letter from Jackson.[77]

Rather surprisingly, it was reported that there was no real crisis atmosphere at LAOOC, and not much interest among the citizenry, in the stifling 34 degrees in the shade then prevailing.[78] Nor were the sponsoring companies thought to be dismayed. ABC, the company with potentially the most to lose, was said not to be worried about the television audience declining. Indeed, some people, one of them Roone Arledge, head of news and sport at ABC, thought it would be bigger because the United States would have a better chance of winning gold medals in the absence of some of the major sporting countries.[79] Nevertheless, the possibility was floated that ABC might pay LAOOC $40–70m less than the $225m agreed. Harry Usher did not think the Soviets' absence would make much financial difference[80] and of course he was right, not only because, as we have seen, Ueberroth took a firm line with the television company, but also because the powerful Arledge was prepared to argue to his board (correctly, as it turned out) that ratings would not suffer.

The courageous Romanians broke the Soviet boycott. As early as 9 May, the day after the boycott was announced, a spokesman for the Romanian embassy in Vienna had said that his country would take part,[81] and it was thought sure to do so, although there would be no decision until the President, Nicolae Ceauşescu, returned from his visit to Pakistan. Ceauşescu had seen Samaranch on the previous Saturday and had reaffirmed the Romanian determination to participate in events organised by the IOC.[82] On 15 May it was reported that the Romanians were continuing in training[83] and the announcement that Romania would attend was made on 24 May. Ueberroth draws attention to the decision's immense symbolic importance. It also brought Romania sporting success. It had been ninth in the medal table at Montreal and seventh at Moscow, but at Los Angeles Romania's 127-person team came third, behind the USA and West Germany. LAOOC contributed $60,000 of the $180,000 cost of bringing the Romanian team to the Games, and the IOC another $60,000.[84] In due course Ceauşescu received the Olympic Order from Samaranch. He plainly saw it as an honour, and accepted with humility and gratitude.[85]

The State Department seems not to have been taken by surprise by the boycott, since it reacted very promptly. The spokesman, John Hughes, rejected the suggestion that the United States could not ensure the Soviet athletes' security; since (he claimed) no notice of their intentions had been given it was difficult to analyse the Soviet motives; he regretted the 'blatant attempt' to play politics with the Olympic Games and stated that the United States government had 'gone the last mile' to accommodate Soviet requests. The only question unresolved was Yermishkin's appointment and the government would be willing to accept another official, but not Yermishkin, who was believed to be a high-ranking KGB officer. He added that the government had given no encouragement to the Soviet emigré groups which had protested against Soviet attendance and vowed to encourage Soviet defectors, but, although it must be difficult for the Soviets to understand, the USA was a free country. The difference between the two boycotts was 'the extraordinary brutality shown by the Soviets in Afghanistan. There is no comparable action by the United States here.'[86]

The salvage operation

Ueberroth complains that he was given little help by the IOC or the United States government in his efforts to salvage Soviet participation. This is probably a fair judgement so far as the government is concerned, since although it was happy enough to use the Olympics if any advantage could be squeezed from them, it naturally did not attach the same value to them as did Ueberroth or Samaranch. However, it would be unjust to claim that the IOC was inactive, though its priorities may have been rather different from Ueberroth's. His concern was to do his best for Los Angeles, whereas Samaranch had to look to the future and ensure that the Olympic movement did not suffer permanent damage, even if the Soviets could not be persuaded to change their minds.

Samaranch's first thought was that he must go to Moscow, although he was determined that he must be received at a level appropriate to his own high office, which meant Chernenko or some other very senior politican. His request for such a meeting was telexed to Gramov on 10 May and thereafter he was warned on various occasions that the President would be unlikely to receive him.

On 17 May Samaranch and Berlioux met the two Soviet members of the IOC, Constantin Andrianov and Vitaly Smirnov, and asked them what had happened since the meeting of 24 April. Having protested their loyalty to the Olympic movement, they alleged that the fault lay with the American administration. They went on to explain that on 27 April an official from the Soviet Embassy in Washington had been invited to a meeting at the State Department (to which Ueberroth was furious not to have been invited), presided over by Edward J. Derwinski, adviser to the Secretary of State and had been told that the charges made by the Soviet NOC were without foundation. Derwinski had re-emphasised that LAOOC was a private organisation which had no right to solve problems and had said that the administration could do nothing about the 'Ban the Soviets' organisation in the USA. Andrianov and Smirnov denied that the boycott was revenge for that of 1980, and to reinforce the point said that they had paid over $2m for television rights. They could not take the risk of another Munich, where Israeli athletes had been assassinated. Furthermore (departing from their conciliatory line), they considered that the IOC President had made too many concessions to LAOOC, and that the IOC rules had even been changed in its favour. Derwinski was to profess himself puzzled by this account of the meeting. He agreed that he had met the Soviet Minister-Counsellor on 27 April, but said that he had emphasised the United States' willingness to co-operate and communicate with the Soviets. 'There were no demands on their part, and therefore no rejections.'

On 18 May the Executive Board and the Commission for the Olympic Movement met in Lausanne. Samaranch made a fighting speech, recalling the great efforts made to allay all the Soviet anxieties at the meeting on 24 April, and deploring the Soviet boycott. Where, he asked, were the noble intentions and devotion to the Olympic ideal which the USSR had proclaimed, particularly in 1980? In reply, Marat Gramov, speaking as President of the Soviet NOC, made much the same points as had been made by Andrianov and Smirnov on the previous day. He emphasised the good relations established with LAOOC, and (perhaps with tongue in cheek) asserted that the Soviets had been relying on LAOOC being able to deliver on the agreement previously made. It was the meeting at the State Department, at which Derwinski had said that Ueberroth had been exceeding his powers, and had repudiated the positive steps made at Lausanne on 24 April, that had decided the Soviets to boycott the Games. However, Ueberroth was able to point out that the Soviets were not at all anxious for their judges, officials and referees to stay away from Los Angeles.

The last meeting of any significance was with the sports ministers of the socialist countries in Prague on 24 May, which Samaranch attended, flanked by Rana and Nebiolo. Samaranch said that the IOC had to act as a bridge between two great political systems; Rana, who had been touring socialist countries 'in order to consolidate relations with them' had no choice, as President of ANOC, but to accept the socialist NOCs' decision gracefully, whereas Nebiolo was free to urge them to reconsider. Again the various sports ministers took the opportunity to rehearse the usual grievances, but the meeting was notable because they also inflamed an open sore by making much of the need for NOCs to play a greater part in the Olympic movement, and in particular in the choice of the Olympic city. They were especially incensed by the choice of Seoul, which many of them thought virtually an American colony, to host the 1988 Games. The meeting was

also unusual in its overt acrimony, and because no agreed communiqué was issued: instead there were two, one put out by the IOC
and the other by the delegates.[87]

While the IOC did its best to limit the damage, LAOOC was not
idle. Intensive persuasion by telephone coupled with visits to key
countries like Romania, China, East Germany and Cuba, brought the
record number of 140 'countries' to the Games (the previous record
had been 123 at Munich, against 81 at Moscow and 88 at Montreal.[88]
Good inducements were offered. For example, LAOOC paid for air
charter for African athletes, and many of the Romanian costs, and the
number of athletes was kept up by such strong Olympic countries
as Britain, France, West Germany and Australia being invited to
increase their teams. The number of countries taking part was inflated
by allowing some territories to participate which were not properly
qualified according to Olympic rules. For example Tonga was
admitted, although it had insufficient affiliations to international
federations, yet after the Games Tonga was told that it was ineligible
for that very reason! (However, the situation was saved by Samaranch, who visited Tonga in March 1987 and promised to facilitate the necessary extra affiliations.)[89]

There followed great efforts, in which Rana played a full part as
President of ANOC, to persuade NOCs not to join the boycott. Rana
journeyed to see Gramov in Moscow, although Ueberroth had little
hope and Viktor Cherkashin of the Soviet Embassy in Washington
had said that the specific Olympic problems were overshadowed by
the much larger one of the United States government's attitude,
specifically that of the State Department.

In Cuba, where Rana and Ueberroth travelled together, they were
well received, but Castro would not break the boycott because during
the United States' boycott of Cuba in the 1960s Cubans had been able
to find no sporting opponents except teams from the Soviet bloc, and
now he felt a debt of loyalty. However, he did agree not to disrupt the
games and to make a public commitment to this effort, Ueberroth
having flattered him by referring to his many troops in Africa and the
great respect in which he was held there. He also agreed that security
at Los Angeles was not a problem and allowed the point to be made for
him at a press conference, after which the Soviets never again used the
security excuse. Samaranch had cautioned against the meeting with
Castro, but in Ueberroth's opinion he had done so only because he
considered it his own prerogative to deal with heads of state.[90]

Samaranch himself eventually went to Moscow on 31 May, despite the warnings he had received that Chernenko would not see him. He saw only Gramov and Nikolai Talysin, one of fourteen deputy Prime Ministers, and admitted after the meeting that no hope remained of saving Soviet participation in the Games.[91] Despite this failure, which he must have realised was inevitable, Samaranch started work on the major task of salvaging the long-term unity of the movement by asserting that the IOC's links with Moscow were not severed. Soviet officials agreed and promised to 'struggle to maintain the Olympic movement's unity and purity'.[92] Back in Los Angeles Samaranch was in tougher mood and said that no excuses would be accepted for non-participation in future Games and that the IOC was to hold an extraordinary meeting in Lausanne in December to decide how to deal with non-participants.[93]

Verdicts on Los Angeles

The boycott definitely had an adverse effect on the athletic quality of the Olympics because the seventeen boycotting states included six of the top ten medal winners at Montreal: the USSR, East Germany, Poland, Bulgaria, Cuba and Hungary. On the other hand the boycott helped to make the Games a success in that the American people became more interested in them than would otherwise have been the case.[94] As Ian Wooldridge tartly put it: 'The corporate sporting knowledge around here is that the filthy, cheating Russians are too scared to turn up.'[95] There were also many protests about the crude bias of ABC's concentration on American exploits, which led Samaranch to issue a stern warning to Roone Arledge.[96]

Though the Games may not have been of the first quality, they had many good points. There was no terrorism and virtually no incidents, bar demonstrations by Sikhs against the Indian hockey team. (Ashwini Kumar, one of the Indian IOC members, and the IOC's expert on security, had protested bitterly to Samaranch about these demonstrations. Ueberroth then investigated, and makes the bizarre allegation that Kumar had acted as agent provocateur!)[97] In Reich's view security, on which over $60m was spent, became one of the Games' triumphs, without being so stringent as to spoil them.[98] David Miller generously summed up the Games as having been memorable.[99] and Samaranch went so far as to say that they had given the Olympic movement a shot in the arm, with half a dozen candidates already in the field for the summer and winter Games of 1992.[100]

That, of course, is the crux. The Games had necessarily become a commercial operation on a scale hitherto unknown, although Harry Usher had claimed that their great achievement would be to return the Games to the athletes.[101] But their greatest achievement was to make a huge profit, which emboldened other candidate cities, and assured the IOC that it would never again be placed in the position of having to give way to a city's excessive demands, simply because no other was available.

Notes

1   Harry Edwards, 'Sportpolitics: Los Angeles 1984 – the Olympic Tradition Continues', in *Sociology of Sport Journal*, 1, 1984, p. 172 and James Riordan, *Sport in Soviet Society*, Cambridge, 1977, p. 364.

2   Lord Killanin, *My Olympic Years*, London, 1983, p. 104.

3   Geoffrey Miller, *Behind the Olympic Rings*, Lynn, Massachusetts, 1979, p.136. I have drawn heavily on Miller's work in this section, especially on his pp. 136–48.

4   Peter Ueberroth, *Made in America*, London 1986, p. 13.

5   *Ibid.*, pp. 14 and 46 and Kenneth Reich, *Making it Happen: Peter Ueberroth and the 1984 Olympics*, Santa Barbara, 1986.

6   Killanin, pp. 104–7.

7   Reich, p. 132.

8   Reich, p. 24.

9   Miller, p. 148.

10   Killanin, pp. 104–6.

11   Killanin and Rodda, *The Olympic Games 1984*, p. 10.

12   Reich, p. 245.

13   Ueberroth, p. 91.

14   Reich, p. 130.

15   Ueberroth, foreword.

16   *ibid.*, pp. 11–13, 21, 37.

17   Reich, p. 246.

18   Ueberroth, p. 60.

19   Reich, p. 101.

20   *ibid.*, pp. 157 and 166.

21   *ibid.*, pp. 88–9, 103, 96.

22   Ueberroth, pp. 53 and 55.

23   Reich, p. 15.

24   Ueberroth, p. 54.

25   *Ibid.*, p. 44.

26   *Ibid.*, p. 118.

27   Reich, p. 130. However, Miller, pp. 73–4, makes the related point that, if the IOC ever tried to reduce the importance of track and field events in the Games, the IAAF would simply drop out of them.

28 Reich, p. 242.
29 Ueberroth, p. 197.
30 *Olympic Review*, March 1981, p. 141.
31 Ueberroth, p. 104.
32 *ibid.*, pp. 47–52 and 57–8.
33 Ueberroth, pp. 158–66, 174, 211.
34 Ueberroth, pp. 191–2 and 211–12. The quotation is at p. 191.
35 *The Times*, 23 February 1984.
36 'The Great Olympic Hype', Ian Wooldridge, *Sport in the 80s: a Personal View*, London, 1989, pp. 78–9.
37 Ueberroth, p. 266.
38 Reich, p. 204.
39 Ueberroth, pp. 102, 108, 112.
40 Reich, pp. 196–8 and 200–3. The quotation is at p. 196.
41 Ueberroth, pp. 97, 98, 100.
42 *The Times*, 5 August 1980.
43 Reich, pp. 208–10.
44 *The Times*, 26 July 1983.
45 Ueberroth, pp. 168 and 77.
46 *ibid.*, pp. 127–30 and Reich, pp. 213–14.
47 Ueberroth, pp. 134 and 138.
48 *ibid.*, p. 146.
49 *ibid.*, pp. 148–54. The quotations are at pp. 151 and 153.
50 *ibid.*, p. 139.
51 *ibid.*, pp. 166–7 and 171. the quotation is at p. 167.
52 *ibid.*, p. 200.
53 *ibid.*, pp. 183–4.
54 *ibid.*, pp. 205–9 and IOC press release, 24 April 1984.
55 *ibid.*, pp. 213 and 218–21.
56 *Le Monde*, 10 May 1984.
57 *UPI*, 8 May 1984.
58 *ibid.*, 10 May 1984.
59 Ueberroth, p. 221.
60 *AFP*, Washington, 9 May 1984.
61 *UPI*, Paris, 9 May 1984.
62 Ueberroth, p. 225.
63 *Le Monde*, 10 May 1984.
64 *AFP*, Moscow, 10 May 1984.
65 *AFP*, Paris, 8 May 1984.
66 *AFP*, Moscow, 9 May 1984.
67 *International Herald Tribune*, 15 May 1984, Leopold Unger.
68 *Le Monde*, 10 May 1984.
69 *International Herald Tribune*, 10 May 1984.
70 *Frankfurter Allgemeine Zeitung*, 15 May 1984.
71 *UPI*, Los Angeles, 10 May 1984.
72 *AFP*, 10 May 1984.
73 *UPI*, 9 May 1984.
74 *ibid.*

75   *AFP*, Paris, 10 May 1984.
76   *AFP*, Moscow, 10 May, 1984.
77   *AFP*, Washington, 10 May 1984 and Ueberroth, p. 249.
78   Gerald Marcout, *AFP*, Los Angeles, 9 May 1984.
79   Ueberroth, p. 224. Interesting light is thrown on Arledge's swashbuckling methods in David A. Klatell and Norman Marcus, *Sports for Sale: Television, Money, and the Fans*, New York, 1988. Chapter 8.
80   *AFP*, Los Angeles, 10 May 1984.
81   *UPI*, 9 May 1984.
82   *AFP*, Vienna, 9 May 1984.
83   *International Herald Tribune*, 15 May 1984.
84   Reich, pp. 229–30.
85   *The Times*, 6 August, 1985, David Miller, Sofia.
86   *UPI*, 8 May 1984.
87   Ueberroth, *passim*; Reich, Chapter 12, IOC Press Release, 24 April 1984, *The Times* (Richard Owen) and *International Herald Tribune*, both 15 May 1984, reporting from Moscow, and *Guardian*, 19 May 1984, John Rodda, Lausanne. Smirnov has since said that he thought the decisions to boycott Moscow and Los Angeles were both bad and that he did all he could to show that they were mistaken. See his interview with Marie-Hélène Roukhadze in *Olympic Review*, March–April 1991, p. 132.
88   Reich, p. 229.
89   David Miller, *The Times*, 5 March 1987.
90   Ueberroth, pp. 248–54.
91   *The Times*, 1 June 1984, Richard Owen, Moscow.
92   *ibid.*, 2 June 1984, Richard Owen, Moscow.
93   *ibid.*, 30 July 1984.
94   Reich, pp. 227 and 232.
95   Wooldridge, p. 78.
96   *The Times*, 6 August 1984.
97   Ueberroth, p. 3.
98   Reich, p. 190.
99   *The Times*, 14 August 1984.
100 *ibid.*, 13 August 1984.
101 Harry Usher, 'The Games in Los Angeles: a New Approach to the Organisational Tasks', *Olympic Review*, May 1982, p. 257.

VIII

The Seoul Games of 1988

The Seoul Games of 1988 were a political exercise for the South Korean government from the beginning, and swiftly became a major political preoccupation internationally. In this respect they certainly achieved the Korean objective of putting the country on the map.

Once the decision had been taken to bid for the Games the campaign to gain the IOC's votes was seen as a means to extend Korea's relations with countries which hitherto had tried to ignore its existence, on the grounds that it was a neo-colonial invention of the Americans; to improve its standing in Asia and world-wide, and generally to increase national prestige and raise the nation's profile from that of a rather backward newly developing country to that of a fully-fledged member of the advanced industrial world, which could reasonably hope soon to be admitted to membership of the OECD. In its pursuit of the Games Korea enjoyed the advantage of a ruthlessly authoritarian government, which was, however, hampered in its dealings with dissenters by the need not to be too obviously indifferent to human rights in the run-up to the Games.

Korea had been divided between North and South since the end of the 1939–45 war, following decisions taken at the Potsdam and Yalta conferences. In August 1945 the United States army, which occupied the southern zone, drew the line as far north as it was thought the USSR would accept, on the 38th parallel some thirty miles north of Seoul. That border remains in place, although the North nearly succeeded in destroying it in the Korean War of 1950 to 1953.

In August 1948 the US handed the South over to President Syngman Rhee and in September the People's Democratic Republic of North Korea was established under Soviet auspices, with Kim Il-sung as President. He remains President to this day, and hopes to assure the succession to his son, who was proclaimed his sole heir in 1984.

In the South President Syngman Rhee and his successors continued the tradition of authoritarian rule. In 1972 Major-General Park Chung-lee, who had been President since 1963, introduced the Yushin (Revitalising) constitution, which effectively made him President for life. He was assassinated in October 1979 and a period of chaos ensued, from which Major-General Chun Doo-hwan emerged as President, and was confirmed in office under a new constitution in February 1981. He governed with a mixture of firmness and reluctant conciliation and after its first direct presidential elections at the end of 1987 the country experienced its first peaceful transfer of power in February 1988. But although it was peaceful it was traumatic, and the run-up to the Olympics was conducted against the background of a continuing political battle.

In the spring of 1987 many middle-class Koreans had joined in active dissent. President Chun reduced his unpopularity by dismissing ministers who might be rivals to his expected successor, Roh Tae-woo. The ruling Democratic Justice Party planned a national convention on 10 June 1987 to choose its presidential candidate, and Chun's views were crucial to their choice. These events took place against the background of public anger over the cover-up of a police inquiry into the death in custody in January of a student who had been tortured, and over a financial scandal. The anger was fuelled by Chun's 'grave decision' in April to call off, until after the Games, talks with the opposition parties about constitutional reform, on the plea that the nation could not afford the risk of instability that continuing political argument could cause.[1] At the convention he duly nominated Roh and, although Roh committed himself to a more democratic approach to government, anti-government rallies turned to violence and thousands of students were detained.[2]

Brian Bridges comments that the nationwide protest that followed the suspension of talks about constitutional change and the nomination of Roh as his successor rested on a broader social base than hitherto, which convinced Roh, and ultimately Chun, that there must be reform. American influence, including a message from President Reagan urging Chun not to use troops against the protesters, played some part in this realisation, but the main factor was the strength of the domestic opposition. In normal circumstances martial law might have been an option, but the times were not normal, because all eyes were fixed on the Games and to have introduced martial law might well have caused the Games to be moved to another city.[3]

Kim Young-sam, president of the opposition Reunification Democratic Party was one of the politicians who saw that the Olympics could be used against the government. 'Now is the time', he said, 'when President Chun must take either democracy or the Olympics. According to the current situation in Korea, it looks almost impossible to have the Olympics unless we have a democratic government.' The government had persuaded ten universities to close early for the summer holidays, hoping that things would calm down once the students had gone home, but this may have been wishful thinking, since 25 per cent of the country's population lived in Seoul.[4]

The Sunday Times reported that Roh had resolved the crisis with a short, emotional speech, and saved the 1988 Games from disaster. Roh, a retired four-star General, had blood-stained hands, and had been hated as much as Chun, but now he had become a national hero, because he had said that Chun must either accept all the opposition's demands, including direct presidential elections (which had not been held since 1971), or Roh would resign. Chun accepted all this in a statesmanlike speech.[5]

During the election campaign Roh promised to carry on democratic reforms, eliminate corruption, release political prisoners and similar measures. He was determined to win the elections by fair means and, although there were almost certainly irregularities, he won for acceptable reasons. The opposition was in disarray; his Democratic Justice Party's machine was more effective than those of its opponents, and it had become possible for him to represent himself as a statesman of international stature following a visit in September to the USA and Japan. He won with 37 per cent of the vote against 28 per cent, 27 per cent and 8 per cent for the three opposition parties, but need not have won at all if the two man opposition parties had been able to suspend their differences and decide upon a single presidential candidate to oppose him. However, in the April 1988 Assembly elections the DJP won only 125 seats, the first time a ruling party had failed to gain a majority over the combined opposition, so that the 'opposition can now provide a real balancing force to the presidency'.[6]

The two Koreas and the IOC

The division of Korea posed problems for the IOC no less difficult than those presented by the two Germanies, but the Korean question, in its sporting context, attracted less public attention and took up less of the IOC's time. Before the Korean War a single Korean NOC had been recognised, with its seat in Seoul, but the North naturally was not satisfied with this lack of representation and made repeated requests for a separate NOC to be recognised. These were rejected, on the ground that there could not be more than one recognised NOC in any one country.

At the 1957 Session the Soviet member, Andrianov, proposed provisional recognition for North Korea similar to that accorded East Germany, whereby the two Koreas would be obliged to form a unified team if they were to compete in the Olympics. In 1958 and 1959 Andrianov, aided by the Bulgarian member, Stoytchev, 'demanded full recognition for North Korea because of the South Korean refusal to consider a unified team'. In 1959 the IOC decided that it would not be practicable to expect the two Koreas to select a single team on the basis of joint competition, but instead asked them to do so by arranging for the international federations to select athletes on the basis of times achieved in separate competitions. The unity of the resulting team would be demonstrated by its having a joint flag, emblem and uniform at the Olympics. South Korea agreed to this proposal, but negotiations broke down, and North Korea did not participate in 1960.[7]

At the 55th Session of the IOC, held in Munich in May 1959, Stoytchev supported his proposal for recognition of North Korea's NOC by stating that it had tried without success to contact its southern counterpart. Avery Brundage countered by proposing a meeting of the two NOCs on neutral territory, since there was no possibility of their agreeing to meet in either Korea. South Korea claimed that it had never received any letters from the North, so Stoytchev was commissioned to obtain copies for the Chancellory (as the central secretariat of the Olympic movement was then called), which would pass them on to the South.

Adrianov proposed that Stoytchev's and Brundage's suggestions be combined by calling for recognition of the North's NOC, to be followed by a meeting on neutral ground, with a view to creating a unified team for the Olympics. He said that he understood the South to have been dodging such a meeting, but Brundage replied that the IOC had a signed statement from the South that it was ready to co-operate in the formation of a unified team. After this discussion the

IOC decided to arrange a meeting between the representatives of the two committees.[8]

At the 58th Session, held in Athens in June 1961, the Romanian member, Alexandru Siperco, spoke in favour of recognising the northern NOC. Brundage agreed that the northern statutes were acceptable to the IOC, but explained that the difficulty lay in promoting any contact between North and South. The South had rejected the earlier proposal for a meeting on neutral territory. Now its representatives asked for the matter to be deferred until the following year because of the recent changes in their government, and the Session duly agreed to postpone further discussion until 1962.[9]

In 1962 the IOC went a step further and granted the North Korean NOC provisional recognition on the same lines as that of East Germany, namely that a unified team should be formed as a result of joint competition. This time North Korea agreed, but the South refused. The IOC then began to lose patience and ruled that either the South must form a joint team, or North Korea would be allowed to compete independently. The South persisted, and the IOC kept its word, so that North Korea participated in the Games for the first time at Tokyo in 1964.

By the October 1963 Session the IOC seems not only to have accepted North Korea into the movement but to have become anxious about the possibility of its boycotting the 1964 Games. This anxiety was apparently caused by the competitive threat of the GANEFO Games (Games of the New Emerging Forces), which were to be held in November.[10] The IFs would not recognise the GANEFO, because they were an attempt to compete with the Olympics and were avowedly political in intention. The IFs therefore warned their members not to compete, and on the whole athletes of less than Olympic standard took part. However some North Korean affiliated members of FINA (swimming) and the IAAF (athletics) did participate, and were therefore not allowed to compete at Tokyo.[11]

In September 1965 there was more trouble with GANEFO. Its Council met in Beijing and decided to hold an Asian GANEFO in Cambodia in December 1966. North Korea took part, and incurred the wrath of the IAAF, which disapproved of the Asian GANEFO as much as it had of GANEFO I. 'The IAAF suspended the North Koreans, preventing their participation at Mexico City in the events under the auspices of the IAAF.'[12]

The run-up to the Games

The *Official Report* produced by the organising committee of the Seoul Games provides a useful, though of course selective, record of events and of official thinking about the Games in Korea, and is interestingly supplemented by an account written by Dr Kim Un-yong, who played a leading part in Seoul's bid. It is perhaps unfortunate that he repeats the standard line that IOC members are 'free from political influence and independent of any pressure', as his book provides first-class evidence for the misguidedness of any such statement, especially in the context of the Seoul Games.[13]

His account is in many ways similar to that given by Denis Howell of Birmingham's abortive bid; indeed, it would be surprising if it were not, since all bidding cities share the objective of gathering as many IOC votes as possible, and there are only a limited number of ways in which lobbying can be conducted. The great difference between the two was that Birmingham was bidding on a low budget and with little help from the government, whereas Seoul's bid was a truly Korean effort and not only supported by the government (albeit after much procrastination by the President, who remained lukewarm right up to the Baden-Baden Congress of 1981), but actually led by it in all but name.[14]

Kim was so highly valued by Samaranch that when he was elected to membership of the IOC at the 91st Session at Lausanne on 17 October 1986 the IOC dispensed with the usual gap of a year between election and swearing-in because Samaranch wanted him in Korea as a fully-fledged member during the two crucial years before the Games. Only two years later, in October 1988 at Seoul, he was elected to the Executive Board, when he and Gunnar Ericsson were chosen from seven candidates.[15]

Korea's sporting ambitions are not new. It put in a bid to hold the Asian Games of 1966, but withdrew it when the government decided that the cost of the Games could better be spent on economic development.[16] It was the success of the World Shooting Championship of 1978 which gave the Korean sports administrators the momentum to consider trying for the Olympics and in March 1979 Park Chong-kyu, President of the Korean Shooting Federation and later of the Korean Amateur Sports Association (KASA) recommended to the Ministry of Education that they make a bid, having already obtained a feasibility study.[17] At the Sport Policy Deliberation Council in spring 1979 Park

Chong-kyu insisted they should try, although the Korean IOC member, Kim Taek-soo, said that they would get only one vote, which would be his own.[18]

The Ministry collected the opinions of other ministries, obtained information about the 1964 Olympics from the Korean Embassy in Tokyo, and in August 1979 passed the question back to the National Sports Promotion Deliberations Committee. This body set up a seven-man committee, whose composition shows that from the start it was assumed that, if Korea were to bid, the campaign would be a national effort with backing from the highest levels of government. It consisted of the Minister of Economic Planning as chairman, Korea's IOC member, the Foreign Minister, the Minister of Education, the Mayor of Seoul, the Deputy Director of the (Korean) Central Intelligence Agency and the President of KASA.

The committee was unanimously in favour of a bid, if the burden on the people would not be too great, as it 'would have a favourable effect on national solidarity, exchanges with communist bloc nations and relations with North Korea'. In September 1979 they decided to bid both for the 1986 Asian Games and for the 1988 Olympics and once President Park Chung-hee's approval had been obtained the leaders of the government and the ruling party decided to throw their weight behind the effort. The Mayor of Seoul announced the bid on 8 October. However the President was assassinated on 26 October and the NOC president Park Chong-kyu had to resign 'for political reasons'.

In the subsequent confusion there was a great reshuffle of political jobs. A new President of the Korean Olympic Committee was appointed, who was also President of KASA, and a new Mayor of Seoul. The KOC after a good deal of doubt, decided to apply (though it would not have gone ahead without a governmental decision) on much the same grounds as before, but with the additional point that even an unsuccessful bid would raise national prestige. However, the City of Seoul said that, 'although it was up to the government to make a final decision', it was against the plan because it felt it could not complete the facilities in time. The new President, Chun Doo-hwan, who had taken office on 1 Steptember 1980, and who was asked for a fresh ruling on the Olympics, pronounced in favour of a bid, having been persuaded by Roh Tae-woo (at that time Minister for Political Affairs), whereupon the Ministry of Education instructed the KOC to apply. The IOC announced on 15 December 1980 that Seoul was the fourth candidate city, after Melbourne, Nagoya and Athens.[19]

In fact, however, no firm decision was to be made until May 1981. The result of this vacillation was that when Seoul was invited to make a presentation in Lausanne it did not even reply, leaving the field open to Nagoya, its only remaining rival, which had been campaigning for two years. Seoul might easily have been ignored after this failure to respond, but Samaranch saved its candidacy by sending an evaluation mission to both cities, because he thought it better to have two cities bidding for the Games than one.[20] (Melbourne withdrew in February, as did Athens, whose bid was apparently linked to the idea that Athens would provide a permanent home for the Games.)

It had been intended that the vast questionnaires which soon arrived from the IOC would be completed by a joint Ministry of Education/City/KOC team, but the sceptical Seoul shunned any participation in the team, so that the work seems to have become largely a project of the Sports Bureau of the Education Ministry, with most of the work being done by the KOC's consultants. Most of the preparation for fact-finding missions from the IOC, the IFs and the Association of National Olympic Committees also had to be done by the KOC.

It now appeared that the cost of holding the Games at Seoul would be $900m compared with the $237m originally reported to the President. This misunderstanding had occurred because the Ministry of Education had given the President figures prepared in haste by the KOC's consultants. At a meeting of officials, at which there was no doubt a good deal of consternation over the new figures, no agreement was reached. The office of the Prime Minister still wanted to go ahead, but the Economic Planning Board favoured reconsideration, with the result that the issue was referred to Cabinet. At what turned out to be the first of a series of cabinet meetings, the Minister of Education, 'under whose control fell the KOC' and the city of Seoul were also against a bid, and it was agreed that a ruling must again be sought from the President.

The answers to the questionnaires (three times as bulky as Nagoya's) were delivered to the IOC in time for the 28 February 1981 deadline. The third meeting was held under the Prime Minister's chairmanship on 16 May, amid persisting differences. But this time Ministers heard that the President was in favour of a bid, and decided that there was no way they could back down without substantial damage being done to Korea's international credibility. It was therefore decided that a campaign must be launched, largely through Korea's overseas missions, in order at least to win enough votes to save face. However, it seems that the President's support was still not unequivocal, because after these three rounds of Cabinet talks a statement of the merits and demerits was forwarded to him in June 1981. The overwhelming view among sports experts was that Nagoya stood a much better chance than Seoul, because Korea lacked experience, was the capital of a divided country and could expect fierce opposition from North Korea and its communist allies. On the other hand, the Education Minister thought they could enlist support from other developing countries.

Despite the Presidential instruction to go ahead, indifferent officials, initially lukewarm support from Korea's overseas missions and lack of budgetary support meant that Seoul's promotional activities were not vigorous–perhaps, indeed, because the President was still seen to be hesitating. The first serious arena in which the Korean bidding team performed was a meeting of the Pan-American Sports Organisation in Caracas in July 1981, where Seoul had the good fortune to find that there was no team present from Nagoya. In the same month Kim Un-yong (who, as well as being a leading member of the bidding team was President of the International Taekwondo Federation) set off on a tour of Europe and North America, during which he had the dedicated help of overseas Taekwondo instructors, and met thirteen IOC members. IOC officials, who until then had thought Korea's bid virtually withdrawn, advised Kim to launch extensive activities immediately.

By early August 1981 sixty IOC members had been met, and an evaluation by the Education Ministry suggested that sixteen were for Korea; sixteen would consider its bid favourably and eighteen were uncommitted. America and Oceania seemed to favour Seoul, and the Middle East and Europe to be more inclined towards Nagoya. The general feeling was interpreted to be that Seoul was the better equipped candidate, but Korea's lack of diplomatic relations with the communist states was a disadvantage, and there was a lingering fear of war with North Korea. Furthermore, Nagoya had begun to invite IOC members to visit it in September 1979, whereas Seoul's late start had made people wonder whether they were serious.

The evaluation led economic ministers to take a more co-operative attitude and to decide on thorough preparation for Baden-Baden, where the Games were to be awarded at the IOC's Session in

September 1981, immediately after the Congress of the Olympic movement. There was a fourth ministerial meeting on the day of the evaluation, 10 August 1981, which the *Report* describes as a breakthrough, although there still was not enthusiasm everywhere in government. Nevertheless, the Education Minister reported to the President that the situation had turned in Seoul's favour. The *Report* now implicitly admits that the favourable opinions previously attributed to the President had not been definitive and records that 'President Chun, who had withheld any express opinion over the Olympic plan for several months since the Cabinet itself had been divided over the plan, made his clear determination known, emphatically saying that the country should do absolutely everything to obtain the Olympic hostship.'

Just before Baden-Baden Seoul's count of the 82 IOC members expected to vote (*sic*: these figures total 84!) was 26 for Seoul; 6 friendly; 36 uncommitted and 16 against. Seoul's targets for lobbying at Baden-Baden were, therefore, the undecided from Latin America and Africa, as well as NOC and IF Presidents and 'those figures who exercised background influence in the international sporting community'. The press were cool and IOC leaders seemed to think Nagoya had as good as won, but 'the atmosphere changed overnight with the opening of the Korean exhibition hall'.[21]

The official leader of the delegation was Seoul's Mayor, Park Young-su, because the IOC sticks to its convention that the Games are awarded to a city even when the bid is conducted as a national and governmental operation, but the real leader was Chiung Ju-yung, chairman of the preparatory committee.

Kim dealt decisively with the rumour that General Choi, a Korean emigré in Canada, would stage an anti-Seoul demonstration, as some citizens of Nagoya had done, on environmental grounds, against their own city's bid. Kim did not believe the rumour, but he put five Taekwondo instructors on stand-by in case of trouble and there was no incident.[22]

So successful was the lobbying that in the early hours of 30 September, the day of the vote, the team was confident enough to be able to cable home that they stood to win with 45 votes. In fact they did even better and won by 52 to 27, after a voting session which lasted one and three-quarter hours, although there were only two candidates.[23]

Why was Seoul chosen?

There is of course a problem. Why should so unlikely a candidate as Seoul have won the coveted accolade of the IOC, and why, once the all too obvious difficulties of sticking to that choice became clear, should the IOC not have changed its mind?

The simple explanation of why Seoul should have been preferred to Nagoya is probably the best, namely that the IOC had to award the Games somewhere, and that at the last minute there was no other plausible candidate. Nagoya had destroyed its own credibility, or rather its environmentalist protesters had done so. Melbourne and Athens had withdrawn: all the IOC could do was accept Seoul, whose bid was at least whole-hearted, and fully in tune with the commercial spirit of the age. There seems also to have been a general feeling in Lausanne that it was time to award the games to an eastern city, as they had been held in the Americas or Europe ever since the Tokyo games of 1964.

Peter Ueberroth, the organiser of the Los Angeles Games and so an experienced, if jaundiced, observer expresses some of these thoughts, and adds a down-to-earth assertion of corruption when he says of the Baden-Baden Congress, and of the movement in general:

All policy and operational decisions are made behind the scenes. Unless you worm your way into the inner circle, you are powerless to affect them . . .

This was obvious as we watched the bid selection for the 1988 Games and saw how leverage is brought to bear on the organizing committee. Before Baden-Baden, it had been assumed that Nagoya, Japan, would get the 1988 Games. The IOC had quietly let it be known it was time the Olympics were returned to that part of the world. Seoul was a serious contender but was clearly the underdog because of its unstable political climate. Each bid city hosted costly receptions . . . and they lobbied IOC members hard for their vote.

As well as trinkets and brochures, 'Seoul also gave away, quietly, two first-class roundtrip tickets to each IOC member. The tickets were easily redeemed for cash; many were.'

After the demonstration against the Games by citizens of Nagoya 'Masaji Kiokawa, Japan's IOC member and an IOC Executive Board member, criticized Seoul in a vitriolic outburst that alienated many IOC members from the Arab–Asian bloc.' In Ueberroth's judgement, Masaji's bad manners, the demonstration and the new-found strength of the Arab–Asian bloc all contributed, 'But the free tickets had already turned the trick'.[24]

These factors may have been present, but it is possible that the IOC, or at least the Executive Board, also had in mind the incalculable political and economic benefits to which siting the Games in Korea could contribute, such as the eventual reunification of the Korean peninsula, the healing of old wounds between Korea and Japan (dating from the Japanese colonisation), and the opening up of relations between South Korea and other Asian countries. It would, however, be disappointing to find that this had in fact been the IOC's calculation, because it could so easily have turned out to be a disastrous mistake. The Games could have led to exacerbation of the already tense relations between the two Koreas, perhaps even to war, and if the Soviet bloc had boycotted the Games nothing would have been done to improve Korea's relations with the wider world, and irreparable damage could have been done to the Olympic movement.

Other explanations for the choice of Seoul can be found. There were observers, like Neil Macfarlane, and for a time David Miller, who believed that the power of Adidas had turned the IOC away from Nagoya. (The role of Adidas has been more fully discussed in Chapter IV.) Those inclined to unverifiable fantasy may even say that it was some kind of reward given by the USA to a faithful neo-colonial servant, but that kind of allegation is impossible to substantiate.

At the political level the choice of Seoul can be argued in two different directions. Either it showed a courageous devotion to the universality of the Olympic movement and a determination to assert the values of sport over those of politics, or it showed overweening pride and a complete misunderstanding of what sport is about and of the movement's proper status. Few in the sports business would nowadays assert that it is possible to keep politics out of sport, but Samaranch himself constantly says that the resolution of political questions must be left to politicians: yet to award the Games to such a country as Korea looks more like an irresponsible importation of politics into sport. To put it charitably, the choice lies between the proclaimed universality of the movement and the relative safety of the advanced capitalist world. But to restrict Olympic hosts to countries deemed safe in that sense must deeply offend the less developed countries, and so threaten the principle of universality.

Once, *faute de mieux*, Seoul had been chosen, its disadvantages became only too obvious, even to those who had not been aware of them in advance. At that point simple pride and the need to save the IOC's face came into play. It was unthinkable that the Games should be cancelled, and in any case the movement, by now accustomed to spending very large sums of money, could not afford it. The alternative was to stick through thick and thin with the sitting candidate, arguing throughout that to support Seoul was to assert the suprapolitical values of sport.

No doubt in a real crisis the IOC would have been able to find some experienced city that had already held the Games to take them over at short notice, and it does seem that Korea's leaders believed that this could happen if they allowed opposition by students and others to become so out of hand that it had to be quelled by unacceptably harsh measures. On the other hand, the IOC has in the past beeen tolerant of harsh measures – one has only to remember Mexico City or, indeed, Berlin. The timing of internal repression in any host city also presents problems for those in the IOC who might be inclined to protest. If it occurs well ahead of the Games it can be argued that it forms part of domestic policy with which it is not the IOC's business to interfere. If firmness becomes necessary in the weeks immediately preceding the festival it may be too late to do more than turn a blind eye.

The diplomatic task

Once Seoul had won it was time to begin worrying about whether the communist bloc and some non-aligned nations would participate in the Games. At this point the *Report*, which has chronicled the events leading up to the Games as though they had been an election campaign on a super scale, excels itself by proclaiming: 'Many IOC members supported Seoul in their lofty effort to protect the Olympic movement from being politically contaminated.' It would be comforting to believe that this absurd sentence had been penned with tongue in cheek, but it plainly was not.[25]

Like Peter Ueberroth's LAOOC at Los Angeles, the Seoul Olympic Organising Committee (SLOOC) had to develop foreign relations of its own, although for different reasons. In Los Angeles's case the United States' government's lack of co-operation (at least as it was perceived by Ueberroth) had forced Los Angeles to act independently: in Seoul there was of course no question of the Korean government failing to co-operate, although not all officials were enthusiastic (and there were always rivalries between SLOOC, the Korean Olympic Committee, the Sports Ministry and the city of Seoul), but Korea had no diplomatic relations with countries in the socialist bloc, and had to use Olympic channels instead. SLOOC set up postboxes in Geneva and Hong Kong; often it used the IOC or GAISF (General Association of International Sports Federations, of which Kim became President in 1986 in succession to Tom Keller) as intermediaries if there was no direct means of sending telex messages.

SLOOC was helped by the fact that some sports leaders in eastern Europe were government ministers as well as Olympic officials. Gradually a number of countries in the Soviet bloc followed the Soviet lead in realising that it would be useful to have consular relations with Korea on a temporary basis for the period of the games, and these proved to be the prelude to full diplomatic relations with Hungary, Poland, Yugoslavia, Bulgaria, Czechoslovakia, Romania and Mongolia, and consular relations with the USSR.[26]

Boycott threats started as soon as Seoul had been chosen at Baden-Baden in September 1981 and calls for the site to be changed began soon after and continued for a considerable time; for example, Kim reports that the powerful presidents of the French and Italian NOCs, Nelson Paillou and Franco Carraro, were making this demand in May 1984.[27] However, Seoul was not without friends: in November 1984 the ANOC Assembly, on Roh's initiative, adopted the 'Mexico Declaration' supporting Seoul as host city and Mario Vázquez-Raña, ANOC's President, helped still further by (after consultation with Samaranch) calling an ANOC meeting in Seoul in April 1986 before the Asian Games. These gatherings gave socialist sports leaders a chance to have a preliminary look at Seoul.[28]

The IOC gave significant help in a variety of ways, of which the most dramatic was to call North/South sports talks in Lausanne on four occasions. It changed the Olympic Charter's rule respecting the sending out of invitations to the games, so that they now emanated from the IOC, not the organising committee, a year ahead and had to be answered within four months. The IOC also raised its contribution to NOCs' expenses by finding airfares and accommodation for up to eight persons per NOC, plus $8,000 for equipment and $500 for each athlete up to six, thus pre-empting the excuse made by some NOCs after Moscow that they could not afford to attend.[29]

On 1 September 1983 a Korean aircraft was shot down by the Soviets and SLOOC had to lower its profile until Korean public opinion had had time to calm down. Meanwhile the SLOOC President Roh Tae-woo, who was later to become President of Korea, overcame his natural feelings of rage against the Soviet Union and kept his eye on his main objectives, which were to keep the Games for Seoul and to ensure that the USSR and its allies attended. He therefore handled the press with great restraint, and refrained from the virulent anti-Soviet explosion that might have been expected.

Soviet bloc opposition to Seoul continued after the Games were awarded and the situation worsened with the boycott of Los Angeles. However, during the Los Angeles Games Horst Dassler of Adidas again demonstrated his considerable influence by arranging the first official meeting between the two sides in which the Soviet Sports Ministry participated. He achieved this by giving a dinner for Kim, Roh, and Valery Syssoev (Vice-Minister of Sports of the USSR), at which Syssoev's sympathy was engaged, although he could not, of course, commit his government.[30] By the time of the 89th IOC Session in Berlin in June 1985 it was still not certain that the socialist bloc states would attend, with the result that Roh and his party received a welcome which was cordial but cautious.[31] Nevertheless, Manfred Ewald, the President of the East German NOC, who was later to take the lead in pressing the Soviets to attend, gave a small reception for Roh at which some progress was made.[32] The supportive East German attitude is not surprising when one remembers how reluctant the East German leader Erich Honecker had been to boycott in 1984, especially as he had been given little or no notice of the Soviet intention.

In his efforts to ease international tension Kim began to talk about Olympic relations, instead of diplomatic relations, once he had realised that part of the difficulty of easing the Soviet bloc into the Games lay in the two sides' very limited personal knowledge of each other.[33] Some of their concerns were very similar to those which had bedevilled Los Angeles, but they seem to have been handled more effectively on the Korean side than they had been by LAOOC and the Soviets also were probably more intent on achieving a satisfactory outcome than they had been in 1984.

The similarities with Los Angeles became apparent at a secret meeting, called in Tokyo at the Soviets' request at the end of June 1987, when Kim found that one of the chief Soviet worries was about whether they would be permitted to dock a ship at Inchon. Kim himself considered the request reasonable, but knew that his government would oppose it. The Soviets were also anxious, again as at Los Angeles, to obtain landing rights for Aeroflot. One further difficulty was that assurances were sought (it seems not only by the USSR) that

Korea would not offer political asylum to defectors. Kim could have given the assurances without contravening Korean policy, which was to refuse asylum, but this could not be admitted without risking accusations of offending against international law and practice.[34]

A few weeks after the Tokyo meeting the first official delegation from the Soviet NOC and Sports Ministry visited Korea, but although the two sides now had official contact, communications had still to go through Kim's GAISF office in Monte Carlo. The Soviets, Kim found, were interested mainly in technical issues, whereas Ewald, who had already paid an unpublicised visit to Seoul, was anxious to promote sports talks between North and South, and believed that a generous offer should be made to the North to allow it to hold six or even more of the Olympic sports.

In December 1987, after talking to the President, Kim was able to give an unofficial assurance that a ship could be moored. Very shortly thereafter the Soviet bloc countries, led by East Germany, began to accept their invitations to the Games.[35] The most important announcement was that made on 11 January by the USSR that it would compete in the interest of 'strengthening the unity of the international Olympic movement' and because of the Games' role in fostering world peace and international understanding. There must also have been some significance in the fact that when they had last met the USA (in 1976) the USSR had won the most medals of any nation, 125, including 49 gold, against 94 by the USA (35 gold).[36]

Kim puts it down mainly to personal contact and good human relations that all but six of the 166 NOCs competed, but there is, of course, more to the story than that.[37] Part of the difficulty for the USSR was that it needed to be seen to have given reasonable support to its North Korean ally in its demand to co-host the Games, yet did not wish to carry that support to the point where it would have to boycott. To have done so would have relegated the USSR to the second rank of sporting powers and perhaps provoked overt discontent, or even outright disobedience, among athletes and their governments in satellite countries.[38]

North Korea's demands

North Korea had made its demand to share the Games in the summer of 1985. President Fidel Castro of Cuba promised to help, and Moscow told Samaranch that a movement towards sharing would help the Soviet bloc to participate. Seoul was at first opposed to any such gesture, but Samaranch went ahead with talks.[39] They were not helped by the memory of the aircraft shot down by the Soviets in the summer of 1983 and there was at least one other serious incident before the talks came to an end, an explosion at Kimpo international airport in September 1986 just before the arrival of the Chinese team for the opening of the Asian Games.

According to *The Times*, it had taken a prolonged initiative by Ashwini Kumar (one of the Indian members of the IOC, a former General who acts as its security expert), 'a man of exceptional sensitivities' to persuade the President of the North Korean Olympic Committee, Yu Sun-kim, to agree to meet a South Korean delegation at Lausanne on 8–9 October. The IOC intended to propose (at separate, and then at joint meetings) that the two teams, integrated, should march side by side behind their two flags, headed by an Olympic flag. It would also be proposed that the marathon and road cycling races should pass through both territories, and that the preliminary rounds of team sports, like football, should be held in the North. There would be no proposal of jointly staged events by Seoul and Pyongyang, because the South Koreans had already rejected this idea. It appeared that Romania and Bulgaria were already in sympathy with these proposals.[40] *The Guardian* was less sanguine and commented that Samaranch had 'perhaps dangerously, agreed . . . to join in the charade of meetings, at all levels, between North and South Korea'.[41]

Despite the bad omens the meetings were held. At the first, in Lausanne on 8–9 October 1985, North Korea insisted on co-hosting what it would have liked to call the 'Pyongyang–Seoul Games' and on a single team for the two countries, but with two organising committees and two opening and closing ceremonies. However, the IOC drew the line at co-hosting and ruled that the issue of a single team was for the two Koreas to settle (it was by no means a new issue, as we have seen), but it did not exclude sharing the games, in the sense that some sports, or some events within sports, might be held in the North. At the second meeting, in January 1986, North Korea persisted in its demand for co-hosting and the IOC continued to say no, but suggested sharing a few more sports with the North than the South had hitherto agreed. South Korea then proposed that four sports, and some events in others, be held in the North. Much the same positions were adopted at the third meeting, held in June 1986.[42]

Even now Samaranch did not give up. In an interview just after Barcelona had been awarded the 1992 Games in October 1986 he said that he was about to see a North Korean delegation, and hoped that the meeting might lead to a fourth North/South meeting in Lausanne. The IOC had already offered the North archery, table tennis, part of the football, and the start of the 100 km cycling and was ready to demonstrate a certain flexibility.[43]

At the IOC Session at Istanbul in May 1987, shortly before the final North/South meeting, North Korea demanded eight sports. Kim, who replied at Samaranch's request, said that the door was still open to negotiations, and the IOC delegated the next steps to its Executive Board, which sent a mission to Pyongyang later in May. The mission (headed by the influential Romanian member, Alexandru Siperco, who was seen in Seoul as too sympathetic to the northern point of view) sought permission to return to the South via the border post at Panmunjom, but visas were refused by the North. The request was widely seen as a test by Samaranch of how far the North would go, and the refusal of visas as a further portent of failure. The fourth and final talks were held in Lausanne on 14–15 July 1987. Seoul was by now ready to give up six sports and Samaranch advised an opening offer of five. North Korea continued to insist on eight sports with their associated television rights and the IOC at last decided that there was no point in further negotiations.[44] However, the socialist countries had been impressed by the efforts that the IOC had made, although experienced observers continued to doubt whether the games would be held at Seoul at all. Many had thought the talks had been doomed from the start, not least because a country like North Korea, accustomed to being hermetically sealed off from its southern neighbour, would not have taken kindly to admitting thousands of athletes, spectators and hangers-on. Yet it could hardly have done otherwise if it had succeeded in co-hosting the Games.

After the final round of talks the door was still open to the North Koreans, but they seem effectively to have signified their own displeasure by blowing up a South Korean aircraft, with 115 people, on the way from Baghdad to Seoul in November 1987. The government did not at first confirm that the North Koreans were the culprits, but in December the incident was, according to *The Scotsman*, coming increasingly to be seen as the beginning of a violent campaign orchestrated by the North. The paper's reporter was baffled by the continuing optimism of Samaranch, whom he dubbed the 'Olympic

Pope'.[45] Eventually it was announced that the aircraft had been blown up by explosives placed by an agent acting on Kim Jong-il's orders, and South Korean officials were commended for delaying the announcement long enough to take the edge off public opinion.[46]

Despite this superhuman restraint by the South, which seems fantastic simply in order to save the Olympics, the North announced on 12 January that it would not participate in the Games, giving as its reason its disappointment with the progress of the talks.[47] Park Seh-jik (another Major-General, who had become President of SLOOC) reacted by saying that the North would still not be banned from the Games, despite the sabotage of the plane (which North Korea denied).[48] However, Britain had formally accepted that North Korea was responsible, and *The Times* reported that the Communist Party newspaper *Rodongja Shinmum* had said on 21 January that North Korea has 'no chance but to make war'.[49]

Such was Samaranch's determination that the Games should be held in South Korea or not at all that he visited Seoul no fewer than eleven times from April 1982 to September 1989 (the last occasion was to celebrate the anniversary of the Games).[50] In April 1988 he told the leaders of South Korea's three opposition parties that the door was still open to the games being shared (but not co-hosted), but it was clear by then that the negotiations had little future. The students were restive because co-hosting was no longer on the cards (if it ever had been), but after Samaranch's visit and his offer to go to Pyongyang if invited (no invitation came), both students and opposition politicians gave up calling for co-hosting. Even President Castro sent Rana to ask President Kim Il-sung to release him from his promise to side with North Korea, but Kim held him to his word.[51]

Television

Kim correctly states that 'the development of television has made TV no more a spectator, but one of the main organizers of the Games'. The IOC thought SLOOC would be doing well to get $400m for the American television rights, whereas SLOOC hoped to sell them for $500 or $600m, despite the fourteen-hour difference between Korean and American east coast time, which made it difficult to schedule events for prime time on United States television (8 p.m. to midnight). SLOOC could not negotiate until the competition timetables had been worked out with the IFs and it appears that the schedules proposed by Barry Frank of TWI (SLOOC's consultants) stirred up trouble among the major sports, although eventually some adjustments were made.[52]

The negotiations with the television companies were not easy, perhaps partly because of the relative weakness of ABC, which had had the contract, 1980 apart, ever since 1968, but whose declining viewers had forced the company to lay off 10 per cent of its staff.[53] CBS, ABC and NBC all made disappointing offers, though Kim claims to have understood that $500m was not a realistic target. 'I was caught between Korea's national pride and the cold reality of a maximum market price.'[54] NBC had offered around $315m, plus profit-sharing which would produce a possible maximum of $450m. Furthermore, NBC, though keen to buy the rights, was wary because it had lost $30m on the Moscow Games, even after insurance. At the second round of negotiations NBC discovered that it was the only serious bidder, and in the end Kim reached a compromise whereby SLOOC settled for $300m with an additional $200m on a risk-sharing basis.

Repayment conditions were the biggest hurdle, should the Games be postponed, cancelled or not held in and around Seoul. It would have been difficult for NBC to arrange insurance and the company wanted a letter of credit instead. The request for a letter of credit was seen in Seoul as an insult: it provoked governmental and popular rage when news of it was leaked and 'As it involved both the Korea Exchange Bank and the Ministry of Finance, no one could make a decision.'[55] However, after a difficult hour Kim persuaded President Chun to give him the go-head; Samaranch helped to get the amount of the letter of credit reduced and it was agreed that NBC would not cover the Games if the United States did not participate. After the deal had been struck both SLOOC and NBC thought they had done badly, but Arthur A. Watson, the President of the Sports Division of NBC, was able to write gracefully to Kim that the people, culture, history and development of Korea would be the centrepiece of their coverage. 'We at NBC Sports are aware of the special bonds which exist between Korea and the United States.'[56]

The Japanese rights attracted great public attention. SLOOC and the Korean government thought they could fetch $80m; the IOC thought about $30m and in the end $52m was achieved. One argument used by SLOOC was that the Games were in the right time zone for the Japanese, to which the latter were able tellingly to reply that they were not, because the events had already been scheduled to fit United States prime time.

Once the North American and Japanese markets had been settled and the European rights sold to the European Braodcasting Union the sale of other rights was a political more than a financial question: in Korean eyes the only important point was to get more than Calgary or Los Angeles. The East bloc rights were also important politically and SLOOC had to be careful not to announce too much of what had already been achieved until the bloc had decided to participate. The domestic rights were almost given away to the Korean Broadcasting System for $3.25m, a figure which Kim wryly contrasts with the $25m paid to the Barcelona organising committee for the Spanish rights. Seoul's final worldwide total, according to Kim, was $408m, against Calgary's $324m and Los Angeles's $288m.

The Games

The security operation was massive: 'Security was not only needed on the ground but also on the water, in the air and under the sea' and the USA, apart from its 40,000 troops along the border and manning the Panmunjom check point, stationed two aircraft carriers off Seoul as a warning to the North.[57] In March Park Seh-jik, now president of SLOOC, was optimistic that the North would not commit atrocities, for fear of worsening relations with their friends. Nor did he expect internal demonstrations directed against Olympic visitors. The student and other protesters were too few, he said, and would be under the control of government security agencies; the political slogans would be largely meaningless to outsiders; and nearly all Koreans were convinced that Korea should host the Olympics. Co-hosting was not an option, but Park still hoped that the North would see the wisdom of participation.[58]

As part of the operation 'The background of 122,043 participants in the Games was examined to eliminate those with criminal records, alcoholic records, mental disorder, etc.', and 81,630 military and police guarded 264 facilities.[59] But despite all the precautions, which many observers have said gave the Olympic areas the feeling of armed encampments, radical students (whose riotous behaviour Kim often attributes to Korea's rapid democratisation) were able to interfere with some of the arrangements. For example, they forced SLOOC to protect the marathon by stationing a plain clothes policeman at metre

H

intervals along its route. On one occasion a demonstration prevented Samaranch and Kim from leaving the main stadium to visit the volleyball; some students were arrested for disseminating anti-Olympic leaflets, and hockey training had to be moved from Kyunghee University. Nor did the operation always proceed smoothly. 'As usual, security agents for VIPs did not follow the necessary procedures for carrying weapons and that caused many misunderstandings' and guards getting up early 'generated some yelling and noise' which caused the athletes to complain. In addition to conventional arms the guards had at their disposal such items as 910 inspection sticks, numerous varieties of metal detector, 415 road blocks and 344 movable flower stands(!).[60]

There were the usual trivial-seeming disputes which, if not dealt with, could have led to disaster. For example, an Israeli gymnast wished to compete at 8.30 a.m. for religious reasons, and was urged by the Games' authorities to compete at 11.00 or abstain altogether. This disregard of the gymnast's religious needs caused the Israeli NOC to threaten to withdraw its entire team.[61]

Numerous national teams, like those of Iran and Iraq, had to be kept apart: the Taiwanese national flag could not be used, for fear of offending the Chinese, although there was no objection to the use of the Taiwanese NOC's flag. Even the electronic scoreboard was an unexpected source of difficulty because it showed Jerusalem, not Tel Aviv, as the capital of Israel. Kim also records an embarrassment of a perhaps novel kind: 'Some media people wanted complete hotel-type services, but some maid personnel, for example, were volunteers from good families and any misconduct was intolerable.'[62]

Kim had a great deal to say about the demands made by IFs on SLOOC. For example, Prince Philip, and later the Princess Royal, as successive Presidents of the International Equestrian Federation (FEI), were able to persuade SLOOC that the individual jumping events should be held, as the FEI's rules provide, on the last day of the Games, and in the main arena. By contrast, at Los Angeles only the equestrian award ceremony had been held in the main stadium. The arrangement in Seoul was made against the advice of Primo Nebiolo of the IAAF, and was not ideal because equestrian events do not attract great crowds in Korea (any more than track and field), and the seats had to be filled artificially.[63] However, Kim seems to have borne no grudge against the Royal Presidents, who were, after all, only doing their best for their sport.

Another event which upset Kim occurred when Korean coaches protested against a Bulgarian beating a Korean at boxing and NBC gave the ensuing fracas live coverage for an hour.[64] It would be naive to expect any news organisation to have done otherwise, but the worldwide unfavourable publicity caused anti-American feeling, which was not dampened down by some American swimmers being caught shop-lifting, NBC crews ordering T shirts with symbols depicting the boxing incident and disorderly behaviour by the Americans at the opening ceremony. The trouble also provoked renewal of the perennial debate about whether so dangerous a sport as boxing should be included in the Olympic programme. Kim was relieved that there was not much anti-American feeling, though he does revive the accusation that the judging at Los Angeles had not been fair. 'Such anti-Americanism as there had been among Koreans had been largely inspired by NBC's inquisitorial televison coverage of boxing, a sore point in light of the blatant American bias in judging in 1984.'[65]

The home front

While Kim and his allies were active on the diplomatic front much was also happening at home. The bidding campaign had been run as a truly national effort and once the bid had been won the preparations for the Games were tackled in a similarly whole-hearted way, although the lukewarm attitude of some officials had to be overcome. In March 1982 the Ministry of Sports was created to take overall charge of both the Asian and the Olympic Games, replacing the Sports Bureau in the Education Ministry; the two organising committees for the Asian and Olympic Games streamlined their secretariats into one in February 1983 and every other ministry created a section to take charge of Olympic projects.[66] In June 1985 the first sponsorship agreements were signed with Coca-Cola and Kodak: the latter had obviously had been quick off the mark, in order not to repeat the fiasco of 1984 when its dilitoriness had caused it to lose the Olympic sponsorship to Fuji.[67] The negotiations with NBC were concluded in March 1986, but the *Report* is putting an unjustifiably high gloss on the results achieved in saying that NBC was to pay up to a further $500m depending on the advertising revenues, on top of the basic $300m. The agreement in fact provided for a further $200m, bringing the theoretically possible maximum to $500m.[68]

A variety of nationwide activities was undertaken. Sports support officers or sections were established in each city and provincial government and the Ministry of Government Administration 'formulated a program called "Orderly Life and Mentality Education", for government employees and their families'. One of the more bizarre programmes, which is recorded in the *Report* without any indication that it was considered in any way odd, was undertaken by the Office of Monopoly, which 'put on sale 200 million packs of Olympic commemorative cigarettes and 90,000 sets of specially wrapped cigarettes to support public relations and revenue-generating projects; the office also marketed red ginseng as an Olympic product'.

Local committees for environmental beautification and consciousness-raising were set up, but tended to be weak, and it became necessary to create a central Council in March 1985. This body organised support committees throughout South Korea and abroad. The purpose was to build on the momentum of the Asian Games for order, cleanliness and kindness and to 'instil civic pride among the people so as to project a good image as modern and cultured people in connection with the Olympic games'. The Council introduced all sorts of activities, of which the most enjoyable sounds a cheerleading contest, which 'contributed to the development of new styles and techniques of cheerleading . . .'.

Minute attention was paid to the improvement of shops, taxis, lodging houses and restaurants. There were campaigns to promote 'the development of a general atmosphere of reliable commercial transactions, eliminating outmoded commercial practices' and 'to serve customers kindly and to avoid altercations'. A major campaign was undertaken to depollute the Han river, which flows through the central part of Seoul. Streets were extensively improved and disorderly street stalls and unauthorised roadside heaps dealt with. No fewer than 224,975 stalls were removed or relocated in 1988 and even the bland language of the *Official Report* suggests that the process may not have been altogether benign 'when their removal was deemed inevitable, stall vendors were ordered to move their stalls to back alleys out of public sight.' Owners of stalls near Olympic sites 'were advised to pull down their stalls and stands on their own accord so as not to deal a crippling blow to their daily living'. There were even lavatories reserved exclusively for foreigners.[69]

Journalists with an eye to human rights naturally did not care for this (it must be said that some aspects of Barcelona's current refurbishment sound rather similar). One commented that along the route that the Olympic torch was to travel a hundred miles of walls had been built to hide the slums and poor quality houses[70] and there were understandably disapproving references to the large number of poor people who had lost their homes during the extensive facelift given to Seoul in preparation for the games.

A successful Games?

The city of Seoul obviously benefited greatly from its refurbishment, which created numerous parks and required architects of buildings to spend one per cent of the construction cost on decorative artwork. Tremendous efforts were made to reduce air pollution and to keep the areas liable to be seen by visitors clean and to decontaminate the yacht-racing course in Suyong Bay. There was a strong emphasis on public health, especially on AIDS control, 'to protect local people against infection with AIDS through incoming foreigners' though in the context of public health it does seem odd that the Olympic family should have been exempt from normal vaccination requirements.[71] Runways were extended; more foreign airlines ran flights to Seoul and the national airline extended its fleet.[72] Kim naturally sees the Games as having been a success, both as a sporting occasion, and as the beginning of a new phase in Korea's existence as a nation, at last free from the inferiority of having been a colony of Japan. 'Korea emerged from its Japan complex in Baden-Baden,' he says. 'Baden-Baden was a start. The Olympic Games were a turning point for Korea to move into the ranks of the world's advanced nations.'[73]

Proud as he is of the Games and their results for his country, Kim does not take kindly to the idea that Seoul may stick in the popular mind largely because a positive dope test caused Ben Johnson to be deprived of his gold medal for the 100 metres, which he had run in the world record time of 9.79 seconds. He points out that out of 1,598 dope tests only ten were positive, compared with twelve at Los Angeles: two were in the modern pentathlon, five in weightlifting, one (Johnson) in athletics, one in wrestling, and one in judo.[74]

The public sector investment was immense at $1.7bn and SLOOC invested $1.5bn 'in direct and private-sector investment and in operation of the Games'.[75] The eventual profit at Seoul was $497m, and handsomely achieved the organisers' ambition to outdo Calgary and

Los Angeles. However the profit figure was not arrived at in an orthodox manner, since most of it did not represent a surplus on operations: instead it included $80m donations and $300m premiums on the sale of apartments.

Seoul was able to make a good deal with the IOC, which normally sets aside 20 per cent of television income for the local organising committee as a TV installation fund before dividing the remainder between the organising committee (two-thirds) the IOC itself, and IFs and the NOCs, via Olympic Solidarity, (one-ninth each). However, Seoul argued that 20 per cent would have amounted to only $80m, and Samaranch agreed to Roh's request that they should instead receive $125m. In total, $320m stayed with SLOOC, and the IOC, the IFs and the NOCs (via Olympic Solidarity) shared the remaining $92m. A further concession was made. It appears from Kim's figures that the IOC would normally have received $4.5m for its share of the profit from marketing the Olympic symbol, yet it consented to receive only $1.75m. This was possible because, although for reasons of pride Seoul was allowed to declare a surplus which included income from donations and from the sale of flats, when it came to dividing the proceeds it was allowed to work on a much lower profit figure, which excluded those items. The Olympic movement as a whole cannot therefore be said to have done as well as it might have done out of the 1988 Games, but Seoul got the best of both worlds.[76]

It is too soon to tell whether holding the Games had a significant effect on Korea's political system. Samaranch was certainly optimistic, though he may have exaggerated when he said at the beginning of the Games: 'Today I can assure you that South Korea is really a democracy where they have the liberty to film and write what they want . .'[77] Just after the Games fifty-two political prisoners were released 'to set a tone of post-Olympic reconciliation'[78] A few days later the Pope spent a weekend in China and added his voice to those urging Korean reunification, warning the South's rulers that he was keeping an eye on their justice and human rights record.[79] The internal picture was further improved by former President Chun's return to Seoul at the end of December 1990 from two years of internal exile at a remote mountain temple. Plans to demonstrate did not materialise, partly because most of the student activist leaders had been arrested over the past few days, and partly because nearly three thousand riot police were mobilised.[80]

Steps towards reunification began with two days' talks at Pyongyang between the Prime Ministers of North and South Korea. They decided to meet again in December and President Kim Il-sung said that he would meet President Roh once progress has been made. There were expectations in Seoul of a non-aggression pact, forced on Kim by the South's improving relations with China and the USSR, which had left the North isolated.[81] In so far as that isolation was accentuated by South Korea's improved network of foreign relations, and if the improvement resulted directly from the Games, then it may indeed be said that the Games played a part in forcing North Korea towards reunification.

In his preface to Kim's book Samaranch sums up the political value of the games: 'Apart from being a tremendous success for the whole Olympic family, one could perhaps even say that the Olympic Games in Seoul were a major factor behind the rapid democratization of the Republic of Korea and the development of an element of international goodwill, cooperation and fraternity, a new hope for peace'.[82]

Notes

1 *Financial Times*, 'Man in the News: Roh Tae Woo: an Heir apparent but not certain', 30 May 1987, Maggie Ford, Seoul.

2 *The Times*, 11 June 1987, David Watts, Seoul.

3 Brian Bridges, 'East Asia in Transition: South Korea in the Limelight', *International Affairs*, vol. 64, number 3, summer 1988, pp. 381–92.

4 *The Times*, 18 June 1987, David Watts, Seoul.

5 *The Sunday Times*, 5 July 1987, Jon Swain, Seoul.

6 Bridges, p. 384. The historical data in this section are taken from Bridges's article and from his book *Korea and the West*, 1986. Chapter 2: 'Political Culture in the Two Koreas', London, pp. 5–20.

7 Richard Espy, *The Politics of the Olympic Games*, Berkeley, 1979, pp. 66–7.

8 55th Session of the IOC, Munich, 25–8 May 1959. *Minutes*.

9 58th Session, Athens, June 1961, *Minutes*.

10 GANEFO had been proposed by President Achmed Sukarno of Indonesia in April 1963, following the suspension of the Indonesian NOC in February for having failed to protest when its government had refused visas to athletes from Israel and Taiwan who had hoped to attend the fourth Asian Games in the summer of 1962. Within the same month the Indonesian NOC had withdrawn from the movement. Espy, p. 80.

11 *ibid.*, pp. 81–3.

12 *ibid.*, pp. 109–10.

13 I have drawn freely on the *Official Report* of the 1988 Games and on Kim Un-yong, *The Greatest Olympics: from Baden-Baden to Seoul*, Seoul,

1990. This quotation is from Kim, p. 23.

14 Denis Howell, *Made in Birmingham: the Memoirs of Denis Howell*, London, 1990, Chapter 14.

15 Kim, pp. 26–7. Elsewhere he states that there were originally seven candidates, but that Robert Helmick had withdrawn.

16 Kim, p. 53.

17 *Report*, p. 33.

18 Kim, p. 54.

19 *Report*, p. 34.

20 Kim, p. 54.

21 *Report*, pp. 35–9.

22 Kim, p. 61.

23 *Report*, p. 42.

24 Peter Ueberroth, *Made in America*, London, 1986, pp. 92–3.

25 *Report*, p. 43.

26 Kim, p. 32.

27 Kim, p. 116.

28 *ibid.*, pp. 46–7.

29 *ibid.*, pp. 30–1.

30 *ibid.*, pp. 116–7.

31 *ibid.*, p. 34.

32 *ibid.*, p. 117.

33 *ibid.*, p. 119.

34 *ibid.*, pp. 48 and 121–2.

35 *ibid.*, pp. 123–7.

36 *AP*, Moscow, 11 January 1988.

37 Kim, p. 127.

38 Horne and others, *The 1988 Seoul Olympics*, North Staffordshire Polytechnic, Occasional Paper No. 5, June 1988, pp. 18.

39 Kim, pp. 133–4.

40 *The Times*, 6 August 1985, David Miller, Sofia.

41 *The Guardian*, 7 June 1985, John Rodda.

42 Kim, pp. 135–6.

43 *L'Equipe*, 20 October 1986.

44 Kim, pp. 137–40.

45 *The Scotsman*, 28 December 1987, Chris Thau.

46 Horne and others, p. 19.

47 *The Guardian*, 13 January 1988, John Rodda.

48 *ibid.*, 19 January 1988, John Rodda.

49 *The Times*, 22 January 1988.

50 Kim, p. 41.

51 *ibid.*, pp. 142–4.

52 *ibid.*, pp. 88, 173 and 177. In David Miller's view, the only sports in which starting times might present problems for US television were athletics, gymnastics and swimming. *The Times*, 9 October 1984, David Miller, Delhi.

53 *The Times*, 14 September 1985, David Miller, Lausanne.

54 Kim, p. 89.

55 *ibid.*, p. 93.

56   *ibid.*, pp. 112–13.
57   *ibid.*, p. 261 and *The Times*, 17 November 1987, David Miller.
58   *The Times*, 8 March 1988, David Miller.
59   Kim, pp. 260 and 261.
60   *ibid.*, pp. 149, 170, 260, 262, 263.
61   *ibid.*, p. 175.
62   *ibid.*, p. 271.
63   *ibid.*, pp. 165–7.
64   *ibid.*, p. 155.
65   *ibid.*, pp. 230–1.
66   *Report*, p. 233.
67   See p. 166.
68   *Report*, p. 217 and Kim, Chapter 4.
69   *Report*, pp. 234–9.
70   *The Guardian*, 30 August 1988, Mike Green.
71   *Report*, p. 241 and Kim, p. 35.
72   *Report*, p. 240.
73   Kim, p. 60.
74   *ibid.*, pp. 291 and 282–3.
75   *ibid.*, p. 287.
76   *ibid.*, pp. 286–8.
77   *The Observer*, 18 September 1988, Christopher Brasher, Seoul.
78   *The Guardian*, 3 October 1988.
79   *The Times*, 9 October 1989.
80   *The Times*, 31 December 1990, Simon Warner, Seoul.
81   *ibid.*, 19 October 1990, Simon Warner, Seoul.
82   Kim, p. 14.

IX

Barcelona and the Games of 1992

The history of Barcelona's bid for the Games of 1992 and of its subsequent preparations for them well illustrates the many difficulties that face an Olympic host. First, support must be gathered not only within the city itself, but throughout the country as a whole. If a country's government and people are not seen to be behind a bid the IOC is unlikely to take it seriously. A good example is provided by Manchester: the lack of conviction that it carried as an Olympic city, even among British people who were well disposed to the idea of the Games being held in Britain, must have contributed to its failure when bidding for the Games of 1996.

Once the bid has been won there is an interval of six years (seven from 1993) before the Games are held. During that long period a multitude of problems arise and it becomes an important task of the organising committee to maintain the support which was gathered earlier and to see that internal rivalries and political disagreements do not prejudice the momentum of preparation for the great event. In Barcelona's case such rivalries have been only too apparent.

The genesis of Barcelona's bid

Barcelona naturally makes much of its pertinacity in seeking to host the Olympic Games. It bid for 1924, but lost to Paris, because Coubertin had asked for the Games as his swan song; it tried again for 1936, and even built the Montjuic stadium in anticipation, but was defeated by Berlin on a confused postal vote. Its third attempt was for the Games of 1972, when it again lost to a German city, this time Munich.

Furthermore, Barcelona had a long sporting tradition. The Barcelona Football Club was founded in 1897 and the Barcelona Swimming Club in 1907; the Spanish National Olympic Committee (Comité Olíympico Español COE) was established in Barcelona, as were numerous Spanish sports federations, and there is a flourishing sporting press. In recent years numerous international contests have been held in Barcelona, so that the city can truthfully say that it has had practice in organising major events.

When it came to bidding for the 1992 Games (against Amsterdam, Belgrade, Birmingham, Brisbane and Paris) the Spanish case was rather different from the British. In Britain the British Olympic Association had had to decide between rival candidates: in Spain there is a traditional rivalry between Barcelona and Madrid, but once Barcelona had announced its candidacy Madrid did not oppose it. Instead, as one observer put it, Madrid's politicians 'played the politics of generosity, though with knives in their pockets'.

The idea of holding the Olympics in Barcelona was the brainchild of, among others, Narcis Serra, a socialist Mayor of Barcelona who later became Minister of Defence, and was succeeded by the present Mayor, Pasqual Maragall. Serra seems first to have thought of Barcelona as a site for the Games as long ago as 1978, perhaps with some prompting from Samaranch himself, and then to have looked into the practicalities with great discretion, in order not to alert Madrid. Serra saw both the Olympics and the International Exhibition to be held at Seville in 1992 as means to give Spain a new focus after the abortive attempt of 23 February 1981 to reimpose dictatorship on the country, and had realised that the best way for a city to promote itself as of worldwide importance was for it to host the Olympics, better even than the old route of holding an international exhibition.

When Maragall became Mayor and took over the prospect of bidding for the Games he had to make sure that the objective of winning the bid become a national, not merely a local, ambition, which would involve the central government without sacrificing Barcelona's control, and, by being above or outside party politics, become a worthy object for the King of Spain's support. To contrive such an image for the bid required considerable political skill, since the next tier of government above the socialist municipality of Barcelona has a distinctly conservative and Catalonian nationalist tinge. The central government in Madrid is again socialist, but the political affinity that one might expect it to have with Barcelona seems often to be strained by the rivalry between the two cities, as well as by the different traditions from which the national and local socialist parties spring.

Gathering support for the bid

Once Barcelona's intention to bid had been formally announced by Serra at a dinner in honour of the best exporters of 1980 on 30 January 1981, the public campaign was under way. It lasted nearly six years until its successful conclusion at Lausanne in October 1986. After the announcement events moved swiftly. In May Serra asked King Carlos for his approval and patronage; at the end of June the Barcelona City Council unanimously approved the initiative and encouraged a first study, and the world's sporting press was briefed on Barcelona's aspirations at the football World Cup of 1982. Barcelona had, of course, been chosen some years ahead to host the World Cup, but once the city had bid for the Olympics the football festival became an obvious promotional vehicle.

In October 1982 a first outline of the project was produced. It met with general approval and was delivered to Samaranch at Lausanne in November by Serra and Josep María Vilaseca, the Director-General of Sport in the Generalitat (provincial government) of Catalonia. In December Serra became Minister of Defence in the Madrid government and was succeeded as Mayor by his deputy, Pasqual Maragall, who became Mayor in his own right when he won the municipal elections of April 1983. In December 1982 the Prime Minister, Felipe González, informed Maragall of his cabinet's total support for Barcelona's candidature. In the following month the President of the Generalitat, Jordi Pujol, and Maragall signed articles of association of the organising committee. This body in turn created an Olympic office to take charge of the candidature, which was approved by a resolution of Spain's Council of Ministers in March 1984.

Early in February 1985 Samaranch saw González for the first time since 1983, when he visited him in Madrid to ask his support for a United Nations declaration against boycotts of the Olympic Games. He pointed out that the new President of the General Assembly in September would be a Spaniard, Jaime de Piniesa, so that the time was propitious for his campaign to gain for the Olympic movement a status akin to that of the Red Cross. (However, it soon appeared that the route to the United Nations was to be via UNESCO.) The meeting was not solely concerned with international manoeuvrings, for afterwards Samaranch told the press that González had asked him for the details of how to formulate a city's candidature, and the meeting ended with a game of billiards. The press made much of this meeting, and of the fact that González had again assured Samaranch of his total support for Barcelona's candidature.

The Catalan Parliament was concerned about the place that would be accorded in the Olympic Games to the Catalan language and national anthem, to which Maragall could only reply that they would be favourably treated within the framework of the Catalan Statute of Autonomy of December 1979 and the laws of Spain.[1] The Catalan question (regarding the degree of autonomy, or even full independence, which Catalonia ought to enjoy) has naturally grumbled on, but is apparently not regarded as a major security problem. Most Catalans are to some extent nationalists, but there are few who seriously expect complete independence. Conservatives concentrate on the need for a more favourable interpretation of the Statute, whereas socialists focus more on the objective of a truly federal Spain. There is, it is true, a small fringe of Catalan separatists, known as Terra Lliure, but they, like the Basque terrorist organisation, ETA (Euskadi ta Askatsuna), are seen as controllable. What the organisers fear more than violence are such demonstrations as Catalan separatists jumping into the swimming pool during the events. Measures of this kind have been threatened by the Esquerra Republicana de Catalyuna, led by a member of the Catalonian Parliament named Ángel Colom, unless a separate Catalonian Olympic Committee is recognised by the IOC in time for the games.[2] However, any such recognition is out of the question.

The King, although always sympathetic to Barcelona's bid, did not rush to receive the organising committee officially. However, once Maragall and Felipe González had sorted out such urgent matters as the date on which work would start on rebuilding the stadium, and González had promised the state's help, especially abroad, he and Maragall were duly received, with members of the committee, including Narcis Serra, the Visconde de Güell (owner of the Barcelona newspaper La Vanguardia), Josep María Vilaseca and representatives of the COE, the Diputación, etc. (The Diputación is a local government body, of which Samaranch was once President, whose powers the provincial government would like to curtail.) At his meeting with González, before going to see the King, Maragall said that he planned a seminar on international politics in February or March 1985 and González said that he would attend. Maragall was also reported to have told González that there was a strong neutralist tendency in Catalonia, which wanted Spain to get out of NATO, because the region had done well in the Second World War, when Spain was neutral.[3]

There continued to be points of dissension. For example, the Press Commission of ANOC made it known that it wanted an experienced Olympic journalist in charge of press relations, instead of Pedro Palacios, who had been brought in from a magazine specialising in crime, rather than sport. Maragall and Ramón Trías Fargas, boss in Barcelona of the conservative Convergencia i Unio (CiU) party which held nearly half the seats in the City Council, accused each other of spoiling Barcelona's image. However, on the whole a very convincing unity was maintained for most of the time. February 1985 was a particularly active season of goodwill. For instance, the Generalitat promised Samaranch that it would do all it could to help the city administration; the Barcelona Diputación unanimously backed the candidature; the city, the Generalitat and the Diputación agreed to spend ptas 140m ($0·825m) equally divided, on getting the sports hall ready for the 1988 World Basketball Championships; Ramón Trías Fargas said that the Olympics were above politics and Don Alfonso de Bourbon (President of the Spanish Olympic Committee – COE) said that all must work together for Barcelona.

Maragall thought 1985 a good year for settling differences between the city and the Generalitat on such matters as municipal law and the territorial division of Catalonia, because it was not an election year, and all parties were united in wishing to project Barcelona for 1992.[4] Javier Solana, the Minister of Culture, called the Games 'A compromise for the whole of Spain'[5] and Jordi Pujol, the President of the Generalitat (who often refers to himself as President of Catalonia), was anxious to strengthen Catalonian relations with Italy and used a visit to the Milan fair to push Barcelona's candidature. Later he was to use the prospect of the Games to strengthen relations between Catalonia and the Rhône–Alpes region of France.[6]

Problems in the Spanish sports establishment

The Spanish Olympic Committee (COE) did not come officially into the picture until June 1983, when its plenary session supported the candidature, and there was another long delay before the Spanish

Committee of Olympic federations ratified the decision in March 1984. There was a continuing crisis within the COE, revolving round its chairman Alfonso de Bourbon, Duke of Cadíz. When he had been elected President of the COE in 1984 he had received a minority of the votes, 29 against 28 and 25 for the other candidates, and thereafter always claimed to have been the first democratically elected president.[7] Another source of trouble in the COE lay in the relations between the Olympic and non-Olympic federations, with the former thinking themselves under-represented. The relations between the COE and the interim organising committee of the Games were never good, not, it seems for any institutional reason but because of Don Alfonso's unusual character and history. He had bid for the monarchy in the 1960s and was closely linked to the Franco regime, and it was even whispered that, as Pretender to the French throne, he had really favoured the French bid for the Games, although he declared that he had played his part in Barcelona's victory. He was credited with some odd notions, having even been thought to have toyed with the idea of posthumously giving Franco the COE's gold medal.[8] Nevertheless, Olympic protocol continued to be observed to the extent that it was Don Alfonso who officially presented the candidature document at Lausanne on 16 May 1985.

In June David Miller reported that Paris, Brisbane and Barcelona were all working hard, and that Barcelona had a $10m promotional budget: but he saw a British bid as way down the list.[9]

The relations between the COE and Maragall's organising committee took a turn for the worse when the COE let it be known that it was ready to sue the committee for unauthorised use of the Olympic logo, probably because of its poverty following a cut-back in its funding from the state.[10] The relationship between the two bodies was clarified on paper in January 1987 when Don Alfonso and Maragall, with visible coldness, signed a document to create the joint committee, which would in turn spawn COOB '92 (see below). The purpose of both Maragall and central government in creating this joint committee was thought to be to relegate the COE to second place until its internal affairs were sorted out and the question of the presidency resolved. The Duke's resignation was predicted daily, but he was determined not to go before the end of his mandate in 1988.

The Duke complained, not without reason, that the Mayor of Barcelona had grabbed all the campaign funds raised from private sponsors, leaving nothing for the NOC.[11] However Miquel Abad,

Chief Executive of the interim organising committee, asserted that the internal crisis of the Spanish NOC would not inhibit the founding of the permanent organising committee. (The latter was to be known as COOB '92 – Comité Organizador Olímpico de Barcelona – '92, usually abbreviated to COOB '92, the natural acronym – COJO – Comité Organizador de los Juegos Olímpicos having had to be rejected because in Spanish it means lame man or cripple, hardly a suitable name for an Olympic Games organising committee.) The new body, Abad said, must be founded by April, but meanwhile there would be a joint liaison committee, and another to write COOB's statutes. This joint committee of the COE and the Municipality was to be the IOC's official interlocutor for the time being.[12]

In May 1987 elections for the presidency of the COE were eventually held, from which Carlos Ferrer Salat emerged victorious. Ferrer Salat, normally known simply as Ferrer, is a prominent businessman who has made his fortune in banking, chemicals and pharmaceuticals and who became a member of the IOC just after being introduced to the existing members as the leader of Barcelona's bid. (John Rodda called this an extraordinary election. 'Perhaps', he commented sourly, 'in the Latin world they do not see a conflict of interests here.')[13] Once Ferrer had been elected President of the COE he became a Vice-President of COOB and relations between the two bodies improved greatly. Don Alfonso died in an accident on 30 January 1989 and *The Times*'s obituary summed up well in recalling that he had been attacked for opposing revision of the COE's rules and that it had seemed to many that he was being used by leftovers from the Franco era to resist a democratisation of Spanish sport, which would make Spain more prepared for hosting the 1992 Games.[14]

The Barcelona 92 Candidature Managing Council (as the interim committee was officially known) was dissolved in December 1986, two months after Barcelona won the contest to hold the Games, and succeeded by COOB. This body has a complicated structure, reflecting the complexity of the political state of affairs. It consists of a General Assembly, containing representatives of the Catalan and Spanish sports federations, and the economic, social and cultural worlds, as well as of the four consortium members – the COE and the three tiers of government. (The COE is in a special position, in that its lack of funds renders it unable to accept any of the financial responsibility.) The Assembly delegates responsibility to an Executive Board and a Standing Committee which deals with the day-to-day work.

These bodies are led by Maragall as President, and four Vice-Presidents, Carlos Ferrer, Javier Gómez Navarro (Secretary of State for Sport in the Madrid government), Josep María Vilaseca and the Chief Executive Officer, Josep Miquel Abad. Beneath this super-structure has grown a rash of companies and directorates, but the principle of political control of COOB, upon which Maragall has always insisted, has been preserved.

COOB itself has not always been a happy ship. The press described it as a battlefield where problems quite unrelated to the Olympics were fought out.[15] In December *Euroletter* summed up the four elements of the crisis in COOB. First, Seoul's success had made COOB realise how much work it had to do; secondly Samaranch's constant involvement in Barcelona's affairs created complications, largely because the organisers did not always fall in with his ideas, especially in the matter of the sale of television rights; thirdly, the central government was displeased by Maragall's bad relations with its Secretary of State for Sport, Gómez Navarro, and finally it was still necessary to delimit the areas of competence of Abad and the new Director-General of COOB, José María Vilá and to give some teeth to the consultative committee of businessmen which had been set up by Maragall, but which had practically never met.

Another of Maragall's projects had also never got off the ground, namely the creation of an effective committee of representatives of the city, the Generalitat and the central government to oversee the financing of the Olympics.[16] The new physical education institute's opening offered an opportunity for some of the continuing political tensions to surface in the neutral context of the Olympic Games. Maragall said, rather sharply, that he was glad that the Generalitat had at last associated itself with the preparations, and that the architect, Ricardo Bofill, might now be able to get on with the Hotel Miramar, the grand hotel being built next to the new yacht basin to accommo-date the IOC during the Games, and that it should now be possible for progress to be made with the construction of an adequate transport system. However Jordi Pujol, the President of the Generalitat, instead of answering in kind seems to have done his best to turn aside wrath and to emphasise the provincial government's constructive role, when he said that the Institute's opening would dissipate any accusations of failure of collaboration between institutions.[17] Later in the year Pujol was less conciliatory, when he taxed Maragall with systematic disin-formation, by accusing the Generalitat of frustrating the organisation of the games.[18]

Even at official level things had not gone smoothly. The unpopularity of the organising committee's first director, Jaume Clavell, led to his replacement by Miquel Abad. It appears that he was dismissed without compensation in November 1988, having left his job with Apple computers in the spring of 1987 but that terms of compensation were agreed in January 1989: according to *El Mundo Deportivo* he received about ptas 100m. ($0·85m). The complaint against him was 'insubordination' at an Executive Board meeting, where had he complained of the limitations placed upon his powers.[19] Another view is that he was dismissed for not being enough of a socialist, or perhaps for not being faithful enough to Maragall.

Another power struggle surfaced in the press when it was reported that there was some doubt about whether Leopoldo Rodés, who was reputed to be a close friend of Samaranch, would continue in charge of COOB's external relations. He said that he would do so, although he had never officially accepted the position because the job outline and degree of independence allowed were vague. He asserted that he was on good terms with all parties, but he did think COOB too large – larger than the corresponding body had been at Los Angeles. COOB denied that this suggestion of Rodes's disaffection was a sign of crisis within it.[20]

However, there was soon a second crisis within COOB (the first having been the Clavell affair) arising from an attack on Abad. It was suggested that in socialist circles this former communist municipal councillor was not considered to have a good socialist pedigree and there were fears that he might be toppled if the crisis were not resolved.[21] Be that as it may, he was saved by Maragall's total support, and the successful sale of the television rights in the games consolidated both their positions and put an end to the crisis.

The international task

Despite Barcelona's rivalry with Paris, which turned out to be the city's most dangerous adversary, Maragall's main energies until mid 1984 had been spent on creating unity of purpose between the three tiers of government in Spain, so much so that when he returned from a trip to Madrid, where he had been selling the Games, all the questions at his press conference were about politics, rather than sport.[22] However, once the decision was announced to send a delegation to promote

Barcelona's case at the Los Angeles Games the campaign entered its international phase, although there was still political rivalry to be handled at home and periodic faction fighting within the organising committee.

Maragall clearly did well in Los Angeles. Samaranch could of course not give open support, but said that all the candidates were good, and that Barcelona's bid would be strong if the city maintained its sporting, political and social unity. His heart, he said, was in Barcelona, but there were five other candidates. Maragall made a big presentation at the Biltmore Hotel, and got Julio Iglesias and Plácido Domingo to sing at a reception given by Barcelona's team. He showed his capacity for saying the right thing by stating that 'Olympic votes are not bought or sold, but won', and seems to have 'won' the South Korean vote by doing a deal whereby he would not try to take the 1988 Games from Seoul if South Korea backed him for 1992.

The first major figure in the sporting world from outside Spain publicly to announce his support for Barcelona was Dr Primo Nebiolo, President of the International Amateur Athletic Federation. He said that as a Latin he would prefer Barcelona to other cities, and that after the problems of Moscow, Los Angeles and Seoul, Barcelona would be ideally quiet. Nebiolo and Joan Mas Conti, the Olympic Commissioner for Barcelona, rejected the idea floated by Nelson Paillou, President of the French NOC, that the 1988 Games might be taken away from Seoul (presumably by a campaign designed to emphasise the physical and political danger to which the Olympic family would be exposed in Seoul) and given to Barcelona, leaving the field free for Paris in 1992.[23] (Barcelona's refusal to take part in any plot may have stemmed from honourable feeings but may also have been the result of knowing that Samaranch would go to almost any lengths to keep the Games at Seoul.)

One important device used by Maragall to familiarise foreign dignitaries with his city was to arrange a seminar in the autumn of 1984 on the impact on major cities of holding the Olympic Games. It was attended by Tom Bradley, the Mayor of Los Angeles, who said Barcelona was well able to hold the Games. Samaranch opened the seminar; Vladimir Rodichenko, Vice-President of the NOC of the USSR, attended and representatives of Munich, Moscow and Los Angeles promised that if Barcelona won they would give any help they could with the organisation.[24] Shortly afterwards João Havelange, the powerful President of FIFA, came out in favour of Barcelona.

In November 1984 Barcelona made a big impression with its presentation to the Association of National Olympic Committees (ANOC) in Mexico. The delegation was led by Joan Mas Conti, and merely accompanied by the embarrassing Don Alfonso. This was the first time Barcelona had met ANOC, and the Mexican press did the delegation proud, which is not surprising when one remembers that much of it belongs to Mario Vásquez-Raña, the President of ANOC, who was probably supporting Barcelona even at this early stage. Later he was to call the 1992 Olympics 'my Games' because he had helped to get them for Barcelona.[25]

The slow process of gathering international support continued, on the whole, to go well. José Beracassa, Honorary President of the Pan-American Olympic Committee, said Barcelona could count on all the countries of Central and South America.[26] The Korean ambassador to Spain made supportive remarks; the Spanish government asked for Japanese support; Barcelona was helped by the fact that unnamed sources in Amsterdam sought crime statistics for the West Midlands in an attempt to undermine the Birmingham bid, and Maragall upstaged Birmingham by obliging it to postpone a reception for IOC members by suddenly holding a civic reception himself.[27] It appeared that Barcelona was worried by the strength of the late bid from Birmingham, for Maragall said of its leader, Denis Howell, that he had good political muscle, and 'must be admired and respected because he knows so many influential people in the international sporting world'.[28]

Despite his international efforts, Maragall did not forget the need to raise Spanish Olympic consciousness. On 29 September 1985 Pujol told the Catalan Parliament how essential it was that Barcelona should get the Games, and an opinion poll showed that 64 per cent of Spaniards, especially those living in big cities, believed that the Games in Barcelona would benefit the whole of Spain. The Barcelona Diputactión (a local government body) voted ptas 1,000m ($6·0m) for infrastructural development and at the fifth anniversary party of *Sport*, a Barcelona newspaper, Maragall said that they could not fail to win if they maintained unity. By early November a correspondent of *Le Martin* in Lausanne was tipping Barcelona as favourite, as were the Barcelona papers *El Mundo Deportivo* and *Sport*.

Note   Pesetas are converted to dollars at the average rates for 1985 and January 1989.

Getting the IOC's votes

Ambassador Ignacio Masferrer was seconded from the Spanish diplomatic service in 1985 to help with the international side of the bid, and
in particular to sell it to IOC members, since it was thought that he
would have a higher standing with them than would a firm of public
relations agents. The international operation, known as the Commission for External Relations, was run by Leopoldo Rodés and Carlos
Ferrer. The third member of the Commission, which was given
complete independence and discretion by the municipality, was
Andreu Mercé Varela, a journalist and another old friend of Samaranch.

Barcelona's bid seems to have cost well above the average, as did
that of Paris. Ferrer was asked by Maragall to raise industrial money
to assist in financing the bid. He and Rodés set up a Foundation and
were able to recruit over ninety other businessmen, each of whose
companies contributed at least ptas 10m ($60,000) to Barcelona's
fighting fund.

As with all bids, it was necessary to persuade as many IOC members
as possible to visit Barcelona. All of them were invited and more than
half accepted. As with other visits, they would have fares and hotels
paid, some would bring their wives or another family member, and
they would be invited to stay with the industrialists who had contributed to the fund.

Ferrer would invite members to visit him at his bank, while Rodés
favoured a more personal touch and asked them to his home. Yet it is
doubtful whether Rodés was the more effective, and after the bid he
did not play the leading part in the preparations for the Olympics
which he would perhaps have enjoyed. It is often said that he would be
worthy of a place on the IOC if Samaranch retires and becomes an
honorary member in 1992, but it is open to question whether it would
be politic to appoint yet a third Spanish member from Barcelona.

The programme for visiting IOC members would include meeting
Maragall and Pujol and seeing Barcelona from the air. They would
also receive gifts, of a personal rather than a luxurious nature (the
most valuable was a lithograph, signed by the artist, of Salvador Dali's
1968 oil painting *The Cosmic Athlete*) though there were, it is said, also
favours rendered which it might have been difficult to justify had the
details been publicly known. It must be added that there was considerable talk, though never of a specific nature, about other gifts

which were alleged to have been given, and there lurked in the background, as no less a sports journalist than David Miller pointed out, the shadow of Adidas.[29] To many of the members money was not important: what mattered was to study the personal psychology of each of them when deciding what programme would be most suitable. Perhaps the master stroke of the exceedingly well-run campaign was that, shortly before the crucial vote at Lausanne, each member of the IOC received a personal letter from King Carlos, worth little in itself, yet a flattering mark of attention.

It was important, as it is in any such campaign, to form an assessment of the degree of independence an IOC member would enjoy from his government. Of course, all IOC members are appointed by the IOC (in practice largely by its President) as independent individuals, but some are more independent than others. Governmental influence may be reduced by the fact that even those members who are willing, or obliged, to listen to their governments would not have time to consult between the rounds of voting. On the other hand, those who are open to influence are probably aware in advance of their governments' second and even third preferences.

Voting day

Although it is often denied that blocs of voters exist, Barcelona felt sure of the Latin American vote, thanks to Spain's historical links. Its relationship to those countries is regarded by Spaniards as similar to that between the United Kingdom and the rest of the Commonwealth, without the structure, but with more affection.

On the day of the vote (17 October 1986) David Miller wrote in *The Times* that Barcelona's strength lay not so much in its promotional budget, as on solid support from the King, and in not having had to sell itself on sentiment, as Paris had done. He could not see Barcelona failing, although the IOC had many members who were only interested in making friends. He did, however, think Barcelona's projected income from radio and television rather high at $293 million, unless, as he acidly put it, they decided to start the 100 metres at two in the morning for the benefit of American prime time viewers.[30] Another article in the same day's *Times* commented that no one could forecast the effect on IOC members of the bombings in Barcelona earlier in the week, but that William Hill, the British bookmakers, had Barcelona as favourite at 3–1 on, with Birmingham at 2–1 against.

As we have seen in the section on Birmingham's bid, Barcelona's footwork was impressively swift and decisive. When it became clear how great an impression the speech by the French Prime Minister, Jacques Chirac, had made, Barcelona was able to divert those IOC members who would have given the winter Games to Falun (Sweden) to voting for the French candidate, Albertville, instead. This extraordinary manipulation ensured that Albertville had a very good chance of being awarded the winter games and rendered it virtually inconceivable that Paris would win the summer competition as well.[31] Reporting Barcelona's decisive win, Miller said that the pattern of voting showed that Samaranch's influence had not been a factor, since Barcelona had got a minority in the first two rounds of voting. (This is rather a surprising remark by Miller, since Samaranch *could*, though there is no suggestion that he *did*, have influenced members's votes in the later stages, once they had cast their first and second votes elsewhere.) Miller goes on: 'How much the Latin-American support guaranteed by João Havelange, the FIFA President, or the clandestine influence of Adidas, which was said to be at work, affected the vote, will never be known.'[32] Once euphoria was over, John Rodda presciently concluded, Samaranch might find it difficult to be strict enough with his native city in relation to the actual organisation of the Games.[33] Meanwhile Barcelona celebrated. Many of its citizens had never believed that they could possibly fail and when the result was announced the city erupted in fireworks.

Since then development has accelerated: at Barcelona new hotels are being built; much of the seafront which was previously obscured by a railway has been opened up by diverting the railway to allow space for the Olympic village, and the flats which are to be built in it were already for sale two years ahead of the Games. A new ring road is under construction and insalubrious parts of the city are being cleaned up: in short, the prospect of the Games has forced the three tiers of government to co-operate on projects which might otherwise have been indefinitely delayed by in-fighting.

Problems of 1992

As we saw at the beginning of this chapter, winning the bid does not guarantee a stress-free life thereafter and Samaranch has justifiably been worried about the failure of some of Barcelona's plans to materialise. For example, an early hope, now abandoned, was to extend the city's metro system up to the Montjuic stadium. (At unofficial level one can hear some rather absurd excuses, to the effect that the lack of a new link really will not matter since it is possible to walk from the centre of Barcelona to the stadium in fifteen minutes. Perhaps a marathon walker could do it in fifteen minutes, but how many ordinary spectators will even want to try in the heat of July/ August?)

The report of ANOC's Commission on the Olympic Games, presented to the ANOC meeting at Barcelona in June 1990, was also not altogether sanguine. One particular worry was about the capacity of the Olympic village. Seoul had had fewer events, and probably fewer participating NOCs than Barcelona. It had provided for more than 9,000 competitors, plus 3,900 officials and 1,500 extra officials who stayed outside the Olympic village. Barcelona was banking on 10,000 competitors and 5,200 officials, which was an increased projection necessitated by the larger programme and the larger number of NOCs, but it was not clear to the Commission where the extra officials were to be accommodated. 'Acknowledging that there has to be some limitation of the total number of participants, nevertheless the matter of capacity was extensively discussed.'

The Commission was not happy with the plan to accommodate 1,500 referees and judges next to the Olympic village. It thought they would be better lodged near to their sports' venues, leaving the accommodation next to the village free for essential support staff. Nor was the Commission pleased to learn that competitors in the finals of demonstration sports (not full Olympic sports, but allowed on the fringe of the Games) were to be housed in the main village, contrary to what had previously been agreed.

The Commission also concerned itself with quite trivial matters of housekeeping. It noted that no daily rate for officials and competitors living in the Olympic village had been agreed, nor the charges for such services as telephone and fax. It even looked at the number of towels to be provided, and at the size of the beds ('for extra tall persons an additional section will be placed at the head'). Its overall view was that 'The planning, construction and organisation of the Olympic village in Barcelona is being competently handled by the persons in charge, however it is recommended to study more closely the needs and requirements of the NOCs as outlined in previous documents.'

The Commission summed up that the preparations for the

Olympics had shown reasonable progress since its visit in July 1989. But it added that there was much concern about the capacity of the Olympic stadium for the Opening Ceremony. Its current capacity was 55,000 and consideration was being given to the feasibility of increasing this to 70,000. The report added, without comment, that there was a plan for the athletes to be sent to the Palau Sant Jordi (Capacity 17,000) sports hall after their parade, when they could watch 'the cultural program of the opening ceremony' on a giant television screen. At the plenary meetings of ANOC some of the complaints were less politely phrased than the Commission's report. COOB was strongly criticised for planning to relegate the athletes to the sports hall and there was bitter talk, particularly by some African NOCs, of meanness on the part of Barcelona. Their complaint was that the athletes alone were to be accommodated free of charge in the Olympic village, and not their entourages, and even the athletes would only be accommodated free on the days on which they were actually competing, plus six further days. Faced with this barrage of complaint Abad remained firm: he regretted the annoyance caused to some NOCs, but insisted that the position had been made perfectly clear in Barcelona's bidding documents. As was noted in Chapter IV, no less a personage than Mario Vázquez-Raña, ANOC's President, remained dissatisfied, and referred darkly to the 'humility with which some people speak when they are presenting their candidature and the pride that they show once they have been successful.'[34]

The remarks made in the ANOC Commission's report and at the meeting itself raised the question of why the Opening and Closing Ceremonies could not have been held in the Barcelona football club's stadium, which, although old and nothing like as magnificent as Montjuic, is larger and more easily accessible. The answer appears to be entirely a matter of politics and 'face'. The Club has always been a centre of Catalonian nationalism, and therefore politically opposed to the socialist administration of Barcelona; consequently Maragall was firmly opposed to its being used. It is one thing to hold some of the football matches in the stadium: it would be quite another to give the Club worldwide publicity by holding the main Olympic ceremonies there, and so giving the world the impression that the city fathers were not capable of providing an adequate stadium of their own.

Worries within the 'Olympic family'

Samaranch, who had tended to be worried and satisfied by turns about Barcelona's preparations for the Olympics, has been perceived in COOB as continually interfering in the preparations for the Games. His visits to the Prime Minister and even to the King to complain about slow progress have naturally annoyed COOB, although the public attitude is one of indulgent tolerance. He has extraordinary access, which he would never be granted in, for example, London, to these high personages, and on the whole his interventions bear fruit.

He visited Montjuic early in April 1987. This time he was impressed and said that everything was going according to time-table.[35] However, his no doubt justifiable tendency to worry showed itself again in late October, when it seemed that central government's participation was insufficient. Fortunately he had reassuring talks with Felipe González, after which it was announced that there would be more direct participation by central government.[36] In November he paid another visit to Barcelona, after which he pronounced himself satisfied with progress, though he was worried that there were only three athletes' entrances to the stadium.[37] He also lamented the absence of the businessmen, who had played such an important part in the candidature. Barcelona would have to find other sources of finance, as the television income was not high.[38]

Others of the multifacious Olympic bodies have expressed worries. For example, the Liaison Commission of the IOC which visited Barcelona in October 1987 was favourably impressed in general, but unhappy with COOB's failure to designate a site for the yachting events. Palma de Mallorca would have been happy to oblige, but the IOC were known to favour Barcelona, where no satisfactory facilities existed.[39] In the end it proved possible to build a yacht basin at Barcelona, which pleased Samaranch, who naturally believed that the events should not be held anywhere except at the Olympic city[40] (though it must be added that the pollution of the Mediterranean will not be agreeable for the yachtsmen).

There were also great difficulties over the equestrian events, which it was feared might have to be moved to a site outside Spain because of outbreaks of African horse sickness. Again, Barcelona would have suffered loss of face if the events were held elsewhere, and the income from television rights would have been seriously affected. The issue was finally decided in Barcelona's favour by the International

Equestrian Federation (of which Britain's Princess Royal is President) in November 1990, subject, of course, to Catalonia remaining free of the disease.

Maragall has occasionally dared to criticise Samaranch, reflecting the dissatisfaction in COOB at what has been seen as his continual interference. Though the criticism has been muted, Maragall has had to pay a price for it in the shape of counter-criticism, against which he has had to defend himself. For example, he felt obliged in November 1988 to attack the provincial government for suggesting that he was not heeding Samaranch's advice, although this particular quarrel seems to have been a storm in a teacup, since by December it was possible for *El Periódico* to report that relations between Maragall and the Generalitat were improving.[41] The powerful Vásquez-Raña also advised COOB that advice given by Samaranch should be followed.[42] Not long afterwards Samaranch showed that he would not be silenced by stating quite firmly that he wanted Taekwondo (the passion of his collaborator, Dr Kim, who had played a great part in the success of the Seoul Games), as a demonstration sport in 1992.[43]

Samaranch drew attention to the lack of progress over building the planned new hotels, and in a good many other directions, at a press conference in Madrid on 1 February 1989, in which he was very hard on Barcelona. The time for ideas and projects was past, he said, and action was needed. The airport extension had not been started; the motorway project was in a lamentable state; the lack of hotel space for journalists was especially grave.[44] A few months later Samaranch was again making his misgivings public. 'With two years and nine months to go before the opening of the Olympics, drastic and urgent decisions have to be taken to sort out current problems.' He had told the Prime Minister about his deep anxiety, but was feeling somewhat better after seeing him. The need for solutions, Samaranch said, was the more urgent for the problems highlighted by the athletics World Cup in September 1989. Reuter commented that the sports facilities looked certain to be ready on time, but there were doubts about the proposed metro line to the Montjuic stadium, a new stretch of ring road, and new hotels.[45] However, Abad said a few days later that COOB had already achieved 90 per cent of the plan.[46]

Samaranch seems never to have stopped putting the men on the spot under pressure. On 27 September 1989 he expressed great anxiety about the state of the preparations, although he again felt better after yet another meeting with the Prime Minister. There had

been open disagreements over some big projects between the conservative nationalists who run Catalonia's local government and
Felipe González's socialist colleagues in power in Barcelona's city
hall. Samaranch said that González had told him that the central
government would involve itself more fully early in 1990, after the
general elections which were to be held on 29 October 1989 and in
which the socialists were expected to retain their parliamentary
majority, albeit a somewhat reduced one. 'Both the Barcelona town
hall and the regional government should leave rancour aside and join
forces for Barcelona '92' Samaranch said. He added that although he
was a native of Barcelona and a good Catalan, the Olympics 'will have
ramifications for all Spaniards'.[47] (Since González had promised
increased involvement by the central government nearly a year
earlier, without any obvious result, Samaranch may well have been
right to return to the attack.)

What is at stake?

There is some doubt, which only became noticeable in 1990, about
whether the Games will make a profit. If they do not, the central
government will pay 20 per cent of the loss by way of compensation for
increased tax revenue generated by the Games and the remaining 80
per cent will be met by the three tiers of government in the pro-
portions 40 per cent central government; 30 per cent Barcelona
municipal government: 30 per cent Generalitat (Catalonian provincial
government).

The financial dangers may be less significant than the political and
personal. Maragall's position was not altogether comfortable until the
1991 municipal elections, because he ran a real risk of losing office if
trends in the national elections of October 1989 were reproduced. The
prospect of the games being held in Barcelona strengthened his position, but they had to be sold to the people of Barcelona as a whole, and
he has been much criticised for the disruption to daily life caused by
the preparations. In fact he returned safely to office: had he not, the
Olympic Games would, of course, still have gone ahead, but it would
have been exceedingly galling for Maragall not to play the leading part
given to the Mayor of the host city, and to feel that the great efforts he
had made to bring the Games to Barcelona had, in a personal sense,
been wasted.

He may have been reassured by a poll conducted for *La Vanguardia* in May 1990, which showed that 70 per cent of Spaniards believed the Games would be a success, and only 9 per cent thought they would be a disaster. Of the people of Barcelona 80 per cent thought the Games would be beneficial for the city, and about the same percentage of Sevillians thought they would benefit from the 1992 exhibition there. Taking the two events together, 72 per cent of Spaniards thought they would be beneficial. Yet 16 per cent of Barcelonans thought the Games would be bad for the city (compared with 10 per cent who believed the exhibition would be bad for Seville). The pessimistic minority is to be found most strongly in the United Right (Izquierda Unida), followed by the nationalist parties, and they are more pessimistic about the Games than about the exhibition.[48]

Samaranch has more to lose than anyone if the Barcelona Games turn out a fiasco. He has not lobbied for his home city in any overt way, but he made no secret of his hope that Barcelona would be chosen, and now that it has been he takes a close interest in the preparations – sometimes too close for COOB. To have the Games in his home town is the culmination of his career, and has made him a popular figure there. He has nothing to lose financially, but a less than perfect Games would cause him incalculable distress and loss of face.

In Barcelona one major worry is about whether the organising committee will prove capable of presenting the Games without mishap. The fear that the preparations may not be on time, partly because of the political differences between the three tiers of Spanish government, has been frequently expressed by Samaranch and has been echoed by other senior sports administrators. It is, of course, impossible to forecast, but it seems likely that the genius for improvisation so often ascribed to the Spanish will be needed to the full in the run-up to the Games. However, although Barcelona may be uncomfortable for enthusiasts who actually attend the Games, they should be a superb television event.

Notes

1 *El Periódico*, 23 November 1984.
2 *El País*, 22 October 1989.
3 *El País*, 27 November 1984 and *La Vanguardia*, 28 November 1984.
4 *El Periódico*, 18 February 1985.
5 *El Mundo Deportivo*, 22 May 1985.
6 *Le Dauphine Libéré*, 9 January 1987.
7 *La Vanguardia*, 25 January 1989.
8 *Libération*, 30 January 1987, Bernard Cohen.

9 *The Times*, 4 June 1985, David Miller, East Berlin.
10 *Diario*, Madrid, 16 September 1985.
11 *Libération*, Bernard Cohen, 30 January 1987.
12 *EFE*, 20 January 1987.
13 *The Guardian*, 7 June 1985.
14 *The Times*, 1 February 1989.
15 For example, *Tribuna*, 21 November 1988.
16 *Euroletter*, 2 December 1988.
17 *Barcelona Olímpica*, 1 June 1988.
18 *Catalunya Política*, 30 October 1988.
19 *El Mundo Deportivo*, 18 January 1989; see also *El Periódico*, 25 January 1989.
20 *EFE*, 13 May 1986.
21 *El País*, 18 November 1988.
22 *El Mundo Deportivo*, 11 July 1984.
23 *ibid.*, 7 June 1984.
24 *La Vanguardia*, 15 September 1984.
25 *Barcelona Olímpica*, 6, Dec./Jan. 1989, p. 21, Antonio H. Filloy.
26 *El País*, 28 August 1985.
27 *Daily Mail*, 27 October 1985.
28 *ibid.*, 21 October 1985.
29 *The Times*, 18 October 1986, David Miller, Lausanne, and see p. 000 above.
30 *The Times*, 17 October 1986.
31 John Rodda in *Running Magazine*, December 1986. Rodda makes the additional point that the voice was Chirac's, but the speech had been written by Monique Berlioux, the former Executive Director of the IOC whom Samaranch had sacked.
32 *The Times*, 18 October 1986.
33 John Rodda, *Running Magazine*, *loc. cit.*
34 *La Vanguardia*, 8 June 1990.
35 *EFE*, 4 April 1987.
36 *La Vanguardia*, 28 October 1988.
37 *Sport*, 14 November 1988.
38 *EFE*, 23 November 1987, reporting an interview in *La Vanguardia*.
39 *AP*, 26 October 1987.
40 *EFE*, 2 December 1987.
41 *El Periódico*, 18 November and 13 December 1988.
42 *El Mundo Deportivo*, 9 December 1988.
43 *El Mundo Deportivo*, 21 January 1989.
44 *El País*, 2 February 1989.
45 *The Times* (Reuter), 28 October 1989.
46 *Sport*, 15 February 1989.
47 *The Times* (Reuter) 28 September 1989.
48 *La Vanguardia*, 4 June 1990.

X

The Olympics in the third millennium

Over the past century the Olympic movement has built up extra-ordinary power, prestige and goodwill, yet it is beset with problems. Some of these are internal. In this category there are some questions which, though time-comsuming, are unlikely to go to the heart of the movement. For example, it is not surprising to find that the United States Olympic Committee is dissatisfied with its share of the money raised from the sale of North American television rights, or that Asia is discontented to be dominated by Arabs in sports administration and with its share of the funds distributed by Olympic Solidarity. These are the types of domestic trouble which any worldwide movement must expect to suffer.

However there are also internal questions which could tear the movement apart at the roots if not dealt with. A further brand of question is linked to national and international politics, and often, as we have seen throughout this book, the domestically and the publicly political interlock.

Olympic dominance

If the Olympic Games are not at the top of the world sporting tree they are nothing, so that one constant preoccupation of the International Olympic Committee is to ensure that the Olympics retain their dominant place. Currently there is no worldwide organisation capable of challenging the Olympic movement's dominance of international sport. Since the IOC headed off UNESCO in the 1970s the only source of danger, short of world catastrophe, is internal dissension which could lead to fragmentation of the movement.

As we saw in an earlier chapter, the effort to maintain unity requires

delicate balancing between the various powerful bodies in the movement, especially between the IOC, the international federations (IFs),
the National Olympic Committees (NOCs) and, once a host city has
been chosen, between the IOC and that city's organising committee.
Other problems are those of 'gigantism', as the Games' permanent
tendency to grow is inelegantly known. With gigantism must be
linked the growing commercialisation of the Games, which still
disquiets some of the more traditionally-minded sports people. There
remain, too, vestiges of the old question of amateurism versus professionalism, although it must be said that this is a problem which lingers
on more in the public mind than in that of athletes or sports administrators. By contrast, doping on its current large scale is a relatively
modern problem, which the movement is tackling to the best of its
ability.

Amateurism and nationalism

Within sport amateurism is more or less a dead issue. The Olympic
Games' reason for existence is to promote the best in human achievement, and to retain the best they have abandoned much that was for
many years thought essential to the Olympic ideal. De Coubertin's
very un-Greek idea was that the ancient Games were strictly for
amateurs and that it was more important to take part than to win. He
was of course more sophisticated than his snobbish Victorian con-
temporaries, who saw sport as a pastime of the leisured class, for
which it was inappropriate to train. His original motive, as was shown
in Chapter I was to promote physical education in schools, and he
originally promoted the Games as a means to that end, though as his
life went on they seem to have become an end in themselves.

It was only in 1981 that the IOC formally abandoned the commitment to amateurism, by saying that eligibility to take part in the
Games must be determined by individual international federations. It
is true that some federations still have great difficulty in defining the
exact conditions of eligibility, but from the point of view of the IOC
the problem is dead.

So, in one sense, is that of nationalism. It has always been said that
the Olympics are contests between individuals, but in fact they are
contests between national teams, chosen by their federations. Of
course there may still be occasions when a competitor of insufficient
standard takes part, but that, again, is not the IOC's problem.

Officially, individual excellence and national fervour sit happily together, since no National Olympic Committee would willingly send a team to the Games which did not have the best possible chance of winning medals. In fact, it is the NOCs which insist on their athletes identifying in the most ostentatious way with their nations, by marching behind their national flags. Any suggestion that national flags be abandoned and replaced with the Olympic flag would be universally rejected by the NOCs, which have no time for the well-meant supra-nationalism of the European Community. It is only traditionalists, like Madame Monique Berlioux, who still wish that individuals could present themselves as candidates for the Games, and this preoccupation with a dead past was very possibly one of the many factors which led to her breach with Samaranch, and to her abrupt retirement.

Gigantism

Gigantism is a problem of a different kind, which has been discussed for many years, since long before the number of athletes, journalists, officials and hangers-on reached its present grotesque size. For example, at the IOC's Session at Helsinki in 1952 various methods of reducing the number of athletes were discussed and J. Sigfrid Edstrom, the outgoing President, said that the number of officials who accompanied the teams and could well be described as tourists was growing alarmingly.[1]

There is constant pressure on the Programme Commission of the IOC to admit new sports, or to enlarge the number of events within a sport. At the same time there is widespread understanding that the Olympic circus has got out of hand. So large are the Games that in practice only the richest of candidate cities, or those under the control of effective authoritarian governments, are plausible candidates to host them. Furthermore, the increasing number of journalists covering them, not to mention the proliferating Olympic family, means that accommodation for ordinary members of the public who would like to attend the Games becomes increasingly difficult to find. Indeed, COOB, Barcelona's organising committee, seems almost to think of ordinary spectators as a nuisance, to be accommodated outside Barcelona in the already crowded coastal resorts.

One important decision that has been taken is that after 1992 'Demonstration Sports' will no longer be included. Some other steps have been taken, some of them ham-handed. For example, in 1991 the Programme Commission reduced the number of medal-winning events in equestrianism, without even consulting the Princess Royal, who as well as being a member of the IOC is President of the International Equestrian Federation. The next steps will be more difficult. One way forward, which is frequently canvassed, is to exclude team games. What, however, would be the reaction of João Havelange and his powerful Football Federation? Would other federations' leaders rejoice at his exclusion, or would they join forces with him, and threaten to do without the Olympic Games altogether? If Primo Nebiolo and his International Amateur Athletic Federation went that way, the Olympics would be finished.

Other candidates for exclusion are those sports where the winning score is determined by subjective judgement, rather than reference to the stop-watch. Richard Pound, a Vice President of the IOC since 1987, has said that other possible casualties are football, boxing and weight-lifting: the first because the upper age limit of 23 imposed by FIFA means that the best players do not take part; the second because of 'continually repeated scandalous decisions' and the third because of the misuse of steroids.[2]

Yet another possible solution is to set quotas for sports. These, however, might lead one country to include inferior representatives, just to fill its quota, and another to exclude some of the best performers in the world because too many of them lived in the same country.

Whatever happens, the problem of gigantism has to be tackled, yet the Olympic movement has to be held together. Both themes were prominent at one of those luxurious Olympic jamborees which so offend commentators who believe that the movement should spend its money on the development of sport. This time it was a meeting at Barcelona in June 1990 of the Association of National Olympic Committees (ANOC). In a *tour d'horizon* of the state of the movement Samaranch asserted that it faced no overwhelming problems at present. He went on:

After the two great successes of the 1988 Games in Calgary and Seoul, we are fortunate in having no fundamental problems before us. There are difficulties, of course, but we also have the means with which to resolve them. We shall be discussing the size of the Olympic Games, as there is a number of participants which we cannot exceed without causing great harm to the Games.

The ground had been well prepared. Samaranch, Vazquez-Rana of ANOC and Nebiolo as Chairman of ASOIF had held a preliminary meeting in Rome after which an IOC circular had asked each NOC how many participants the Barcelona Games might reckon with. By the time of the ANOC meeting it had become generally accepted that there must not be more than 10,000 athletes in 1992. This figure is still an increase over the 9,417 athletes at Seoul in 1988 (9,002 if demonstration sports are excluded). Rather less attention seems to be paid to the excessive numbers of officials accompanying the team and journalists covering them, though of course it might be difficult to limit the latter now that the Olympics live to so large an extent off television. Yet the figures are alarming. At Seoul cards of accreditation were issued to 3,887 officials (there were a further 1,529 'extra' officials), and to no fewer than 15,740 journalists (5,380 press and 10,360 television).[3]

The trend of opinion favouring limitation of the Games' size has probably gone so far that it cannot be reversed, at least while Samaranch is President of the IOC. But there are still opponents of limitation, who scoff at the popular catchphrase of 'gigantism' and recall Philip Noel-Baker's remark that 'giant' is a word used to frighten children, and 'gigantism' has the same function in the adult world of sport.

It is ironic that, despite the preoccupation with gigantism, it was reported that the Barcelona programme was expected to be the fullest in the history of the Games and that the Spanish team at Barcelona was to consist of 660 men and women, compared with 363 at Seoul (269 athletes and 94 officials and others). The justification was that it was considered logical for the host country to be well represented, and to expect that a corresponding number of places would be dropped by Korea. However, there were to be more events than in Seoul, more countries taking part (167, if all accepted their invitations, against 161 at Seoul) and the IOC was paying $8,000 to each NOC for general expenses as well as $800 per athlete.[4] In the speech quoted above Samaranch also took the opportunity to emphasise the unity of the movement, which depended upon respect for the autonomony and independence of each of its pillars (the IOC, the IFs and the NOCs). But he did not fail to assert the essential role of the IOC: 'Let us not forget that at the head of this Olympic Movement there is its creator, the International Olympic Committee, whose strength is automatically channelled to each of the members of the Movement.'

In the same speech he reverted to another preoccupation, the control of sport:

in short, what we must succeed in doing is achieving complete control over our spectacular development. The leadership of Olympism and sport must always remain in the hands of sports leaders, and likewise all the financial resources we may obtain must return to the world of sport.

These were brave words in the context of the frequent complaints that are made about the ruthlessness of sponsors, who are prone to treat sport as a commodity like any other, and who have already had some success in arranging the timing of events to suit television, and in changing some games' rules to make them more attractive spectacles for the mass audience.

Doping

Common sense suggests that doping's dramatic growth must be at least in part a by-product of professionalism, so that it may be fairly said that in embracing money the world of sport has invited the growth of drug taking. But that once said, the Olympic movement has taken the lead in measures, both at the Games and between them, to stamp the problem out. It must be said, however, that all good intentions notwithstanding, it seems unlikely that it ever will be stamped out, for it appears that many athletes take drugs for granted, and would continue to take them, even in the knowledge that they were thereby inviting early death.

The Olympic movement is thus somewhat in the position of an industrialist, who having made a great fortune spends some of it in his old age on charitable works. Having grown rich by selling the movement, the IOC can now afford to spend a great deal on counteracting one of the unfortunate by-products of riches. The comparison is not entirely just, since the effort to eradicate drug taking is not solely a matter of charity. If unchecked it reduces the value of the product that is for sale. No one wants to know, as they watch their favourite athletes, that they are drugged automata, testing the latest concoction of some pharmaceutical company, and setting up records which are nonsensical.

National and international politics

There remain the numerous problems of national and international politics, on which the Olympic movement cannot avoid taking a view, however much it would like to leave politics to the politicians. An exhaustive list would be long, but some of the most obvious items on it include South Africa; terrorism; choosing the host city; and the insistence of various territories that they are worthy of separate recognition and should be allowed to set up separate National Olympic Committees.

South Africa

It may seem surprising to include South Africa in such a list, now that the Republic has been welcomed back into the Olympic fold, and is expected to compete at Barcelona in 1992. It has certainly been a triumph of diplomacy on the part of the IOC and its friends to produce sufficient unity in South Africa's sports establishment for it to have been possible to grant recognition to a single Olympic committee. Perhaps it is ungenerous to suggest that the IOC has acted precipitately in reversing the policy of over twenty years, or over thirty, if one dates South Africa's exclusion from its appearance at the Rome Games of 1960, rather than from the formal withdrawal of recognition (suspension was not in those days an option) in 1970.

Ungenerous or not, there are certainly South Africa watchers who point out that there's many a slip 'twixt cup and lip. Although President F. W. de Klerk has succeeded in removing the statutory framework of apartheid with extraordinary speed, attitudes will take much longer to change, and progress towards holding a constitutional conference will be slow, especially since the revelation (in itself not surprising) in July 1991 that the South African government had been secretly funding Inkatha, the main black rival of the ANC, and may even have been directly responsible for deaths in the African townships. Nor can anyone forecast the duration or extent of the white backlash which manifested itself in a dramatic confrontation between the police and white extremists in August 1991.

Once a constitutional conference does begin, it will drag on for a long time; rival leaders, who seem to have no difficulty in being on reasonable terms when removed from the Republic to the calm of a conference abroad, may find it difficult to restrain themselves from playing the card of violence once they have gone home, or may even be unable to restrain their followers. Nor is it likely that any conference will produce a lasting settlement which will both satisfy the whites', and particularly the Afrikaners', demands for safeguards for their national identity, whilst giving the ANC the 'one person one vote' which it demands. There is therefore some reason to suppose that South Africa's triumphant return to the Barcelona Games (if it in fact occurs) may be marred by a background of unrest, unless, of course, some modern version of the ancient Olympic truce comes into play.

Yet it is not difficult to understand the IOC's reasoning in readmitting South Africa. Samaranch said at the ANOC meeting in June 1990: 'We were the first sports organisation to close the door on South Africa, and we shall be very happy if we are the first to open it.'[5] To open the door in time for the 1992 Games can easily be seen as a risk worth taking. Furthermore, the Olympics aspire to be universal, and if there is no boycott (arising perhaps from the aftermath of the Gulf War of early 1991), Barcelona may stage the first universal Games. This would be the summit of Samaranch's career, so that to stay on as President after a successful Games in his own home city would be an anti climax. It might even bring him the Nobel peace prize, perhaps the only international honour which would finally persuade him that his place in history was assured.

Terrorism

Meanwhile, quite apart from the continuing doubts about the competence of the Barcelona organising committee, and about whether the Games will make a profit, there can be no guarantee against terrorism, although of course Spanish and other agencies will be fully alert. As we have seen, the authorities profess not to be worried that Catalonian separatists may resort to violence, but they are obliged to take seriously the threat posed by the Basque ETA, for which an Olympic festival on its home territory offers an unrivalled opportunity to obtain worldwide publicity. Life would perhaps be easier for the Spanish authorities if they were not still anxious to live down the authoritarian reputation so richly earned during the Franco era.

Choosing the host city

Much has been written since the IOC chose Atlanta, Georgia, in hot competition with Athens, to host the Games of 1996, about the need for some change in the voting procedure. Now that the Games have for good or ill become as much desired as an engine for growth as for any sporting reason, and the potential for wealth creation has become so enormous, it is widely felt that the IOC's methods of making a choice on which billions of dollars hang should in some way or another be made more rational and open.

This is primarily a matter for the IOC to decide, but it cannot be denied that the choice of city not only has developmental and financial effects, but more straightforwardly political ones as well. To revert to an earlier example, if the IOC were to choose Beijing, which has announced its intention to bid for the year 2000, it might on the one hand be argued that that it was playing into the hand of a coldly authoritarian regime, or on the other that it was seeking to bring the world's most populous country into the comity of nations.

In the past the IOC has managed to ignore questions of human rights when making friends: one has only to think of Nicolae Ceauşescu; but if it again allows the Games to be master-minded by a government which ignores human rights, it may well find itself suffering the disapproval of western governments. In an age when the provision of aid to poor countries is beginning to be linked with those countries' records in the matter of how they treat their populations, it would be odd if the IOC, which can in a sense be seen as an aid-giver on a vast scale, were allowed to feel comfortable if it gave the Games to a country whose government displayed indifference to human rights. Although not responsible to any higher authority, even the Olympic movement cannot afford to create a mood among governments that it needs to be cut down to size.

On the other hand the IOC's mission is universality, not uniformity. It does not wish to be seen as an agent of cultural imperialism – rather as a bridge between different social and political systems – and it is true that western concern about human rights can sometimes seem unpleasantly holier than thou to politicians who have somehow to govern disastrously poor countries. Nor can the IOC afford endlessly to grant the Games to conventionally democratic countries. To argue that there is only one worthwhile kind of democracy may itself be seen as a facet of cultural imperialism.

Yet, now that the IOC has become so unequivically the agent of world capitalism it may become hard for it to continue to ignore the humanitarian demands of capitalist governments. To give the Games to China would in some quarters be seen as the prelude to opening up new markets for the developed nations of the west, but at the same time there may be liberal concern that a gift so valuable should not be given to a regime about whose credentials there are so many, and justifiable, doubts.

It may therefore be less easy than in the past for the IOC to stick to its robust independence of judgement. To insist on independence in the name of the autonomy of sport while continuing with its current voting procedure may come to be seen as a handicap in the new political and economic climate, in which even the IOC may be held accountable for its actions.

New territories

The IOC'S official position on its response to requests for recognition by breakaway territories is that it will not consider an application without first canvassing the opinion of the existing NOC. Thus, the IOC would not even contemplate any claim from, for example, Catalonia or Ukraine without first holding discussions with the NOCS of Spain and the Soviet Union and it has managed to avoid discussing the extremely embarrassing case of Gibraltar.

From the legal point of view the fact that the IOC is a non-governmental body preserves its freedom to recognise NOCs whose territories do not coincide with the boundaries of states. The relationship between the IOC and an NOC is something like that between a company and its local agent. Because the relationship is private the IOC could reduce the area covered by an NOC, though it would not do so without its consent, without any loss of face for the government of the country whose NOC's territory was reduced and without any implications for the boundaries of the state.

That, however, is a legal approach to an essentially political problem. To take Catalonia first, the IOC would never wish to be thought to have contributed to the dismemberment of Spain. Fortunately, Catalonia's case will look far less urgent once the Barcelona Games are safely over, and it seems unlikely that the region will ever formally receive recognition for a separate Olympic committee, though there is nothing to prevent the Spanish NOC itself establishing regional sub-committees and consulting them to whatever degree it judges necessary. Perhaps some similar expedient will be adopted if Yugoslavia regains the outward appearance of unity as a nation state.

The atmosphere in the Soviet Union is as delicate from the Olympic point of view as from the conventionally political. In September 1991 the IOC recognised the three Baltic States of Estonia, Latvia and Lithuania. Meanwhile, a number of Republics, still precariously within the Union, had established their own Olympic organisations, to which the Soviet NOC had no choice but to listen.[6] Some of these Republics may achieve internationally recognised political recognition, and in that case the IOC will be obliged to recognise separate Olympic committees.

At some point it may even come to the conclusion that there are simply too many NOCs. So far it has always seemed to believe that more is better – that it is better, for example to have 170 nations invited to Barcelona than 161 to Seoul – but there must be some limit. Not only does the representation of vast numbers of minuscule territories eventually become absurd, but the proliferation of territories will itself contribute to the gigantism which has at last come to be taken seriously as a threat to the movement.

A gigantism of the spirit

There is one quality above all of the Olympic movement which makes it reasonable to return to the unthinkable question 'Are the Olympic Games really necessary?' which was posed in the introduction, and that is the movement's overweening sense of its own importance.

In many senses it indubitably is important, as is any organisation whose decisions can affect the social, economic and diplomatic fates of whole countries. It is important, too, to sports people, particularly in poor countries, who would not without its help be able to practise and promote the sports they love.

But in the richer countries there is room for ambiguity and paradox. On the one hand it is they who are responsible for the Games' commercialisation, but on the other they can afford the luxurious feeling 'It's only a game'. There is something both ludicrous and offensive about seeing the best hotel in whatever city is holding an Olympic meeting reserved entirely for sports administrators, with all the apparatus of sniffer dogs and diverted traffic which nowadays is unhappily necessary for meetings of heads of state and government.

But it is important to remember that there is a difference between an IOC Session and a G7 summit meeting.

There is, too, a feeling that the endless lobbying to be host city is not merely distastefully extravagant, but rather absurd. Nor have the opening and closing ceremonies of the Games much to do with sport – though it must be admitted that they are popular spectacles for which the tickets sell out and which attract enormous television audiences.

Even those students of sport (nowadays no doubt the majority) who admit that there is nothing wrong with being a professional athlete, and that there was much wrong with some versions of the cult of amateurism, must be a little disgusted by the extremes of commercial activity into which the Olympic movement has fallen. The money, of course, is recycled for the good of sport, but one cannot help wondering if there are any limits to commercialism.

The official answer to that question is that there certainly are. As Samaranch repeatedly says, the sticking point is that the control of sport must remain in the hands of sports people. But his is a cry from the last ditch, and there must be many who wonder whether it is not already too late.

The future

It is, in short, reasonable to feel that the whole thing has got out of hand. It does not, however, seem likely that the Olympic movement will reform itself to any significant degree, and there is no external authority that can force it to do so, although, as has been suggested, governments may show disapproval if 'bad' choices of host cities are made. Internally the forces making for conflict and division are immense, but it is probable that self-interest, diplomatic skill, wealth and ideals will continue to hold the movement together.

So long as it does hold together, there will still be a market for the Games: that is, there is no reason to suppose that they will not continue to hold the attention of millions world wide. The world needs the Games, because it needs to be reminded of what human beings can do. But the world also needs to be reminded, as does the Olympic movement, that in a sense sport is a triviality. It is foolish to try to put back the clock, but it is still worth saying that the world may need the Games, not as they are, but as they might have been.

Notes

1 47th Session, Helsinki, 16–27 July 1952, *Minutes*.
2 *Sport Intern*, 11, 16, 25 August 1990, p. 4.
3 Kim Un-yong, *The Greatest Olympics: from Baden-Baden to Seoul*, Seoul, 1990, pp. 188, 195, 205 and 217.
4 *La Vanguardia*, 6 June 1990.
5 *La Vanguardia*, 8 June 1990.
6 Interview with Vitaly Smirnov, IOC member and president of the Soviet NOC since June 1990, *Sport Intern*, 11, 18/19, 15 September 1990, p. 7.

Postscript

On 17 January 1992 the IOC's Executive Board acknowledged the fragmentation of Yugoslavia by granting provisional recognition to the Olympic Committees of Croatia and Slovenia, subject to ratification at the IOC's Session in February at Courchevel.

On 25 January Samaranch and President Boris Yeltsin agreed on provisional recognition for the NOCs of the twelve Republics of the Confederation of Independent States, provided that they agreed to field joint teams at Albertville and Barcelona.

Select bibliography

ANOC Commission on the Olympic Games, *Review of the Preparation of the Olympic Games of Barcelona '92*, presented to the ANOC conference in Barcelona, June 1990.

Aris, Stephen, *Sportsbiz: Inside the Sports Business*, Hutchinson, 1990.

Barcelona '92 Olympic Organising Committee (COOB '92), *Press Dossier. Report to the ANOC General Assembly*, Barcelona, June 1990.

Bridges, Brian, *Korea and the West*, London, Royal Institute of International Affairs, 1986.

'East Asia in Transition: South Korea in the Limelight', *International Affairs*, vol. 64, no. 3, Summer 1988, 381–92.

Carter, Jimmy, *Keeping Faith: Memoirs of a President*, New York, Bantam House, 1982.

Coubertin, Baron Pierre de, *L'Education en Angleterre, Collèges et Universités*, Paris, Librairie Hachette, 1888, reprinted in Norbert Mueller (ed.), *Pierre de Coubertin: Textes Choisies*, Zurich, Weidmann, 1986, vol. I, pp. 39–56.

——'Une Compagne de Vingt-et-un Ans (1887–1908)', 1909, *Textes Choisies*, Vol. II.

——'Pédagogie Sportive', Paris, 1922, reprinted in *Textes Choisies, vol. II*.

Mémoires Olympiques, Bureau Internationale de Pédagogie Sportive, Lausanne, n.d., but 1931.

——New Year message, repudiating the proposed boycott of the 1936 Games, *La Revue Sportive Illustré*, 32nd year, numéro spécial, 1936:38, reprinted in *Textes Choisies*, pp. 440–1.

Coubertin, Baron Pierre de, and others, *The Olympic Games in 776 BC to 1896 AD: The Olympic Games of 1896*, Athens and Paris, 1896. Fascimile edition (with English translation), 1966.

Czula, R., 'Sport as an Agent of Social Change', *Quest*, vol. 31, 1979.

Diem, Carl, *Pierre de Coubertin* (speech on the fiftieth anniversary celebration of the IOC), 17 and 18 June 1944.

Eede, A. Vanden, 'The National Olympic Committees and Marketing', *Olympic Message-Marketing and Olympism*, International Olympic Committee, 24 July 1989.

Edwards, Harry, 'Sportpolitics: Los Angeles 1964 – the Olympic Tradition Continues', *Sociology of Sport Journal*, 1984, vol. 1, 172–83.

——'The Free Enterprise Olympics', *Journal of Sport and Social Issues*, vol. 8, no. 2, Summer/Fall 1984, i–iv.

Espy, R. *The Politics of the Olympic Games*, Berkeley, University of California Press 1979, (new edition, *with an epilogue 1976–1980*, 1981).

Finley, M. I. and H. W. Pleket, *The Olympic Games: the First Thousand Years*, London, Chatto and Windus, 1986.

Games of the XXIVth Olympiad Seoul 1988, *Official Report*, vol. 1, 'Organization and Planning'.

Guttman, Allen, *The Games Must Go On: Avery Brundage and the Olympic Movement*, New York, Columbia University Press, 1984.

Hazan, Baruch A., *Olympic Sports and Propaganda Games: Moscow 1980*, London, Transaction Books, 1982.

Horne J., and others, *The 1988 Seoul Olympics*, North Staffordshire Polytechnic, Occasional Paper no. 5, June 1988.

Howell, Denis, *Made in Birmingham: the Memoirs of Denis Howell*, London, Macdonald, Queen Anne Press, 1990.

International Olympic Committee, *Bulletin*, nos. 1, 2, 3, Jan. 1894, July 1894, Jan. 1895.

——*TOP – The Olympic Programme: The National Olympic Committees' Manual of the Olympic Marketing Programme*, 1988.

——*Olympic Charter*, 1989, 1990, 1991.

——*Olympic Biographies*.

——*Olympic Movement Directory*.

Kanin, David B., 'The Olympic Boycott in Diplomatic Context', *Journal of Sport and Social Issues*, vol. 4, no. 1, Spring/Summer 1980.

Killanin, Lord, *My Olympic Years*, London, Secker and Warburg, 1983.

Killanin, Lord, and John Rodda (eds.), *The Olympic Games 1984*, Willow Books, London, 1983.

Kim Un-yong, *The Greatest Olympics: From Baden-Baden to Seoul*, Seoul, Si-sa-yong-o-sa, 1990.

Klatell, David A. and Norman Marcus, *Sports for Sale: Television, Money and the Fans*, New York, Oxford University Press, 1988.

Lovesey, Peter, *The Official Centenary History of the Amateur Athletic Association*, London, Guinness Superlatives, 1979.

MacAloon, John J. *This Great Symbol: Pierre de Coubertin and the Origins of the Modern Olympic Games*, Chicago, University of Chicago Press, 1981.

Macfarlane, Neil, *Sport and Politics: a World Divided*, London, Collins (Willow Books), 1986.

Manchester Olympic Bid Committee, *Manchester 1996: the British Olympic Bid*, n.d., but 1990.

Miller, Geoffrey, *Behind the Olympic Rings*, Lynn, Massachusetts, H. O. Zimman, Inc., 1979.

Mullins, Sam, *British Olympians: William Penny Brookes and the Wenlock Games*, London, Birmingham Olympic Council in Association with the British Olympic Association, 1986.

O'Neill, Tip, with William Novak, *Man of the House: the Life and Political Memoirs of Speaker Tip O'Neill*, London, Bodley Head, 1987.

Payne, M., 'Sport and Industry', *Olympic Message-Marketing and Olympism*,

International Olympic Committee, 24 July 1989, pp. 37–43.

Polignac, Marquis Melchior de, *Baron Pierre de Coubertin, 2 Septembre 1937 – 2 Septembre 1947* (speech on the tenth anniversary of Coubertin's death), *Bulletin du Comité Olympique,* new series, col. 6, September 1947, pp. 12–15.

Pujol, Jordi, *Afirmacio catalana d'europeisme: Paraules del President de la Generalitat a Aquisgra i Estraburg,* Barcelona, Generalitat de Catalunya, 1985.

——*The political and economic importance of the north-western Mediterranean: Statement by the President of the Generalitat in Stockholm,* Generalitat de Catalunya, Barcelona 1988.

Rees, C. Roger, 'The Olympic Dilemma: Applying the Contact Theory and Beyond', *Quest,* Vol. 37, 1985.

Reich, Kenneth, *Making it Happen: Peter Ueberroth and the 1984 Olympics,* Santa Barbara, Capra Press, 1986.

Riordan, James, *Sport in Soviet Society,* Cambridge, Cambridge University Press, 1977.

——'Elite sport policy in East and West', in Lincoln Allison (ed.), *The Politics of Sport,* Manchester, Manchester University Press, 1986.

Sipes, Richard G., 'War, Sports and Aggression: an Empirical Test of two Rival Theories', in D. Stanley Eitzen (ed.), *Sport in Contemporary Society: an Anthology,* New York, St. Martin's Press, 1984 (first published 1979).

Tyler, Martin and Phil Soar (eds.), *The History of the Olympic Games,* London, Marshall Cavendish, revised ed. 1980 (first published 1969).

Ueberroth, Peter, *Made in America* (with Richard Levin and Amy Quinn), London, Kingswood Press, 1986.

Usher, Harry L., 'The Games in Los Angeles: a New Approach to the Organisational Tasks', *Olympic Review,* no. 175, May 1982, pp. 257–60.

Wilson, Neil, *The Sports Business: the Men and the Money,* London, Mandarin, 1990 (first published 1988).

Wooldridge, Ian, *Sport in the 80's: a Personal View,* London, Centurion, 1989.

Young, David C., *The Olympic Myth of Greek Amateur Athletics,* Chicago, Ares Publishers Inc., 1984.

Index